FOUNDATION
FUNDAMENTALS

FOUNDATION FUNDAMENTALS

A Guide for Grantseekers
5th Edition

Edited by Mitchell F. Nauffts

CONTRIBUTORS: Althea Ashman, Sharon Braude, Timothy Carens, Sarah Collins, Margaret Derrickson, Charlotte Dion, Sara Engelhardt, Margaret Mary Feczko, Daniel Hodges, Francine Jones, Ruth Kovacs, Steven Lawrence, Elizabeth McKenty, Ben McLaughlin, Judith Margolin, William Matthews, Lorna Mehta, Carlotta Mills, Margaret Morth, C. Edward Murphy, Stan Olson, Loren Renz, Richard Romeo, Patricia Ryan, Rick Schoff, Alyson Tufts, Mare Valgemae, Heather Willey

THE FOUNDATION CENTER

ISBN 0-87954-543-7
Printed and bound in the United States of America.
Cover design by Greg Apicella.

Library of Congress Cataloging-in-Publication Data
Nauffts, Mitchell F.
    Foundation fundamentals : a guide for grantseekers /
edited by Mitchell F. Nauffts.—5th ed.
        p.   cm.
    Rev. ed. of: Foundation fundamentals / edited by Judith B. Margolin.
4th ed. 1991.
    Includes bibliographical references.
    ISBN 0-87954-543-7 : $24.95
    1. Endowments—Information services—United States.
2. Research grants—Information services—United States.
I. Margolin, Judith B. Foundation fundamentals. II. Title.
HV41.9.U5M37   1994   94-71440
361.7'632—dc20   CIP

Contents

List of Figures and Charts

List of Figures and Charts

Foreword

When the Foundation Center was established in 1956, it was to endeavor, first and foremost, to be a useful resource for anyone seeking funds from grantmaking organizations. Today, 37 years later, that remains our primary goal.

Our charter suggested that this goal might best be achieved if the Center were to "collect, organize and make available to the public reports and information about foundations...." It was almost an afterthought that, "to the extent deemed advisable by its board of trustees," the Center might "compile and publish periodically a general directory of foundations." Thus, while our goal remains unchanged, the manner in which we accomplish it has evolved substantially. Although we continue to collect and make available through our libraries substantial amounts of existing information about individual foundations and the foundation field, we are today best known for our directories, in particular *The Foundation Directory*.

But then, the foundation field has itself changed significantly in the past four decades. There are many more foundations. And many more now recognize the value of making accurate and up-to-date information available to the grantseeking public. Since the first Foundation Center library opened its doors in New York City in the mid-fifties, patterns of foundation type, size, geographic location, and giving priorities have shifted, sometimes dramatically. The information collected and made available by the Center has expanded along with the field.

Staying abreast of the changes and burgeoning information can be overwhelming, and so the Center has taken an additional step in recent years. Now, not only do we collect the information and make it available in free libraries around the country as well as in published directories, we also help grantseekers navigate a course through the sea of information. All our libraries and many of our Cooperating Collections offer orientation programs on a regular basis. We also publish *The Foundation Center's User-Friendly Guide: A Grantseeker's Guide to Resources,* which helps the first-time grantseeker get a fast start in foundation research. *Foundation Fundamentals,* in contrast, is intended for those who want a more in-depth orientation to the field, the foundation research process, and the many resources for grantseekers available at Foundation Center libraries.

We hope you'll find this guide of value in your work. Please call on our other resources as well as you make your way through the challenging and exciting process of seeking foundation support.

Sara L. Engelhardt, President
The Foundation Center
December 1993

Introduction

A s the '90s unfold, the role of the nonprofit sector in society grows increasingly prominent. From AIDS to homelessness, drug abuse to youth violence, nonprofit organizations staffed by dedicated individuals are leading the charge against a wide range of social ills. The philanthropic community has responded in kind, donating ever larger sums of money to a broad spectrum of causes.

And yet the demand for philanthropic dollars far exceeds the supply. With all indications pointing to a continuation of this trend through the remainder of the decade, the message for grantseekers is clear: In an increasingly competitive environment, the bulk of foundation and corporate giving will go to nonprofits that combine creativity and resourcefulness with a thorough knowledge and understanding of prospective funding sources.

As first-time grantseekers quickly discover, there is no dearth of information on grantmakers. If anything, in fact, the problem often is one of information overload. Fully revised and updated, the fifth edition of *Foundation Fundamentals* is designed to help grantseekers make sense of the wealth of information available to them. Building on previous editions developed by Carol M. Kurzig, Patricia Read, and Judith B. Margolin, it introduces the grantseeker to the resources of the Foundation Center, the oldest and most authoritative source of information on grantmaking and grantseeking, and then outlines a number of research strategies designed to help grantseekers develop a list of potential funders.

The organization and arrangement of the book, with one or two exceptions, follows that of earlier editions:

Chapter 1 describes the various types of foundations and the regulations that govern their activities. Chapter 2 looks at support from foundations in relation to other funding sources, including government grants, earned income, and individual donors.

Chapter 3 reviews the issue of nonprofit tax exemption and includes a brief discussion of program-related investments (PRIs).

Chapter 4 discusses in detail the importance of planning your funding research strategies and includes a number of worksheets designed to facilitate the process.

The resources the Foundation Center makes available to grantseekers—many of them derived from the Center's ever expanding database—are described in Chapter 5. The numerous changes in, and additions to, the Center's lineup of publications over the last three years are noted and, where appropriate, discussed in detail, making the chapter a must-read for first-time grantseekers and more experienced fundraisers alike.

Chapters 6, 7, and 8 introduce the reader to three research strategies designed to identify potential funders. The subject, geographic, and types of support approaches are based on the content of the general reference directories discussed in Chapter 5 and may be employed sequentially or simultaneously (although novice grantseekers are likely to find the sequential approach less confusing than a simultaneous one).

Chapter 9 is devoted to the ins and outs of corporate grantmaking, with an emphasis on the trend toward increased "in-kind" support by corporate giving programs and company foundations. Chapter 10 describes in detail the crucial process of presenting your ideas to a funder, be it a private foundation or a corporate giver.

This latest edition of *Foundation Fundamentals* also includes a number of modifications that make it easier to use than previous editions of the book. The appendices have been streamlined and an index has been added to help grantseekers reference unfamiliar terms and concepts. The design of the book has been modified as well, enhancing the readability of the text. And, of course, the illustrations and worksheets have been completely updated to reflect the many changes in the form and content of the Center's resources, both printed and online. As before, repetition and overlap have been kept to a minimum, making it possible to read *Foundation Fundamentals* from cover to cover or, using the index, to zero in on items of specific interest.

The list of people who contributed to the preparation of this edition includes almost every member of the Foundation Center's public services, research, and editorial divisions. As a newcomer to the field of foundation research, the end result of my labors would have been much diminished without their encouragement and splendid professional help.

I especially want to thank Judith Margolin, who edited the previous edition of the book and offered advice, encouragement, and guidance in equal measure. A good deal of what I was able to accomplish was made possible by the collaborative model Judi developed for the last edition of *Foundation Fundamentals*, and the final product is as much a reflection of her efforts as mine. I also want to thank Sara Engelhardt, president of the Foundation Center, who contributed the Foreword and took time out from a busy schedule to review the final manuscript with a copy editor's eye. Cheryl Loe handled the desktop publishing chores with aplomb and deserves most of the credit for the improved design of the book, while Rick Schoff gets the credit for keeping the whole enterprise firmly on track.

Last but not least, I want to thank my wife, Lisa, who, over the course of an eventful autumn, juggled the demands of a career, newborn twins, and a sometimes ornery husband, and made it look easy.

Mitchell F. Nauffts
Editor

Chapter 1

What Is a Foundation?

The Foundation Center defines a private foundation as a nongovernmental, nonprofit organization having a principal fund that is managed by its own trustees and directors, and that maintains or aids charitable, educational, religious, or other activities serving the public good, primarily by making grants to other nonprofit organizations.

Some private foundations are organized as operating foundations that conduct their own research programs or provide a direct service. Operating foundations generally make few, if any, grants to other organizations. Community foundations function in much the same way as private foundations, but because their funds are drawn from many donors they are usually classified as "public charities." Foundations may use different words in their names, such as "fund," "trust," or "endowment," without having legal or operational differences. Similarly, there are organizations that use the term "foundation" or "trust" in their names that do not operate as foundations, although in some cases they may make grants to other organizations. The nomenclature can be confusing, but the significant distinction is that those nonprofits actually classified by the IRS as private foundations must be organized and operated under specific regulations.

Foundations are usually created and organized as corporations or charitable trusts under state laws and receive their federal tax-exempt status under the Internal Revenue

Code. The Tax Reform Act of 1969, the first major legislation dealing with foundations, introduced the term "private foundation" and defined the phrase only by the exclusion of other nonprofit organizations. David Freeman, former president of the Council on Foundations, explains the Code's definition in his book, *The Handbook on Private Foundations*:

> Starting with the universe of voluntary organizations described in Section 501(c)(3), the code excludes broad groups such as churches, schools, hospitals, government, and publicly supported charities and their affiliates. (Publicly supported charities derive much of their support from the general public and reach out in other ways to a public constituency.) The code refers to all of the above kinds of excluded organizations as *public charities*. Section 501(c)(3) organizations remaining after these exclusions are considered private foundations.[1]

Within the category of private foundations, the 1969 Tax Reform Act distinguishes between operating foundations—that is, foundations established primarily to operate specific research, social welfare, or other charitable programs—and nonoperating foundations. The category of nonoperating private foundation includes independent grantmaking foundations, company-sponsored foundations, and a variety of nongrantmaking organizations that function much like operating foundations or "public charities" but do not meet the legal criteria established by the tax code to qualify as either.

Types of Grantmaking Foundations

Foundations are classified in a number of ways, with the differences in terminology generally implying certain operational differences.

Independent foundations, which comprise the largest segment of the foundation universe, are grantmaking organizations whose funds are generally derived from an individual, a family, or a group of individuals. They may be operated under the direction of the donor or members of the donor's family, a type often referred to as "family foundations," or they may have an independent board of trustees or directors that manage the foundation's program.

Typically, independent foundations have broad charters, although in practice they often limit their giving to a few areas of interest. Their broad charters, however, allow

1. Freeman, David F., and the Council on Foundations. *The Handbook on Private Foundations*. New York: The Foundation Center, 1991, p. 9.

them to move into new areas in response to changing social priorities. Depending on the range of their giving, they may also be known as "general purpose" or "special purpose" foundations.

Company-sponsored foundations, also called corporate foundations, are created and funded by business corporations for the purpose of making grants and performing other philanthropic activities, which they do as separate legal entities. Generally, they are managed by a board of directors composed of corporate officials, although the board may also include individuals with no corporate affiliation. (In some company-sponsored foundations, local plant managers and senior officials are also involved in grantmaking and policy decisions.) Their giving programs usually focus on communities where the company has operations and on research and education in fields related to company activities.

Company-sponsored foundations should not be confused with corporate contributions or direct-giving programs that are administered within the corporation. Direct-giving programs are under the full control of the corporation, with funds drawn solely from the corporation's pretax earnings. Direct-giving programs may also encompass noncash "in-kind" contributions, such as donations of equipment, office space, supplies, or the labor of volunteer employees, as well as monetary grants. Despite its close ties to the parent company, a company-sponsored foundation, in contrast, is an independent organization. It is classified as a "private foundation" under the Internal Revenue Code and is subject to the same regulations as any other private foundation. The foundation receives funds from the parent company's pretax earnings, which it then "passes on" to nonprofit organizations in the form of contributions. It may also maintain its own endowment, however small. A company-sponsored foundation therefore makes it possible for a corporation to set aside funds for use in years when earnings may be reduced and the needs of charitable organizations may be greater.

Many corporations maintain both a company-sponsored foundation and a direct-giving program, with the two often coordinated under a general giving policy. For more information on corporate grantmaking, see Chapter 9.

Operating foundations are established to operate research, social welfare, or other charitable programs deemed worthwhile by the donor or the governing body. Although some grants may be made outside the programs operated by the foundation, the majority of the foundation's funds are expended on its own programs. Endowment funds are generally provided by a single source, although many operating foundations also receive contributions from the general public or from other foundations and grantmakers.

Community foundations are supported by and operated for the benefit of a specific community or region. They receive their funds from a variety of donors; in fact, their endowments are frequently composed of a number of different trust funds, some of which bear their donors' names. Their grantmaking activities are administered by a governing body or distribution committee representative of community interests. Investment funds are managed professionally, usually by trustee banks.

Owing to the nature of their support and philanthropic activities, nearly all community foundations qualify as "public charities" under the Internal Revenue Code. As such, they are not subject to regulatory provisions that apply to private foundations, and their donors are able to claim maximum tax deductions for their contributions.

See Figure 1 for the general characteristics of four types of foundations.

Historical Background

The concept of private philanthropy dates back to ancient times, but legal provision for the creation, control, and protection of charitable funds (the forerunner of today's foundations) was not established until 1601, when England's Statute of Charitable Uses granted certain privileges to private citizens or groups of citizens in exchange for support and/or performance of charitable acts intended to serve the public good. Since then, legal doctrines in the common law countries have generally preserved this status for all types of charitable organizations, including foundations, churches, hospitals, and colleges, ensuring their existence in perpetuity as well as their right to tax exemption as long as they serve a charitable function.

Most early foundations were established for the benefit of particular institutions or to answer specific social problems, such as feeding or housing the poor. But in the late nineteenth and early twentieth centuries a different kind of foundation began to emerge in the United States. Exemplified by the Carnegie Corporation of New York (1911) and the Rockefeller Foundation (1913), these "general purpose" foundations were given broad charters enabling them to address the causes of and seek solutions to major social problems. This approach to philanthropy has led foundations to support, among other things, research to determine the causes of disease instead of, or in addition to, providing support for the operation of clinics or hospitals.

The number of foundations established in the United States has grown significantly since those early days, with a large portion of that growth occurring in the decade immediately following World War II. This growth has been attributed to the high tax

FIGURE 1.   General Characteristics of Four Types of Foundations

Foundation Type	Description	Source of Funds	Decision-Making Activity	Grantmaking Requirements	Reporting
Independent Foundation	An independent grant-making organization established to aid social, educational, religious, or other charitable activities.	Endowment generally derived from a single source such as an individual, a family, or a group of individuals. Contributions to endowment limited as to tax deductibility.	Decisions may be made by donor or members of the donor's family; by an independent board of directors or trustees; or by a bank or trust officer acting on the donor's behalf.	Broad discretionary giving allowed but may have specific guidelines and give only in a few specific fields. About 70% limit their giving to local area.	Annual information returns (990-PF) filed with IRS must be made available to public. A small percentage issue separately printed annual reports.
Company-Sponsored Foundation	Legally an independent grantmaking organization with close ties to the corporation providing funds.	Endowment and annual contributions from a profit-making corporation. May maintain a small endowment and pay out most of its contributions received annually in grants, or may maintain endowment to cover contributions in years when corporate profits are down.	Decisions made by board of directors often composed of corporate officials, but which may include individuals with no corporate affiliation. Decisions may also be made by local company officials.	Giving tends to be in fields related to corporate activities or in communities where corporation operates. Usually give more grants but in smaller dollar amounts than independent foundations.	Same as above.
Operating Foundation	An organization that uses its resources to conduct research or provide a direct service.	Endowment usually provided from a single source, but eligible for maximum deductible contributions from public.	Decisions generally made by independent board of directors.	Makes few, if any, grants. Grants generally related directly to the foundation's program.	Same as above.
Community Foundation	A publicly sponsored organization that makes grants for social, educational, religious, or other charitable purposes in a specific community or region.	Contributions received from many donors. Usually eligible for maximum tax-deductible contributions from public.	Decisions made by board of directors representing the diversity of the community.	Grants generally limited to charitable organizations in local community.	IRS 990 return available to public. Many publish full guidelines or annual reports.

Source: The Foundation Center, 1993.

rates that prevailed after the war, the emergence of corporate foundations, and an increase in family foundations with living donors.

After the rapid growth of the 1950s, the rate of foundation creation slowed in the 1960s and then declined sharply in the 1970s, a trend some have attributed to the increased regulation and taxation of foundations following passage of the 1969 Tax Reform Act, a preference among corporations for giving programs over company-sponsored foundations, and changes in the overall economy.[2] According to the Foundation Center's most recent analysis of active grantmaking foundations holding assets of $1 million or more or awarding annual grants totaling at least $100,000, only 945 foundations were established in the 1970s, compared with 1,614 in the 1960s and 1,880 in the 1950s.

As government regulations eased after the mid-1970s, the rate of foundation formation began to increase. In fact, the Foundation Center estimates that more than 3,000 larger foundations were created between 1980 and 1990, making the 1980s the decade of most rapid foundation growth. Establishment rates were highest for independent foundations but also strong for corporate foundations. Factors contributing to this resurgence included an unprecedented rise in personal wealth, increased incentives for giving as regulations were relaxed, and a more positive view of the role of foundations. Still, after 1986, the establishment rates appear to have slowed as lower personal tax rates took effect and the economy fell into recession.

The development of community foundations differs somewhat in its particulars from those of other types of foundations. The community foundation movement in the United States began in the early twentieth century. The first community trust, the Cleveland Foundation, was established in 1914 by Frederick H. Goff, who believed "that better results and greater efficiency could be secured if the management and control of the property dedicated to charitable use in each community could be centralized in one or at most a few governing bodies." According to F. Emerson Andrews in *Philanthropic Giving* (Russell Sage, 1950), "the idea of the community trust was accepted enthusiastically, especially by the officers of trust companies, and organizations were set up at the initiative of banks in many town and cities." The rate of formation of community foundations jumped in the 1970s, when tax policies began to discourage philanthropy through private foundations. Growth remained strong in the 1980s, and the more than 340 community foundations across the country and in Puerto Rico have developed into a significant force in the philanthropic community.

---

2. See *America's Wealthy and the Future of Foundations,* edited by Teresa Odendahl. New York: The Foundation Center, 1987.

Regulation of Foundations

Nonprofit organizations defined as private foundations by the IRS must be organized and operated under specific regulations laid out by the Tax Reform Act of 1969, with some significant modifications as a result of the 1976 Tax Reform Act, the Economic Recovery Tax Act of 1981 (ERTA), and tax legislation enacted in 1984, 1986, 1987, and 1988. The Tax Reform Act of 1969 established the criteria for distinguishing private foundations from public charities and created a separate category with a more favorable tax status for operating foundations.

The 1969 Act set forth special rules that, among other things, prohibit self-dealing between foundations and "disqualified persons," including their donors; restrict foundation ownership and simultaneous management of profit-making businesses; limit the percentage of an individual's annual income that can be donated to a private foundation as a tax-deductible contribution; and regulate foundation giving to individuals, other foundations, nonexempt organizations, and activities that influence legislation or political campaigns. To offset costs incurred by the IRS in regulating tax-exempt organizations, the 1969 Act imposed an excise tax on foundations at the rate of four percent of net investment income. After it was proved that this excise tax generated revenues that greatly exceeded the annual budget of the exempt organizations branch of the IRS, the Revenue Act of 1978 reduced the tax to two percent. With tax revenues still many times greater than regulatory costs, the Deficit Reduction Act of 1984 reduced the tax from two to one percent for any foundation that, in a given fiscal year, makes qualifying distributions meeting certain requirements.

In addition, the 1969 Act required a private foundation to distribute for charitable purposes all its "adjusted net income" or a percentage, to be set each year, of the market value of that year's investment assets (whichever was higher). This "payout requirement" was later set at five percent of the market value of that year's investment assets.

Also enacted as part of the 1969 Act was a reporting stipulation that required foundations to file two annual information returns with the IRS (Forms 990-AR and 990-PF), to make the forms available for public inspection, and to file two copies of the forms with authorities in the state where the foundation is incorporated and maintains its principal offices. Since 1982, foundations have been required to file only one form, a revised version of the 990-PF form that incorporates all information previously required on the separate forms and which also asks for additional information on the foundation's grantmaking activities.

The Tax Reform Act of 1969 further prohibits or circumscribes a number of activities by private foundations, including attempts to influence legislation, intervention in political campaigns, and making grants to individuals or to other private foundations or non-501(c)(3) organizations. Making grants in these areas entails a certain amount of paperwork for foundations. For instance, a foundation must have an IRS-approved individual grants program in order to make grants to individuals for the purpose of study or travel, and it must follow up such grants with special reports. A foundation may make a grant for a charitable purpose to an organization that does not qualify as a public charity so long as it takes "expenditure responsibility," which entails a grant contract and follow-up reports to the IRS as part of the 990-PF. A foundation may also support groups that include lobbying or voter education and registration in their activities, provided that it and the grantee follow the regulations governing these areas.

The IRS is responsible for enforcing the federal regulations on foundations, and it accomplishes this primarily through review of the 990-PF reports as well as through audits of individual foundations. At the state level, regulation is typically the concern of the state attorney general, who enforces the state's not-for-profit corporation law and any statutory or common laws governing charitable trustees. The federal regulatory system was designed to encourage more active state regulation of foundations. The 990-PFs, for instance, must be filed with appropriate state authorities as well as with the IRS. Thus, in many states, the office of the attorney general and/or the charities registration office is another source of information for those interested in researching a foundation located in that state. (See Appendix B.)

How Many Foundations Are There?

The Foundation Center's analysis of IRS annual information returns (Form 990-PF) filed by private foundations in 1989, 1990, and 1991 shows that there were more than 33,000 active private and community grantmaking foundations in the United States.

Among foundations filing 990-PF tax returns in 1991 but not included in this total were: 724 independent foundations that did not award any grants (including many newly established funders); 1,650 operating foundations that had either terminated operations, merged into another foundation or corporate-giving program, been reclassified as public charities, or become inactive; and several thousand organizations that were intended to operate as "publicly supported" charities but failed to attract the required amount of support and were therefore classified as private foundations under the tax laws. These organizations were not intended to and do not fulfill the philanthropic function commonly ascribed to private foundations and therefore are excluded from the Foundation Center's statistical analyses.

From 1985 to 1991, the number of active grantmaking foundations tracked by the Center increased from more than 25,000 to more than 33,000, up by 30 percent. The reasons for this increase included improved tracking methods employed by Foundation Center staff (who now verify records directly from more than 40,000 990-PF information returns received annually from the IRS); the formation of new foundations; and the inclusion in the IRS file of nonexempt charitable trusts (NECTs), a type of trust that was required to file Form 990-PF beginning only in the mid-1980s.

In fiscal year 1991, grantmaking foundations held combined assets of $162.9 billion and awarded grants totaling nearly $9.2 billion (Figure 2). Independent or family foundations are by far the largest group and account for nearly 86 percent of the total assets and 76 percent of the grant dollars awarded by foundations. An additional 16 percent is contributed by the nation's corporate foundations, which hold less than 4 percent of total assets.

FIGURE 2. Analysis of Grantmaking Foundations by Type
(Dollar figures expressed in thousands)

Foundation Type	Number of Foundations	%	Assets	%	Total Grants	%
Independent	29,476	88.4	$139,335,317	85.6	$7,032,930	76.4
Corporate	1,775	5.3	6,037,821	3.7	1,490,114	16.2
Community	335	1.0	8,045,642	4.9	544,721	5.9
Operating[1]	1,770	5.3	9,487,778	5.8	142,800	1.6
Total	33,356	100.0	$162,906,559	100.0	$9,210,565	100.0

Note: Figures may not add up due to rounding.
[1]Does not include 1,650 private operating foundations that did not award any grants in the most current reporting year.

Foundations are located in every state of the Union, Puerto Rico, and the Virgin Islands, with a major concentration in the Northeast. New York foundations alone account for 22 percent of all foundation assets, while Middle Atlantic and East North Central foundations combined control more than 54 percent (Figure 3).

The relatively unequal distribution of foundation assets across the country is rooted in past economic and industrial developmental patterns as well as in the personal preferences of the donors. This is offset to some extent by the funding policies of large national foundations, which give substantial amounts outside the states in which they are located. Moreover, since 1975, changing demographic patterns and relatively rapid economic and industrial growth in the Southeast, Southwest, and Pacific regions have stimulated a higher rate of growth in the number of foundations and foundation assets in those areas. Pacific foundations, for example, have doubled their share of assets since 1975, up from 7 percent to nearly 14 percent, while the Middle Atlantic states' share of assets has dropped from 47 percent to 34 percent over the same period. In the late 1980s, the most significant surge in the growth of foundations occurred in the South Atlantic states, which now account for close to 12 percent of assets.

FIGURE 3. Distribution of Foundation Assets by Region in 1991

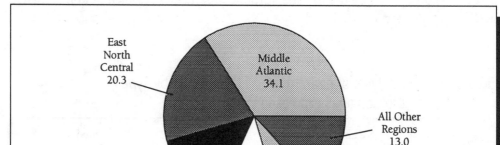

Chapter 2

Where Foundations Fit in the Total Funding Picture

Although the foundation statistics presented in the preceding chapter are impressive, it's important to keep them in perspective. Private foundation giving represents only a small portion of all private philanthropic contributions, which in turn account for a relatively small percentage of the total support for nonprofit organizations.

According to estimates in *Giving USA*, published by the AAFRC Trust for Philanthropy, private philanthropic contributions in 1992 totaled $124.3 billion (Figure 4). The largest portion of these contributions—$110 billion or 88.5 percent—came from individual donors through gifts or bequests. Independent foundations accounted for 6.7 percent of this total, while corporations and corporate foundations were responsible for 4.8 percent of total estimated private giving.

Foundation giving as a proportion of total private philanthropic giving grew rapidly during the 1960s and peaked at 9 percent in 1970. Inflation and restrictive regulations during the 1970s caused the proportion of giving coming from foundations to decline to a low of 5.1 percent in 1979. With the easing of some restrictions, the runup in the stock market, and a robust economy, foundation giving as a share of all philanthropy recovered somewhat in the 1980s, yet still fell far short of 1970 levels. With corporate contributions flat in the early 1990s, the share of foundation giving rose to 6.7 percent. The outlook for the rest of the '90s remains uncertain.

Changes in corporate philanthropy hint at very different patterns of growth. Between 1970 and 1980, contributions from corporations showed the greatest growth after individual giving. As a percentage of total philanthropic giving, corporate contributions peaked at 6.6 percent in 1985, after which they declined to 4.8 percent in 1992.

FIGURE 4.   Private Philanthropic Contributions in 1992

Source	Amount (in Billions)	Percent
Individuals	$101.83	81.9%
Bequests	8.15	6.6
Foundations	8.33	6.7
Corporations	6.00	4.8
Total	$124.31	100.0%

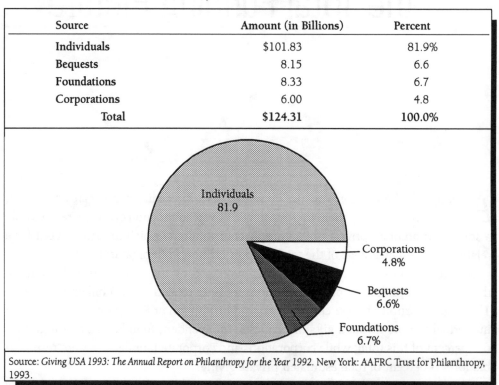

Source: *Giving USA 1993: The Annual Report on Philanthropy for the Year 1992*. New York: AAFRC Trust for Philanthropy, 1993.

In *Dimensions of the Independent Sector* (Washington, D.C.: Independent Sector, 1992), Virginia Hodgkinson reported that private contributions accounted for only 27 percent of the total support for nonprofit organizations in 1989. Religious organizations and arts and cultural groups were heavily dependent on private contributions for support, receiving, respectively, 81 and 63 percent of their total funding from private gifts, while educational institutions and social service agencies received only 15 percent and 34 percent of their funding, respectively, from private contributions, and health organizations received less than 6 percent of their total funding from private contributions (Figure 5).

FIGURE 5. Percentage Distribution of Annual Sources of Support for Independent Sector Organizations, 1989

Source of Funds	All Independent Sector Dollars[1]	Percent	Religious Organizations	Arts/ Culture	Health Services	Education/ Research	Social Services
Government Sector	$105.3	25.8%	—	10.8%	36.2%	17.2%	42%
Private contributions	111.0	27.2	80.8%	62.5	5.5	14.6	33.9
Dues, fees, charges	154.8	37.9	7.4	12.5	50.3	54.3	14.1
Endowments	20.0	4.9	2.6	5.0	1.3	5.6	3.3
Other receipts	17.0	4.2	9.2	9.2	6.7	8.3	6.7
Total	$408.1	100.0%	100.0%	100.0%	100.0%	100.0%	100.0%

[1]in billions of dollars.

Source: *Nonprofit Almanac 1992–1993: Dimensions of the Independent Sector*, pp. 147 (Table 4.2) and 150 (Table 4.3). Virginia Ann Hodgkinson, et al. Washington, D.C.: Independent Sector, 1992.

Reductions in federal spending in the 1980s had a great impact on the funding patterns of many nonprofit organizations, especially those in the human services subsector. In 1977, government provided 54 percent of total annual funds in social and legal services, compared with only 42 percent in 1989. In response to these drastic cuts, private contributions as a share of total annual funds for this subsector increased from 32 percent in 1977 to 34 percent in 1989. Revenues from dues, fees, and other charges also increased, from 10 percent to 14 percent. Across the entire independent sector, the share of annual funds represented by dues, fees, and other charges rose from 36 percent in 1977 to a high of 39 percent in 1987, and stood at 38 percent in 1989, reflecting nonprofits' need to develop new forms of income.

The reductions in federal funding during the 1980s focused increased attention on private philanthropy. Although private giving increased during the decade, it is clear that the increases equaled only a small portion of the shortfall created by federal cutbacks. A study by economist Lester Salamon revealed that between 1982 and 1987 the growth in private giving was enough to offset approximately 22 percent of the cumulative reductions in overall federal spending in education, training, employment, and social services; community and regional development; international affairs; income assistance; and health (excluding Medicare and Medicaid).[1]

In a more recent report Salamon noted that "Although private giving did grow, by about 53 percent in inflation-adjusted terms [between 1977 and 1989], its growth lagged behind that of most of the other sources of income."[2] In fact, the major source of nonprofit growth during the 1980s was in service fees and other commercial income, which accounted for more than half of new growth.

Independent Sector's *Dimensions* report reveals that dues, fees, and other charges for services and goods combined with income earned on endowments accounts for 47 percent of the support for nonprofit organizations. This is most true for health care organizations and educational institutions, which, respectively, derive 58 percent and 68 percent of their support from earned income. Social services and arts organizations derive only 24 percent and 27 percent, respectively, of their total support from earned income.

Government is a key source of support for many nonprofit organizations, according to the Independent Sector report. Government funding accounted for 26 percent of the total revenue of nonprofits in 1989, with health organizations and social service agencies receiving 36 and 42 percent, respectively, of their total support from government sources.

Government Grants

Despite cutbacks in federal spending, government is still a key source of support for nonprofit organizations. Support may come in the form of direct grants or contracts for specific services. Most nonprofits will want to become familiar with the activities and

---

1. *Nonprofit Organizations and the FY 1990 Federal Budget.* Lester Salamon and Alan Abramson, 1990, unpublished.
2. Salamon, Lester. *America's Nonprofit Sector: A Primer.* New York: The Foundation Center, 1992.

funding programs of the federal, state, and local government agencies with responsibility for their service areas.

Information about federal government programs is available through a variety of sources. *The United States Government Manual*, issued by the Office of the Federal Register, describes the broad program responsibilities of all government departments and affiliated agencies, including the National Endowments for the Arts and Humanities and the National Science Foundation. Although grantmaking and contract programs are not outlined specifically, most agency descriptions include information on the publications and brochures available to the public and how to obtain them. You can also write to the agencies working in your field and have your name added to their mailing lists for program announcements and other funding information. To order the *Manual*, write the Office of the Federal Register, c/o National Archives and Records, 8th and Pennsylvania Avenue, N.W., Washington, D.C., 20408.

The primary resource on federal funding is the *Catalog of Federal Domestic Assistance*, issued annually in June by the General Services Administration and updated in December. The catalog lists all federal funding programs available to for-profit and nonprofit institutions as well as individuals. Descriptions of each program provide detailed information on the purpose of the program, eligibility requirements, and application procedures. Indexes by sponsoring agency, subject, functional categories, and eligible applicant groups enable users to identify the funding programs most suited to their needs. Copies of the catalog are available in many public libraries, as well as from the Government Printing Office; Tel: (202) 783-3238.

In addition to the *Catalog*, the General Services Administration maintains the Federal Assistance Programs Retrieval System (FAPRS), a computer database that provides rapid access to federal assistance program information. The GSA has designated access points where computer searches of FAPRS may be requested; grantseekers with their own PCs may arrange for direct access to the system through commercial time-sharing companies. For further information on FAPRS, write or call:

Federal Domestic Assistance Catalog Staff
General Services Administration
Ground Floor, Reporters Building
300 7th Street, S.W.
Washington, DC 20407
Tel: (800) 669-8331

There are two other important sources of information on federal funding. Published weekdays, the *Federal Register* lists proposed and final rules and regulations developed by all federal agencies in addition to information on program deadlines and application procedures. Each issue of the *Register* has a highlights page that can be skimmed for pertinent material. Government agencies also contract for a wide variety of goods and services, from the manufacture of office supplies to the training and education of personnel. Bid requests for federal contracts are published in *Commerce Business Daily*, which, despite the acronyms and abbreviations scattered through its listings, is an invaluable resource for anyone interested in marketing their goods and services to the government.

In addition to publications issued by the federal government, several other useful guides to government funding may be tapped. Information on these and a number of guides and handbooks is included in Appendix A.

In contrast, information about state and local governments is not always readily available. Most state and large municipal governments issue some type of guidebook or manual listing the addresses of departments and agencies along with brief descriptions of their program responsibilities. Sometimes the offices of state senators and congressional representatives will also guide you to appropriate sources of local funding information. You'll want to check with your local public library for the specific resources available in your area.

Corporate Grants

As the federal government cut back its funding for social services, education, and arts programs in the early 1980s, the call went out for private sources, notably businesses and corporations, to pick up the slack. The tax deduction limit for charitable contributions was raised from 5 percent to 10 percent of a company's pretax earnings in an effort to increase corporate giving levels, and a special Task Force on Private Sector Initiatives was established to explore ways to encourage private giving and the greater involvement of corporations in their communities.

The incentives worked. Corporate contributions increased dramatically through 1985, in part because of a healthy business climate. Since then, however, corporate giving as a portion of all private giving has declined, falling prey to corporate buyouts and mergers, the downsizing of operations and staff, and changes in goals and policies ushered in by a new breed of CEOs. Moreover, in this leaner corporate environment, contributions are expected to reflect more closely the interests of the company and perhaps even yield a tangible return—for example, a more skilled labor force. Still, corporate contributions reached $6 billion in 1991, and many nonprofit organizations have come to regard both major corporations and local businesses as important sources of support.

As noted in Chapter 1, corporations may make charitable contributions through a direct-giving program administered within the corporation, through a separate corporate foundation, or through both. Corporate foundations are classified as private foundations under the Internal Revenue Code and are subject to the same rules and regulations as other private foundations. They are often used by parent companies as a way of setting aside funds to maintain a certain level of charitable giving in years when profits are off. Direct-giving programs, in contrast, are subject to fewer regulations. But because the funds for them generally are drawn directly from the corporation's pretax earnings, they are more vulnerable to the ups and downs of an organization's yearly performance.

Many corporations choose to make charitable contributions through both a separate foundation and a direct-giving program. There is often little difference in the giving interests and procedures of the two vehicles, and they may even be administered by the same staff and board. There *are* significant differences, however, in the type and amount of information available to the public about these two funding vehicles.

By law, corporate foundations must report annually on their activities and grant programs to the IRS on the same Form 990-PF used by all private foundations. Many corporate foundations also issue annual reports or informational brochures detailing their program interests and application procedures. In contrast, corporations are *not* required to inform the public about contributions and grants made directly through the corporation. As a result, even with a growing number of corporations choosing to publicize their giving interests, restrictions, and application procedures, it is generally much more difficult to research direct corporate giving programs.

Information on more than 1,700 corporate foundations and 600-plus direct-giving programs is provided in the 3rd edition of the *National Directory of Corporate Giving*. Many of the Foundation Center's other directories and guides also highlight corporate giving. Chapter 9 of this book covers the do's and don'ts of corporate grantseeking in some detail. In addition, Appendix A provides an extensive bibliography of directories and monographs on corporate funding.

To find out about corporations in your community and/or in a specific industry, check with the business reference department of your local public library for sources such as *Standard and Poor's Register of Corporations*, the *Dun and Bradstreet Reference Book of Corporate Management*, Chamber of Commerce directories, and corporate annual reports. Another readily available but commonly overlooked resource is your local Yellow Pages.

As corporate budgets become leaner, many companies will increase their donations of goods and services to offset reduced cash support. These "in-kind" contributions can include product overruns or obsolete models manufactured or distributed by the company, office space or furniture and equipment, paper and printing services, and management or technical advice from company employees. Again, the information provided in subsequent chapters outlines some of the approaches and resources nonprofit organizations can use to tap this important funding source.

Individual Donors

Individual support is an essential component of most fundraising efforts. In fact, according to *Giving USA*, individuals are by far the largest single source of private philanthropic dollars—$110 billion in 1992. The 1980s were characterized by a steady and substantial increase in per capita individual giving, reversing a declining trend in the 1970s. This reversal can be attributed to lower inflation, sharply lower income tax rates after 1986, and increased fundraising efforts prompted by cutbacks in federal funding for social and human services.

Individual contributions range from a few pennies to millions of dollars and from used appliances and clothing to priceless art collections. Many individuals also contribute another priceless resource—their time—although it's seldom counted in dollars and cents.

The list of techniques used by nonprofit organizations to raise money from individual donors is long and varied, and includes direct-mail appeals, door-to-door solicitation, membership programs, special fundraising events, and deferred-giving programs. A good many guides and handbooks detailing these approaches have been published, and a number of them are listed in the bibliography in Appendix A.

Earned Income

With the retrenchment in federal funding of the nonprofit sector since 1980, more and more nonprofits have turned to income-producing ventures and new dues and fees structures to cover their operating costs. For many nonprofit organizations this simply has meant establishing a fee structure for goods and services they had previously supplied free of charge. Others have looked to capitalize on their existing resources by renting out unused office or meeting space; leasing computer time, services, or equipment; or offering consulting or information services to businesses and clients who can afford to pay. Still others have adopted a more ambitious approach to raising funds through ventures such as gift shops, publications, travel services, and the like.

Religious Organizations

Churches, temples, and other religious organizations are more often thought of as recipients of charitable contributions than as potential funding sources. Yet according to a 1992 survey commissioned by Independent Sector, *From Belief to Commitment: The Activities and Finances of Religious Congregations in the United States,* $6.6 billion of the $47.6 billion in expenditures reported by congregations in 1991, or some 14 percent, was spent on donations to organizations, both within and outside specific denominations.

While many religious institutions operate their own service programs, the same survey revealed that, on average, congregations contributed about one-fifth of their total donations to organizations outside their denomination for activities they wished to promote. These activities include a range of direct social service programs, grassroots and advocacy programs, and education and research.

While relatively little has been written about how best to approach religious institutions for funding support, a few directories and guides have appeared in recent years. The *Church Funding Resource Guide,* edited by Mary Eileen Paul and Linda Clements, is one of many respected publications in the field. Information on other religious funding sources is included in Appendix A.

Chapter 3

Who Gets Foundation Grants?

The overwhelming majority of foundation grants are awarded to nonprofit organizations that qualify for "public charity" status under Section 501(c)(3) of the Internal Revenue Code. An organization may qualify for this tax-exempt status if it is organized and operated exclusively for charitable, religious, educational, scientific, or literary purposes; monitors public safety; fosters national or international amateur sports competition (but only if its activities do not involve the provision of athletic facilities or equipment); or is active in the prevention of cruelty to children or animals. These tax-exempt organizations must also certify that no part of their income will benefit private shareholders or individuals and that they will not, as a substantial part of their activities, attempt to influence legislation or participate in political campaigns for or against any candidate for public office.

Under federal law, foundations are permitted to make grants to individuals and organizations that do not qualify for "public charity" status if they follow a set of very specific rules covering "expenditure responsibility." Essentially, the rules for expenditure responsibility involve a number of financial and fiduciary reports certifying that the funds were spent solely for the charitable purposes spelled out in the grant agreement, and that no part of the funds was spent to influence legislation. Provisions for grants to individuals require advance approval of the program by the IRS and prohibit giving to "disqualified persons"—a broad category covering contributors to the foundation and their relatives, foundation managers, and certain public officials. Although some foundations have instituted such giving programs, they represent a small segment of the foundation universe.

Nonprofit Organizations

Foundations award grants to a wide variety of nonprofit organizations. The majority confine their giving to nonprofits that provide services in the foundation's home community. Others restrict their grants to specific types of institutions or organizations active in a particular subject area, such as medical research, higher education, music, or youth services. Still others limit their giving to specific purposes, such as capital campaigns, providing seed money, or bolstering endowments. The research strategies outlined in the chapters that follow are designed to help nonprofits identify funders that are likely to fund organizations similar to their own.

Virtually every grantmaker you identify through these research strategies will want to know that your organization is recognized as a 501(c)(3) organization by the IRS, and most will ask to see a copy of your IRS exemption letter. Depending on the particular state in which your organization is located, the foundation may also wish to see that you've received the appropriate state certification for tax-exempt charitable organizations. If your organization has not yet received tax-exempt status, you'll want to read the IRS booklet *How to Apply for and Retain Tax-Exempt Status for Your Organization* (IRS Publication 557), which includes the actual application forms for Section 501(c)(3) organizations as well as most other tax-exempt organizations. Copies of the booklet can be obtained by calling the tax information number listed under "United States Government, Internal Revenue Service" in your phone directory.

The process of incorporating as a tax-exempt nonprofit organization is regulated under federal, state, and sometimes local law. It is advisable to consult an attorney, preferably one with nonprofit experience, to guide you through the process. There are also a number of handbooks that explain the application procedures and examine the legal ramifications and issues involved in structuring your organization in such a fashion. The bibliography in Appendix A lists publications that can be examined free

FIGURE 6.   How to Form and Operate a Nonprofit Corporation

	Steps	Applicable Form	Results
Articles of Incorporation	Reserve the name of your organization. Prepare Certificate of Incorporation. Includes: purposes and incorporators of the corporation and any other clauses that are required by your State Not-for-Profit Law.	File application for reservation of name with appropriate agency in your state. Obtain necessary consents for name where required. File Articles of Incorporation with your Secretary of State.	Reserves your name so that no other organization can, for a limited period of time, incorporate under that same name in your state. The State recognizes your organization as an Incorporated Nonprofit Organization (i.e. one conducting non-profit activities for charitable, educational, religious, scientific, literary or cultural purposes.)
Federal Employer Identification Number	File with the IRS as a nonprofit, even if you do not have employees.	IRS Form SS-4.	Your organization has an identification number so the IRS can track your reports and 1023 tax exempt application (see below).
Federal Tax Exemption	Determine which section of Internal Revenue Service (IRS) code you are applying under. File with the IRS as a tax exempt organization preferably within 27 months of the date of incorporation.	IRS Publication 557 and IRS Form 1023 or 1024. IRS filing fee is a maximum of $465. See Form IRS 8718.	Recognized by the IRS as exempt from paying income tax on most revenues related to your charitable functions. Donations made to your organization are tax deductible only if you are a 501(c)(3) organization.
State Registration/ and Reporting	Contact the Secretary of State (Corporate Division) and Attorney General (Charities Division)	Registration forms and fiscal annual reports (e.g. New York State/NYCF-1 and New York State G750-497); fee will vary with size of a group's Operating Budget.	Your organization is officially registered as a charity to solicit funds, do business or to own property in your state. You may have to apply for separate exemption under your state's regulations.
Reporting to the IRS	Annually report to the Internal Revenue Service.	Form 990	Provides the IRS with a report of income receipts and disbursements of your income.

of charge at Foundation Center libraries. Figure 6 outlines the basic steps involved in forming a nonprofit corporation.

Although it's often difficult, organizations that do not have tax-exempt status can still participate in the grantseeking process. You may receive funds, for example, from an organization that already is eligible to receive foundation grants and is willing to assume fiscal responsibility for your project on a contract basis. Many of the general fundraising and nonprofit management guides listed in Appendix A outline this and other options in detail.

Individuals

Under the provisions of the 1969 Tax Reform Act, private foundations may make grants to individuals for "travel, study or similar purposes" if they obtain, in advance, approval from the IRS of their selection criteria and procedures. These procedures must ensure an objective selection process and usually involve extensive follow-up reports that demonstrate adequate performance and appropriate expenditures of the grant funds by the individual receiving the grant.

The Foundation Center's research indicates that about 2,250 of the more than 35,000 active private grantmaking foundations currently operate grant programs to individuals. Many of these programs are described in the Center's publication, *Foundation Grants to Individuals*. Nearly two-thirds of these funding programs are for educational aid, including scholarships, fellowships, and loans.

Students seeking financial aid for their education should be sure to consult with the financial aid office at their school. In addition, there are a number of guides and directories that describe grant programs operated by local and state governments, corporations, labor unions, educational institutions, and a variety of trade associations and nonprofit agencies. Many high school and university libraries maintain, and make available free of charge, collections of these funding information resources.

Individuals seeking funds for research or special projects not related to their education may wish to affiliate with a nonprofit organization that can act as a sponsor for a foundation grant. Universities, hospitals, churches, schools, arts organizations, and theaters are just a few of the many types of nonprofits that have received and administered foundation grants for work done by individuals.

There are, as well, a wide variety of funding sources other than foundations that make grants to individuals. Several general reference books (e.g., *The Annual Register of Grant Support*, *The Grants Register*, and *Awards, Honors and Prizes*) describe grant programs run by government agencies, corporations, associations, and nonprofit groups in such diverse fields as sports, religion, medicine, and the performing arts. Foundation Center libraries also maintain a selection of specialized funding guides for individuals interested in specific subject areas or population groups. A comprehensive bibliography of sources on individual scholarships and grants can be found in the Center's publication *Foundation Grants to Individuals*.

Profit-Making Organizations

While foundations generally cannot award grants to profit-making groups, they are permitted under the 1969 Tax Reform Act to make grants to organizations that are not tax-exempt, or have not yet received their exemption, for projects that are clearly charitable in nature, so long as the funders exercise "expenditure responsibility." Foundations may also offer loans or "program- related investments" (PRIs) if a for-profit organization's program or project supports the foundation's funding interests.

Both for-profit and nonprofit organizations may receive PRIs in the form of loans, guarantees, or equity investments, and these allocations may be used to support a variety of projects. PRIs have been made to increase low-income and minority owner-ship of business and property, to aid businesses that cannot find adequate commercial support but whose existence is an important component of the foundation's program goals, and to provide training or employment opportunities for women and in disadvantaged communities. Beyond their immediate benefits, PRIs also help nonprof-its leverage support from more traditional funding sources.

Unlike grants, PRIs must be repaid—generally with interest—and are governed by strict regulations that mandate greater administrative attention than conventional grants. In addition, foundations must prove that PRI funds are spent only for the designated charitable purpose and that the loan recipient could not have secured funding through traditional financial channels. Despite these restrictions, a number of foundations report an interest in, or have a history of making, program-related investments.

Grantseekers interested in program-related investments should contact the Coop-erative Assistance Fund (CAF) and the Local Initiatives Support Corporation (LISC) for further information. CAF represents several foundations that pool their funds to make program-related investments for the economic development of low-income urban and rural communities in the metropolitan Washington, D.C., area. Its annual report and criteria for investments can be obtained by writing to the Cooperative

Assistance Fund, 655 15th Street, N.W., Suite 375, Washington, D.C., 20005. LISC is a nonprofit lending and grantmaking institution that assists experienced community development corporations in improving the physical and economic conditions of their communities. You can obtain a basic information packet by writing to Local Initiatives Support Corporation, 733 Third Avenue, 8th Floor, New York, NY 10017.

Two Foundation Center publications, *The Foundation 1000* and *The Foundation Directory*, identify foundations interested in program-related investments in their types of support indexes. Further information on how to use these resources is provided in subsequent chapters of this guide.

Chapter 4

Planning Your Funding
Research Strategies

Grantmakers receive thousands of requests for funding every year, as the competition for foundation resources grows ever more intense. It is estimated that less than 7 percent of these requests actually result in support. Many requests go unfunded because there are simply not enough resources to go around; others are denied because the proposal clearly falls outside the funder's interests. Proposals may also fail because they are poorly prepared or do not reflect a careful analysis of the applicant organization's needs, its credibility, or its capacity to carry out the project as proposed. (See Chapter 10 for detailed recommendations on proposal writing.)

The key to any successful fundraising effort is homework, beginning with a careful analysis of your organization, the formulation of a clear idea of where it's going, and the development of a concrete plan for getting there. Once you have completed such an assessment, you're ready to begin tracking those foundations whose stated objectives and grantmaking priorities are directly related to your organization's goals and needs. All this takes time.

Faced with this reality, many grantseekers look for ways around the funding research process. They mail copies of their proposal to such easily targeted groups as the largest foundations in the United States or their own geographic region, or to foundations whose names are well known. Rarely does this approach work. Most funders are only too familiar with the mass-mailing technique, and groups that employ it do their causes harm. Grantseekers are well advised, instead, to do their homework carefully and be sure to let it show. Explore all the resources described in this guide, and let the funders you approach know exactly why you believe your program matches their interests.

Know Your Program

The importance of program planning cannot be overstated. Yet far too many nonprofit organizations get so caught up in their daily tasks and problems that they give the process short shrift. Simply stated, there is nothing more important than the careful analysis and planning of your organization's programs and financial needs. Without it, no amount of funding research will save the day. Scores of useful guides and handbooks on program planning and nonprofit management are available. Many of these publications are listed in the bibliography in Appendix A. Whatever procedures you adopt, however, there are several items you need to take care of *before* you can plot your research strategy.

1. You need to see that your organization is structured so it is eligible to receive foundation and corporate grants. As we noted in Chapter 3, most foundations limit their giving to organizations that have received 501(c)(3) tax-exempt status from the IRS; the procedures outlined in this section will focus on such groups. Individuals seeking grant support should refer to the resources mentioned in the previous chapter.

2. You need to be able to transmit verbally and in writing a clear picture of the purpose of the program for which you are seeking support.

3. You need to delineate the type of support required (e.g., general operating, capital, seed money).

4. You need a formal budget indicating the precise amount of money you hope to raise and how it will be spent.

Research Strategies

Once you have analyzed and pinpointed your organization's funding needs, you can begin to develop a strategy for identifying potential funders. Although there are a variety of approaches to uncovering appropriate funding sources, all of them boil down to three basic steps:

1. Developing a broad list of prospects—that is, foundations and/or corporate grantmakers that have shown an interest in funding programs or some aspect of programs similar to your own.

2. Refining your list of prospects to eliminate those grantmakers that seem unable or unlikely to fund projects in your subject field or geographic area, or that do not provide the type or amount of support you need.

3. Investigating thoroughly the funders remaining on your list to determine which ones are most likely to consider your proposal favorably.

Again, the key to success is *doing your homework*. Identifying potential funders requires serious, time-consuming research, but it is not so difficult as to be beyond the reach of most grantseekers.

STEP ONE: DEVELOPING A BROAD PROSPECT LIST

The first step in funding research is to identify foundations and corporate grantmakers that have indicated in their statements of purpose or by their recent grantmaking activities an interest in funding programs or organizations similar to your own. In analyzing your organization and its funding needs, you should look at the subject fields in which your group is active, the geographic area it serves, and the type and amount of grant support you need. To help you determine the best research approach for your funding needs, see the checklist "Know Your Program" (Figure 7). Our experience at the Foundation Center has led us to recommend three basic strategies when developing a broad list of funding prospects:

1. The **subject approach** identifies funders that have expressed an interest in your specific subject field or population group focus.

2. The **geographic approach** identifies grantmakers that fund programs in a specific city, state, or region.

29

FIGURE 7.   Know Your Program

A successful funding research strategy must be based on a realistic appraisal of the types of funders that are most likely to be interested in your project. Your first step, then, is to get all relevant aspects of you own program clearly in focus.

1. Is your organization structured to receive foundation and/or corporate support? (Note date of IRS ruling or agreement with qualified sponsoring organization.) _____

_____

_____

2. What is the central purpose of the activity for which you are seeking funding? _____

_____

_____

    (a) What is the *subject* focus of the activity? _____

    _____

    _____

    (b) What *population groups* will benefit from the activity?

    _____

    _____

    (c) What *geographic* area will be served by the activity? Will this project have an impact beyond that geographic area?

    _____

    _____

FIGURE 7.   Know Your Program (continued)

3. How does this activity fit into the central purpose of your organization?

_____

_____

4. What are the unique qualifications of your organization and/or staff to accomplish the proposed activity?

_____

_____

5. What is the total budget for the project? _____

(a) What *type of support* (e.g., building funds, equipment, operating support) are you seeking? _____

_____

(b) How *much* grant support are you seeking? _____

(c) What *other sources* of support will be used to meet the project costs?

_____

(d) How will the project be funded for the *long term?* _____

_____

6. Who has supported or expressed an interest in your organization's programs? (Note past and current funders, members of the board of directors, volunteeers, community leaders, etc.)

_____

_____

The Foundation Center

31

3. The **types of support approach** identifies foundations that provide specific types of support (e.g., construction or renovation funds, research funds, endowment money, program-related investments, and so on) to nonprofit organizations.

We'll examine each of these strategies in greater detail in later chapters. The Foundation Center recommends that you conduct both a subject search to identify funders with an interest in your field and/or the population group you serve and a geographic search to pinpoint grantmakers likely to support your organization because of the service it provides to the funder's home community. If your fundraising campaign is geared to a specific type of support, you should pursue that approach as well.

During the initial phase of your research you should focus on certain basic facts about the funders you uncover. While you may want to develop your own prospect worksheet, the contents should include the following elements: the funder's name and location; the subject and geographic focus of its grantmaking activities; any stated restrictions or limitations it places on its grants; the size and type of grant it typically awards; and its application procedures, if any. The "Prospect Worksheet" (Figure 8) is the format the Foundation Center recommends to grantseekers using its libraries.

STEP TWO: REFINING YOUR LIST

Once you have developed a broad list of funding prospects, you need to narrow it down to those grantmakers whose interests are similar to your own and therefore warrant further research. You should eliminate funders on your list that:

1. do not fund projects in your geographic area, even though they may have an interest in your subject field;
2. do not fund projects in your subject field, even though they are located in your community or provide the type of support you are seeking;
3. do not provide the type of support you need (e.g., they do not fund general operating expenses or endowment campaigns).

If you follow the research strategies presented in this guide, you should be able to compile a manageable list of funders that merit in-depth investigation without overlooking potential prospects.

FIGURE 8.   Prospect Worksheet

Date:	Funder	Your Organization
1. Name, Address, Contact Person		n/a

2. Financial Data
    Total Assets
    Total Grants Paid
    Grant Ranges/Amount Needed
    Period of Funding/Project
		n/a
		n/a

3. Subject Focus (list in order of importance)	1. 2. 3.	1. 2. 3.
4. Population(s) Served		
5. Geographic Limits		
6. Type(s) of Support		
7. Type(s) of Recipients		
8. People (officers, donors, trustees, staff)		
Application information: Does the funder have printed guidelines/application forms? Initial approach (letter of inquiry, formal proposal): Deadline(s): Board meeting date(s):		
Sources of above information: ❏ 990-PF (Year:) ❏ Directories and grant indexes ❏ Annual report (Year:) ❏ Other ❏ Requested ❏ Received		
Notes:		
Follow-up:		
The Foundation Center		

STEP THREE: FINDING YOUR MOST LIKELY PROSPECTS

The final phase of your research will focus on identifying those prospects that seem most likely to consider your proposal favorably. During this phase you will be gathering information on the funder's staff and trustees, its current financial status, its application procedures, and its most recent grantmaking activities. Background information on the foundation's donors or sponsoring company, financial and institutional history, current guidelines, and future plans will not only help you to eliminate prospects that are unlikely to provide funding for your proposal but will also aid you in coming up with a more compelling case for that particular funder.

Learning More About Your Funding Prospects

As you work your way through each of the three approaches for identifying potential funding sources, you will gather names of grantmakers that, on the basis of the initial evidence, appear to have an interest in some aspect of your project. Then you will eliminate those that, on closer examination, seem unlikely to consider your proposal favorably.

Finally, you will need to gather the most up-to-date information on those grantmakers you consider to be your best bets. You'll want to note the funder's address, officer and trustee names, assets, gifts received, application procedures, and, most importantly, actual grants awarded in a recent time period. As you assemble these facts, you'll also be looking for answers to the following questions.

Has the funder demonstrated a real commitment to funding in your subject field? You may have noted one or more grants by a particular foundation in your subject field. Upon examining the full grants list, however, you may find that these were the exceptions rather than the rule. They may have been made for reasons other than a true commitment to the field—perhaps because of a special relationship between the recipient organization and a foundation board member, for example. Some foundations have historic and continuing relationships with particular institutions (e.g., ties to the donor's family or some specified interest of the donor) that may cause them to fund activities that do not fall within their normal giving patterns. In other cases, grants may have been awarded because the funder is committed to the recipient's location rather than its field of endeavor.

Does it seem likely that the funder will make grants to organizations in your geographic location? Although it isn't necessary for a foundation to have actually made grants in your state or city to remain on your list, you should examine grant records carefully for either implied or explicit geographic restrictions. Be on the lookout for local or regional giving patterns or concentrations in rural or urban areas that might exclude your project. Corporate grantmakers, of course, almost always restrict their funding to locales where they do business or have plants, subsidiaries, or corporate headquarters.

Does the amount of money you are requesting fit within the funder's typical grant range? Obviously you should not request $25,000 from a foundation that has never made a grant larger than $10,000. At the same time, look for more subtle distinctions. If a foundation's arts grants range from $10,000 to $20,000 and its social welfare grants are in the $3,000 to $5,000 range, consider what that says about its emphasis. About 50 percent of this "weeding out" process is common sense; the rest is intuition.

Does the funder have a policy prohibiting grants for the type of support you are requesting? Many foundations will not make grants for operating budgets. Others will not provide funds for endowment, physical plant, or equipment. Be sure the funder is willing to award the type of support you need.

Does the funder like to make grants to cover the full cost of a project, or does it favor projects where other funders share the burden? "Partnerships" is one of the buzz words among today's funders. Look for evidence of two or more grantmakers joining forces to fund a project. The trick, of course, is to secure the initial interest. Once the first supporter signs on, others tend to fall into place.

Does the funder put limits on the length of time it is willing to support a project? Some foundations favor one-time grants, while others will continue their support over a number of years. It is rare to find grantmakers that will commit funding to an organization for an indefinite period of time, however. Be sure you can point to possible avenues of support for the future before approaching funders. Many funders will expect you to have thought through a long-term funding plan for any project in which they might be asked to participate.

What types of organizations does the funder tend to support? Does it favor large, well-established groups such as symphonies, universities, and museums, or does it lean toward grassroots community groups? A funder's past recipients will give you an excellent feel for its focus. Look carefully at the mix of its recipients for clues that may not be stated explicitly in its printed guidelines.

Does the funder have application deadlines, or does it review proposals continuously? Note carefully any information you uncover about deadlines and board meeting dates so you can submit your proposal at the appropriate time. Be aware, as well, that the time elapsed between the submission of your proposal and notification of actual receipt of a grant may be considerable—rarely less than three months and often up to six months or more. In planning your program, be sure to allow enough time to obtain the necessary funding.

Do you or does anyone on your board know someone connected with a potential funder? You'll want to gather background information on the foundation or corporate funder's sponsoring company as well as its current staff and trustees. In doing so, you may find some unexpected connections between your organization and a potential funder that will make it easier to approach the funder. Make a list of individuals that have supported or expressed an interest in your organization and its programs. Include past and current donors, board members, volunteers, and "friends." See if there are any obvious links between these individuals and the funder's board and/or staff. The savvy fundraiser is constantly working to establish these kinds of connections. While "knowing somebody" who is affiliated with a prospective funder usually is not enough to win you a grant, it does tend to facilitate the process.

Large and Small Foundations

When we described the world of foundations in Chapter 1, we noted that of the more than 35,000 active grantmaking foundations, only 6,700 or so (those qualifying for inclusion in *The Foundation Directory*) have assets of more than $2 million or annual giving totaling at least $200,000. Even among these 6,700 foundations, the number of large, staffed foundations is relatively small. The distinctions we make between "large" and "small" foundations are similar to those one would make between staffed and unstaffed or national versus locally oriented foundations. Although it's risky to make generalizations, the differences between these two categories of grantmakers should be kept in mind as you research and approach particular funders.

By definition, **larger foundations** have more money to give away. Their grants also tend to be larger. In many cases, they have paid staff to review and investigate proposals, develop programs, speak with grantseekers, and carry out the directives of the board of trustees. They usually have well-developed statements of interests and make information on these interests, as well as their application requirements, available to the public through annual reports or brochures. The existence of a staff generally permits them to respond to requests for information about their particular programs. Foundation staffers may also participate in panel discussions, attend conferences or workshops, and act as spokespersons for the field as a whole.

Together, these factors give larger, staffed foundations greater visibility than smaller, unstaffed foundations. This visibility, in turn, ensures that they receive a greater number of proposals than smaller foundations, which results in increased competition for their grants. Because of the wide range of proposals they receive, large foundations may be highly selective even within their own narrowly defined areas of interest. Wishing to maximize their investments, their decision makers tend to be particularly interested in funding model or prototype projects with the potential for national or regional impact within their particular areas of interest.

It is easier to learn about larger foundations for a variety of reasons. Many of the larger foundations publish materials describing their interests and activities. More than 900 foundations state that they issue an annual report, usually the most complete and up-to-date source of information available. More than two-thirds of the foundations currently publishing such reports can be considered large foundations, with assets of more than $2 million or annual grant programs totaling more than $200,000.

Published directories also tend to focus on the larger foundations, describing anywhere from 100 to 8,000 of the top foundations, depending upon the criteria for inclusion. Newspaper articles and journals that cover foundation-related subjects generally concentrate on the largest foundations as well. It is usually best to begin researching large foundations by the subject areas in which they have made grants or stated an interest. Your research strategy should be to identify all large foundations with a demonstrated interest in your subject area and then to thoroughly investigate each one of them to be sure your particular project fits their general funding pattern in terms of (a) the size of the grant, (b) the geographic scope of the project, (c) the type of support needed, and (d) the type of recipient organization you represent.

Smaller foundations usually are oriented toward giving in their own geographic areas, which may be defined as a city, county, or state. Within these stated boundaries, however, they often support a wide range of activities. Although their grants are smaller, they are more likely to give general operating support as opposed to grants for specific projects; they also may be inclined to continue their support for longer periods of time and to award repeat funding. With smaller foundations, geographic location tends to be a more significant factor than the subject focus of your proposal. And the lack of staff makes personal contact with foundation board members more desirable when seeking funds from smaller foundations.

If your organization seems likely to fit the interests of a smaller foundation because of the size of your grant request or the local impact of your proposed project, your research strategy should begin with the development of a complete list of foundations that make grants in your geographic area. Your next step should be to investigate each foundation in your area to find those that (a) make grants of a size that fits your needs, (b) make grants for the type of support you are seeking, (c) are not restricted to funding designated or "preselected" recipient organizations, and (d) are not restricted to funding subject areas different from your own.

Financial Data

Carefully examine the available financial data. Although it's often mystifying to first-time grantseekers, data from foundation 990-PF forms, annual reports, and published directories generally include information on assets, grants awarded, and gifts received. Learning to interpret these figures can provide important clues about the funding patterns of a particular grantmaker. Has the foundation or corporation received any large contributions in recent years that might increase its grantmaking potential? Has there been an increase or decrease in the funder's assets in recent years? Might it be going out of business? These are the factors that can affect the amount of money available for grants, as well as the size and type of grants awarded. Of course, general economic conditions will also affect a foundation's assets and gifts received (especially true for corporate grantmakers), which in turn will have a substantial impact on the amount of money it has to give away.

Record Keeping

Throughout the research process you should gather as many pertinent facts about your funding prospects as possible. Develop careful files. Each record of a potential funder should include the following information:

—address
—telephone/fax numbers
—names of trustees and officers
—names of staff
—financial data
—funding patterns

—sample grants

—any prior contacts between your organization and the funder

These records should be updated on a regular basis to provide a dynamic, consolidated base of funding information for your organization. Developing such a system helps to compensate for one of the biggest problems nonprofits face—the lack of continuity in fundraising efforts resulting from staff turnover.

It is important to document your research at every step along the way. As you gather facts about a funder, note the source and date of the information so that later on, if you come across conflicting information, you can quickly determine which is more current. While such attention to detail at the outset may seem needlessly time consuming, careful record keeping is guaranteed to save you and your organization time and money in the long run.

You also need to keep track of each and every contact between representatives of your organization and a staff or board member at a funding institution. Such contacts might include letters of inquiry, formal proposals, and supporting documents; informational and follow-up phone calls; interviews and site visits; and reports, press releases, and invitations to events. Each record should include the date and the initials of the individual who made the contact. Figure 9 is a sample all-purpose form for keeping track of contacts with potential funders. It can also serve as a "tickler" or reminder sheet to let you know when the next steps need to be taken.

FIGURE 9.   Record of Funding Contacts

Funder (name & address): _____

_____

Principal Contact (name & title): _____

_____

Telephone Calls   Type of Call

                                    Appointment [ ]   Status   [ ]
Date(s): _____   Mat'ls Rec'd [ ]   Submit   [ ]
                                    _____ [ ]   Rejection [ ]
Time(s): _____   (Other)

Call from: _____

Spoke to: _____

Comments: _____

_____

MEETINGS	Date: Time: Outcome:	
PROPOSALS	Date submitted: Format: Signed by: Board meeting date(s):	For project: Amount requested:
TICKLER	Deadline: To do: Follow up:	By whom: By whom:
DECISION Notification date: Reason for rejection:		NEXT STEP Resubmit Cultivation: Special activities: Send report:
The Foundation Center		

Chapter 5

Resources for
Funding Research

A wide range of materials is available to help you identify sources of support for your organization or project. The types and number of resources you use will depend upon the type of support you are seeking and the search strategy you adopt to identify appropriate funding sources. Before you can plan an effective search strategy, however, you have to become familiar with the basic resources available to you.

Materials that describe the grantmaking universe fall into four general categories: indexes to grants awarded in the recent past; general reference directories; specialized funding directories or guides; and materials generated or published by grantmakers, including annual reports, brochures, and information returns filed annually by foundations with the IRS.

Indexes to foundation grants provide listings of actual grants awarded, enabling you to determine the specific subject interests of a foundation, the types and locations of the organizations it funds, the size of the grants it makes, and the types of support it awards.

General reference directories may be national or local in focus and can vary widely in the amount of information they provide. In this chapter we focus on the national directories published by the Foundation Center and the state and local directories available at our Cooperating Collections (see Appendix D). When possible, your research should encompass all pertinent reference books.

Specialized funding directories or guides enable you to concentrate on a particular aspect of your fundraising needs, be it a specific field (e.g., the arts, health), population group (e.g., women, minorities), or type of grantmaker (e.g., corporations, community foundations). Some of the more specialized directories are listed in the bibliography in Appendix A, but you should check with your colleagues or local library to learn about others related to your field. A number of journals, periodicals, and newsletters, particularly those issued by professional, educational, and alumni associations, include features or columns on funding opportunities in specific fields, so be sure to check for such listings as well.

The annual information returns filed by private foundations (Form 990-PF) are often the only source of information on the grantmaking activities and interests of smaller foundations. Other materials issued directly by funders can be used to secure detailed information about those grantmakers you have identified as potential funding sources for your project.

As already noted, our primary focus in this chapter is on foundations. For a more detailed discussion of corporate grantmaking, please see Chapter 9.

Some Important Considerations

Once you have a general overview of the available resources, we'll explore the ways you can put those resources to work for you. Most, if not all, of the materials described here can be consulted at the five Center-operated libraries or the 197 Cooperating Collections listed in Appendix D. Although some of the directories and publications described may be useful additions to your organization's library, we recommend that, initially, grantseekers invest their time rather than their money. Visit one of our library collections and examine the materials relating to your area of interest before making any decisions as to which publications to purchase.

When you are examining a publication, pay attention to the quality of the information as well as its relevance to your funding search. It is especially important to:

- note the date the book was published and whether or not it's the most current edition available;

- read the introduction and any instructions on how to use the book, paying particular attention to how the information was obtained, how current it is, and what verification procedures, if any, were used in obtaining it;

- familiarize yourself with the book's format, indexes, and the kinds of information about potential funding sources it contains.

Taking the time to evaluate resources for their accuracy and thoroughness prior to using them can save you countless hours that might otherwise be wasted.

The Foundation Center's Databases

The Foundation Center implemented the use of a computerized database in 1972. Since that time the database has grown both in size and quality. Currently, its nearly 2 million records provide detailed information on 663,856 grants and 56,981 currently operating and terminated foundations. Online editorial screens permit Center staff to access any grantmaker entry in the system, including background data on the grantmaker; its purpose, programs, and donors; the names of its officers and trustees; its current financial data; and its grantmaker publication records.

In addition to the foundation database, the Center also maintains a bibliographic database that contains listings for some 10,000 books and articles pertaining to philanthropy, fundraising, foundations, and the nonprofit sector.

The Center makes the foundation information in its database available to a broader public through two online files managed by DIALOG Information Services (Tel: 800-334-2564). The comprehensive Foundation Directory file (File 26) includes descriptions of more than 35,000 grantmakers, including foundations, company-sponsored foundations, corporate giving programs, community foundations, and operating foundations. This file, which is updated twice a year, corresponds to the following Foundation Center publications: *The Foundation Directory*, *The Foundation Directory Part 2*, the *National Directory of Corporate Giving*, and the *Guide to U.S. Foundations, Their Trustees, Officers, and Donors*. (See below for detailed descriptions of these publications.)

The Foundation Grants Index file (File 27) provides information on grants of $10,000 or more (going back to 1983) made by some 1,000 foundations, including the 300 largest. The file, which is updated five times a year and does not include grants awarded directly to individuals, corresponds to the following Foundation Center publications: *The Foundation Grants Index*, *The Foundation Grants Index Quarterly*, and the *Grant Guide* series (covering 30 separate funding areas).

THE *USER MANUAL AND THESAURUS*

To search either of these files efficiently, grantseekers should refer to a copy of the *User Manual and Thesaurus for The Foundation Directory and The Foundation Grants Index*. Using controlled vocabulary and descriptor codes, the *User Manual* offers helpful advice and examples of search strategies that will aid you in refining, mapping, and broadening your search. The *User Manual* is available through the Foundation Center; for further information, call (212) 620-4230.

ADVANTAGES OF A COMPUTER SEARCH

Searching the Center's database on DIALOG can save you countless hours of painstaking research. In a relatively short amount of time, thousands of foundation profiles and grant records can be scanned. Those relating to a specific search can then be downloaded with a few simple keystrokes.

Flexibility is another advantage of a DIALOG search. You can combine several elements—for example, year, subject, type of support, geographic constraints, and intended population group—in one search statement. Or you can search for potential corporate grantmakers by asset size, specifying geographic constraints and/or a company foundation's past grantmaking activities.

QUESTIONS ABOUT DIALOG

Grantseekers interested in becoming DIALOG subscribers can call (800) 334-2564 for further information.

DIALOG users seeking general information about File 26 or File 27 should call the Reference Desk at the Foundation Center in New York; Tel: (212) 620-4230.

Experienced DIALOG users with specific questions relating to search strategies in either file can receive assistance at the same number through the Foundation Center's online file support.

The Grants Classification System

The Foundation Center began to record and categorize grants in 1961. It established a computerized grants reporting system in 1972. From 1979 to 1988 the Center relied on a "facet" classification system, employing a fixed vocabulary of four-letter codes that permitted categorization of each grant by subject, type of recipient, population group, type of support, and scope of grant activity.

In 1989, following explosive growth in the number of grants indexed annually, the Center introduced a new classification system with links to the National Taxonomy of Exempt Entities (NTEE), a comprehensive coding scheme developed by the National Center for Charitable Statistics that established a unified national standard for classifying nonprofit organizations while permitting a multidimensional structure for analyzing grants. Equally important, the new system provided a more concise and consistent hierarchical method with which to classify and index grants.

The new system uses two- or three-character alpha-numeric codes to track institutional fields and entities, governance or auspices, population groups, geographic focus, and types of support awarded. The universe of institutional fields is organized into 26 "major field" areas (A to Z), following the divisions established by the NTEE. The first letter of each code denotes the field, such as "A" for Arts and "B" for Education. Within each alpha subject area, numbers 20 to 99 identify services, disciplines, or types of institutions unique to that field, organized in a hierarchical structure. These sub-categories cover most activities in the nonprofit field. As a result, hundreds of specific terms can be researched with consistent results and grant dollars can be tallied to determine distribution patterns.

While based on NTEE, the Center's system added indexing elements not part of the original taxonomy, including the ability to track awards to government-sponsored organizations such as public schools, state universities, and municipal or federal agencies; a secondary set of codes to classify 34 specific types of grant support; and a third set of codes to track 40 different grant beneficiary populations. More evolutionary than revolutionary, the new system does introduce two new fields not previously tracked by the Foundation Center: Auspices (NTEE's governance codes are used) and Country of Activity (not part of NTEE). This last field is used to track the foreign locations of grant activities—for example, an award to the New York office of UNESCO for relief services in Ethiopia.

Indexes to Foundation Grants

Indexes to foundation grants help you identify funders with a demonstrated interest in your subject or geographic area by listing the actual grants they have awarded. Studying listings of grants a foundation has recently awarded will give you a better understanding of a foundation's giving priorities in terms of the types of programs and organizations it likes to fund, the amount of money it awards for specific programs, the geographic area in which it concentrates its grantmaking activities, the population groups it serves through its grants, and the types of support it offers.

The Foundation Center currently maintains computer files on reported grants of $10,000 and more awarded by about 1,000 major foundations, including the nation's 500 largest. The Center's database currently contains more than 600,000 grant records. Some 5,000 new records are added to the database every three months and an additional 40,000 records are added at the end of the year. The information included in the database is made available to grantseekers in a wide variety of formats designed to facilitate their individual funding searches.

Each grant record includes the name and state location of the grantmaker as well as that of the recipient organization, the amount of the grant and its duration, and a brief description of the purpose for which the grant was made. When applicable, a statement outlining geographic, subject, or other restrictions on the grantmaker's giving program is also provided (see Figure 10). Foundation Center editors analyze and index each grant by subject focus, type of recipient organization, population group served, and the type of support awarded (e.g., endowment, research, building and equipment).

There are four types of grant-based publications produced from the Center's database: *The Foundation Grants Index* annual volume, *The Foundation Grants Index Quarterly,* the *Grant Guide* series, and *Who Gets Grants/Who Gives Grants*. Each type of publication is designed to offer a different mode of access to the grants information in the database. As you become more skilled at foundation research, you'll be able to determine which of the formats will be most useful, but in the beginning it's a good idea to use and become familiar with all of them.

FIGURE 10.   Sample Grant Record from the Foundation Center's Database

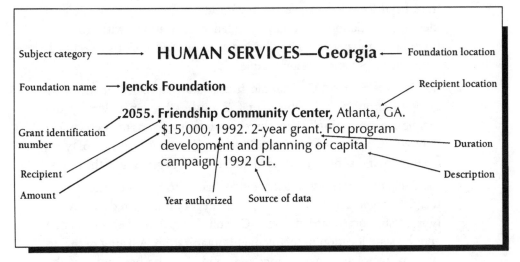

THE FOUNDATION GRANTS INDEX

During the course of a year the Foundation Center receives information about thousands of grants. This information is entered into the database and compiled for inclusion in *The Foundation Grants Index.* To date, this is the most comprehensive subject index to actual grants made by major U.S. foundations.

The Foundation Grants Index offers access to information on approximately 54 percent of all grant dollars awarded annually by private foundations. The volume is divided into major subject fields, under which grants are arranged by state, then alphabetically by foundation name. Grants are listed alphabetically under the appropriate foundation by the name of the recipient organization. The volume's several indexes enable you to customize your search according to your needs:

■   the Subject Index identifies grants by keywords and phrases describing a specific subject focus (e.g., "Ballet," "Environment," "Physics"), the population group served (e.g., "Aging," "Hispanics," "Women"), the type of recipient organization (e.g., "Museum," "Boys Club," "Hospital"), or the type of support (e.g., "Fellowships," "University Endowment," "Publication"). Each grant may be indexed under a number of different keywords and phrases.

- the Recipient Name Index helps you to locate records of grants that have been awarded to specific organizations, making it possible to identify foundations that have funded organizations with goals or programs similar to yours. The index is divided into two sections: domestic (U.S.) and foreign recipients.

- the Type of Support/Geographic Index is an alphabetical index by types of support and subject that is further broken down by the recipient organization's state, thereby providing access to grants made in broad subject fields and specific geographic areas. A listing of types of support and subject fields is included at the beginning of the index.

- the Recipient Category Index provides access to grants by the type of recipient organization. Each recipient category is broken down by the type of support awarded (e.g., "Capital Campaign," "Endowment") and the state location of the recipient organization. A listing of the 36 types of recipient organizations is included at the beginning of the index.

- the Index to Grants by Foundation allows you to access a foundation's complete grants list. The index is arranged alphabetically by state, then by foundation name. For each foundation, grants are listed alphabetically by subject field.

The Foundation Grants Index can be used to get a broad overview of a specific foundation's giving priorities, to survey foundation giving within a state, to evaluate giving to a particular recipient or recipient type, and/or to identify the subject areas that currently are most attractive to private foundations.

GRANT GUIDES

Because many grantseekers want to focus their funding search on a particular subject, the Foundation Center publishes a series of books that lists grants from the annual Grants Index in a more specialized format. Grant Guides are available in 30 subject areas. Each Guide is a "mini" Grants Index, listing grants of $10,000 and more arranged by foundation name and location, as well as by subject keywords. Grant Guides are currently available in the following areas:

1. Aging
2. Alcohol & Drug Abuse
3. Arts, Culture & the Humanities
4. Children & Youth
5. Community Development, Housing & Employment
6. Crime, Law Enforcement & Abuse Prevention
7. Elementary & Secondary Education
8. Environmental Protection & Animal Welfare
9. Film, Media & Communications
10. Foreign & International Programs
11. Health Programs for Children & Youth
12. Higher Education
13. Homeless
14. Hospitals, Medical Care & Research
15. Libraries & Information Services
16. Literacy, Reading & Adult/ Continuing Education
17. Matching & Challenge Support
18. Medical & Professional Health Education
19. Mental Health, Addictions & Crisis Services
20. Minorities
21. Physically & Mentally Disabled
22. Public Health & Disease
23. Public Policy & Public Affairs
24. Recreation, Sports & Athletics
25. Religion, Religious Welfare & Religious Education
26. Scholarship, Student Aid & Loans
27. Science & Technology
28. Social & Political Programs
29. Social Services
30. Women & Girls

THE FOUNDATION GRANTS INDEX QUARTERLY

Foundation grants are reported to the Center and entered into the database throughout the year. Every three months that information is gathered and published in *The Foundation Grants Index Quarterly*. Approximately 5,000–7,000 recently awarded grants are listed in each edition of the *Quarterly*, which includes indexes to the recipient organizations as well as the subject focus of each grant. Because the *Quarterly* provides timely grants data, it is an ideal way for grantseekers to keep abreast of the changing giving priorities of major funders.

The *Quarterly* also includes two other features that have relevance to your funding search:

■   "Updates on Grantmakers," which notes changes in name, staff, address, telephone numbers, giving interests, and application procedures at the nation's major foundations (see Figure 11).

FIGURE 11.   "Updates on Grantmakers" from *The Foundation Grants Index Quarterly*

The Clara Abbott Foundation, IL
  Telephone: (708) 937-1090
  Officers and Directors: Eugene L. Worock has replaced Charles S. Brown
    as Pres.; Dale E. Stavlo is now V.P.; Robert N. Beck (new); Joseph G.
    Miller (new); James W. Milne (new); David A. Thompson (new).
  Board meeting date(s): Apr. and Oct.

The Abelard Foundation, Inc., CA
  Board meeting date(s): May and Nov.

Akron Community Foundation, OH
  Officers and Trustees: Jody Bacon is now Exec. Dir.; Lolita K. Adair (new);
    Jennifer Blicke (new); Stuart Giller (new); Richard L. Hardgrove (new);
    Kathryn M. Hunter (new).

Alabama Power Foundation, Inc., AL
  Directors: Kenneth A. Deal (new); J. Bruce Jones (new); Anthony J. Topazi
    (new); Christopher C. Womack (new).
  Application information: Applicants for employee-related scholarships
    should contact foundation after Jan. 15 for applications and submission
    guidelines.
  Deadline(s): 1 month prior to board meetings
  Board meeting date(s): Quarterly
  Officers: Charles D. McCrary has replaced Travis J. Bowden as Pres.

AlliedSignal Foundation, NJ
  Address: The zip code is 07962-2245
  Telephone: (201) 455-5877
  Officers and Directors: Lawrence A. Bossidy has replaced Edward L.
    Hennessy as Chair.; Peter M. Kreindler has replaced Brian D. Forrow as
    V.P.; Daniel P. Burnham has replaced Roy H. Ekron.
  Deadline(s): Sept. 1
  Board meeting date(s): Dec.

Alsdorf Foundation, IL
  Application information: Currently not soliciting new grant applications.

American Conservation Association, Inc., NY
  Officers and Trustees: R. Scott Greathead has replaced Franklin E. Parker
    as Secy.

American President Companies Foundation, CA
  Contact: Maryellen Cattani, Sr. V.P. and General Counsel, or Lora Breed,
    Prog. Coord., V.P.
  Telephone: (510) 272-8703
  Limitations: Applications not accepted.
  Purpose and activities: The foundation has two grants programs: a
    Matching Grant Program whereby the foundation will match any
    donation made by an employee to a nonprofit up to $5,000 per
    employee, per year; and a Volunteer Service Program, which will
    award a grant of $500 per year to a nonprofit that an employee is
    involved with on a volunteer basis. Occasionally small one-time gifts
    are granted for special events (school auctions, girl guide projects,
    races, etc.) that have employee participation. The foundation has a
    United Way campaign that matches employee contributions at 55
    percent. Any discretionary funds are directed at youth programs in the
    city of Oakland but the foundations's policy is that donations are not
    made without employee involvement.
  Types of support awarded: Employee matching gifts, in-kind gifts
  Officers and Directors: John M. Lillic is now Pres. and C.E.O.; Maryellen
    Cattani is now Sr. V.P. and General Counsel.

American Skin Association, Inc., NY
  Officers and Directors: Edward O. Cole has replaced George W.
    Hambrick, Jr. as Pres.; Mimi W. Coleman has replaced Edward O. Cole
    as V.P.; John B. Lowry has replaced D. Martin Carter as Secy.

■ "Grantmakers' Publications," which lists brochures, newsletters, corporate giving programs, associations of and annual reports issued by grantmakers. Many of these are available to any organization on request and can be useful additions to your files (see Figure 12).

WHO GETS GRANTS/WHO GIVES GRANTS

With the publication of the second edition of this directory, grantseekers can easily answer a crucial question: Where do other nonprofits get their funding? *Who Gets Grants* provides direct access to grant recipient information, an excellent way to pinpoint new funding prospects for your organization. The second edition lists more than 50,000 grants recently awarded to some 17,000 nonprofit organizations across the country, information that can help you determine which foundations are awarding grants to organizations like yours.

FIGURE 12.   "Grantmakers' Publications" from *The Foundation Grants Index Quarterly*

ANNUAL REPORTS

Alcoa Foundation. 202 Alcoa Bldg. 425 Sixth Ave., Pittsburgh, PA 15219-1850
1992 Annual Report, 54p.

The Aspen Foundation. 400 East Main St., Aspen, CO 81611
1992 Annual Report, 24p.

The Vincent Astor Foundation. 405 Park Ave., New York, NY 10022
1992 Annual Report, 24p.

Baton Rouge Area Foundation. One American Place, Suite 610, Baton Rouge, LA 70825
1992 Annual Report, 48p.

Battle Creek Community Foundation. (Formerly Greater Battle Creek Foundation). One Riverwalk Ctr., 34 West Jackson St., Battle Creek, MI 49017-3505
Annual Report for Year Ended Apr. 30, 1993, 16p.

Greater Battle Creek Foundation (*see* Battle Creek Community Foundation)

Bemis Company Foundation. 222 South Ninth St., No. 2300, Minneapolis, MN 55402-4099. National.
1992 Community Relations Report, 24p.

The William Bingham Foundation. 1250 Leader Bldg., Cleveland, OH 44114. National.
1992 Annual Report, 12p.

The Greater Birmingham Foundation. P.O. Box 131027, Birmingham, AL 35213
1992 Annual Report, 10p.

The Boehm Foundation. 500 Fifth Ave., Suite 2107, New York, NY 10110-0296. National.
1992 Annual Report, 5p.

Community Foundation of Boone County, Inc. P.O. Box 92, 410 West Oak St., Suite 8A, Zionsville, IN 46077
Annual Report for Year Ended Mar. 31, 1993, 5p.

The Lynde and Harry Bradley Foundation, Inc. 777 East Wisconsin Ave., Suite 2285, Milwaukee, WI 53202-5395. National.
Report for Period Aug. 1, 1990 to Dec. 31, 1992, 74p.

Otto Bremer Foundation. Suite 2000, 445 Minnesota St., St. Paul, MN 55101-2107
1992 Annual Report, 40p.

Cabot Family Charitable Trust. c/o Cabot Corp., 75 State St., Boston, MA 02109-1806. National.
1992 Annual Report, 11p.

James & Abigail Campbell Foundation. 828 Fort St. Mall, Suite 500, Honolulu, HI 96813
1992 Annual Report, 20p.

Carlsbad Foundation, Inc. 116 South Canyon St., Carlsbad, NM 88220
Annual Report for Year Ended June 30, 1993, 40p.

Who Gets Grants makes your fundraising research easier by:

- targeting the funders of specific nonprofits;
- listing grants awarded within your field;
- listing grants awarded in your geographic area.

The more than 18,000 nonprofit organizations included in the book are listed alphabetically by state in each of 19 subject areas. Each entry then lists the grants of $10,000 or more that the nonprofit has received. Finally, an index of the grants awarded by each foundation gives you an overview of the funding priorities of the grantmaker you have targeted.

General Reference Directories

General reference directories vary widely in the number of foundations they cover, in their geographic focus, and in the type and amount of information they provide. They can include everything from simple listings of foundations to detailed descriptions of the activities and interests of particular grantmakers. Some directories are national in focus and define the criteria for inclusion by size or type of foundation. Others focus on foundations that are active in a particular subject field or geographic area. As you undertake your search for funding sources, you will probably use a number of different types of directories to identify and find out more about potential funders before submitting your grant request.

GUIDE TO U.S. FOUNDATIONS, THEIR TRUSTEES, OFFICERS, AND DONORS

The *Guide to U.S. Foundations, Their Trustees, Officers, and Donors* is the only directory published by the Center that lists all currently active grantmaking foundations in the United States. Published annually, the *Guide* lists some 29,000 independent foundations, 300 active community foundations, 1,775 corporate foundations, and more than 1,700 grantmaking and 1,600 nongrantmaking operating foundations. For a sample entry from this publication, see Figure 13.

The directory is divided into two separate volumes. Volume One contains five sections. Section One contains all independent, company-sponsored, and community foundations arranged by state and in descending order by total grants paid (see Figure 14). Section Two contains operating foundations arranged by state and in descending order by total assets. Section Three is an appendix of all recently terminated foundations. Section Four is an index of all foundations (see Figure 15). Section Five lists community foundations. Sections Four and Five are arranged alphabetically, giving the state and sequence number for each entry.

Entries in Volume One of the *Guide to U.S. Foundations* may contain any or all of the following: the foundation's name, address, and telephone number; separate application address(es) and contact person(s); establishment date; donors; current financial data, including fiscal year-end date, total grants paid, total assets and asset type, total expenditures, and total gifts received; geographic limitations; publications that the foundation makes available; a listing of officers, trustees, and/or directors; the IRS Employer Identification Number (EIN); and a series of codes that indicate: 1) the type of foundation (CS for company-sponsored, CM for community); 2) its grantmaking status (SE for single-purpose endowment, SB for specified beneficiaries, TN for a

FIGURE 13. Sample Entry from the *Guide to U.S. Foundations*

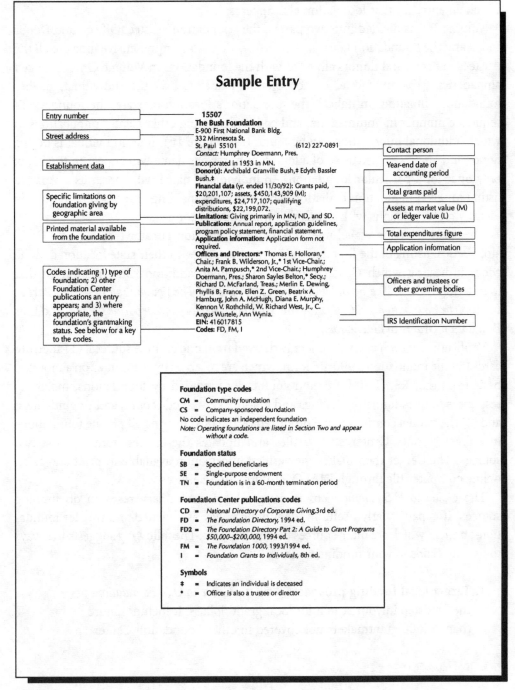

Sample Entry

Entry number — **15507**
The Bush Foundation
E-900 First National Bank Bldg.
Street address — 332 Minnesota St.
St. Paul 55101   (612) 227-0891 — Contact person
Contact: Humphrey Doermann, Pres.

Establishment data — Incorporated in 1953 in MN.
Donor(s): Archibald Granville Bush,‡ Edyth Bassler Bush.‡

Year-end date of accounting period

Financial data (yr. ended 11/30/92): Grants paid, $20,201,107; assets, $450,143,909 (M); expenditures, $24,717,107; qualifying distributions, $22,199,072.

Total grants paid

Specific limitations on foundation giving by geographic area —

Assets at market value (M) or ledger value (L)

Limitations: Giving primarily in MN, ND, and SD.

Printed material available from the foundation —
Publications: Annual report, application guidelines, program policy statement, financial statement.

Total expenditures figure

Application information: Application form not required.

Application information

Officers and Directors:* Thomas E. Holloran,* Chair.; Frank B. Wilderson, Jr.,* 1st Vice-Chair.; Anita M. Pampusch,* 2nd Vice-Chair.; Humphrey Doermann, Pres.; Sharon Sayles Belton,* Secy.; Richard D. McFarland, Treas.; Merlin E. Dewing, Phyllis B. France, Ellen Z. Green, Beatrix A. Hamburg, John A. McHugh, Diana E. Murphy, Kennon V. Rothchild, W. Richard West, Jr., C. Angus Wurtele, Ann Wynia.

Officers and trustees or other governing bodies

Codes indicating 1) type of foundation; 2) other Foundation Center publications an entry appears; and 3) where appropriate, the foundation's grantmaking status. See below for a key to the codes. —

EIN: 416017815

IRS Identification Number

Codes: FD, FM, I

Foundation type codes

CM = Community foundation
CS = Company-sponsored foundation
No code indicates an independent foundation
Note: Operating foundations are listed in Section Two and appear without a code.

Foundation status

SB = Specified beneficiaries
SE = Single-purpose endowment
TN = Foundation is in a 60-month termination period

Foundation Center publications codes

CD = *National Directory of Corporate Giving,*3rd ed.
FD = *The Foundation Directory,* 1994 ed.
FD2 = *The Foundation Directory Part 2: A Guide to Grant Programs $50,000–$200,000,* 1994 ed.
FM = *The Foundation 1000,* 1993/1994 ed.
I   = *Foundation Grants to Individuals,* 8th ed.

Symbols

‡ = Indicates an individual is deceased
* = Officer is also a trustee or director

foundation in a 60-month termination period); and 3) other Center publications in which an entry for that foundation also appears.

Volume Two is divided into two parts—the Foundation Trustee, Officer, and Donor Index and the Foundation Locator. The first section is a comprehensive index to all the trustees, officers, and donors affiliated with the foundations in Volume One. Arranged alphabetically by individual or corporation name, it lists the individual, his/her foundation affiliation (in italics), the foundation's location by state, the foundation's sequence number in Volume One, and codes identifying other Center publications in which additional information can be found (see Figure 16). If an individual is both a donor and an officer or trustee of a foundation, his/her name will appear in the index only once for a particular foundation. An individual's name will appear as a separate listing for each foundation affiliation, however, thus enabling grantseekers to quickly identify all foundations with which that individual is connected.

The second section of Volume Two is the Foundation Locator (see Figure 17), an alphabetical listing of the foundations in Volume One with their state location and the codes indicating which Center publications contain additional information on that foundation (FD for *The Foundation Directory*, FD2 for *The Foundation Directory Part 2*, FM for *The Foundation 1000*, CD for the *National Directory of Corporate Giving*, and I for *Foundation Grants to Individuals*).

Verification of each entry is generally derived from one of three sources: (1) aperture cards* of the foundation's 990-PF form, which are received by the Center on a monthly basis from the IRS; (2) information voluntarily provided by foundations, including responses to questionnaire mailings and grantmaker-issued reports and/or guidelines; and (3) the annual computer tape produced by the IRS covering all private foundations in a given period. Center staff verifies and updates the entries from the first two sources. The Center then makes the verified information available in print and as an online computer file through DIALOG Information Services.

The *Guide to U.S. Foundations* is designed for preliminary research on funding sources. It is particularly useful in identifying newly established and smaller foundations, both of which are often sources of local support. The following suggests five ways to use the *Guide* in your funding research.

1. **Target local funding prospects.** Use the *Guide to U.S. Foundations* as the first step in your search for local grant dollars. It includes more than 20,000 grantmakers not covered in other Foundation Center

---

*a form of microfiche.

publications. Arranged by state, Volume One helps you identify both large and small foundations in your geographic area. You can also check for familiar family names in the Trustee, Officer, and Donor Index to learn more about the giving vehicles of wealthy individuals in your geographic region.

2. **Find a foundation.** Use the Foundation Name Index and Community Foundation Name Index in Volume One to locate the entry for any private or operating foundation.

3. **Follow up giving leads with access to foundation facts.** The foundation entries provide the data you need to decide whether or not to pursue a grant source you've heard mentioned, but need more information on. You can quickly determine the giving potential of a foundation by the current assets and grants listed under each entry. Many entries also list a grantmaker's stated geographic limitations, if any.

4. **Find new philanthropic connections for your organization.** The Trustee, Officer, and Donor Index can help you discover connections between your board members, donors, and volunteers and grantmakers that might be interested in supporting your organization. Using this index, you can determine if an individual has affiliations with other foundations and also uncover the names of people who serve on the same boards.

5. **Locate even more information.** A series of codes in each entry in Volume One and in the indexes in Volume Two shows you which Foundation Center directories include more detailed information on the grantmaker you're researching.

THE FOUNDATION DIRECTORY AND *FOUNDATION DIRECTORY SUPPLEMENT*

The Foundation Directory is the most authoritative and widely used directory of private foundations. It includes descriptions of all grantmaking foundations in the United States with assets of $2 million or more or that award grants totaling at least $200,000 annually. The sixteenth edition of the *Directory*, published in March 1994, includes more than 6,700 foundations, which together account for approximately 90 percent of the total assets and 90 percent of the total grant dollars awarded annually by private foundations.

Each *Directory* entry includes the foundation's name and address; telephone number; establishment data; donors; current financial data, including assets, gifts received,

FIGURE 14. Sample Page from the *Guide to U.S. Foundations*

　　　　　　　　　　　INDEPENDENT, COMPANY-SPONSORED, AND COMMUNITY FOUNDATIONS

CALIFORNIA

752
W. M. Keck Foundation
555 South Flower St., Suite 3230
Los Angeles 90071　　　　(213) 680-3833
Contact: Sandra A. Glass for sciences, engineering, and liberal arts; Joan DuBois for medical research, medical education, law and legal administration, arts and culture, health care, pre-collegiate education, and community services

Established in 1954 and incorporated in 1959 in DE; sole beneficiary of W.M. Keck Trust.
Donor(s): William M. Keck.‡
Financial data (yr. ended 12/31/92): Grants paid, $44,000,000; assets, $844,713,589 (M); expenditures, $47,025,555; qualifying distributions, $44,000,000.
Limitations: Giving nationally in all categories except arts and culture, civic and community, health care, and pre-collegiate education, which is restricted to Southern CA.
Publications: Annual report (including application guidelines), informational brochure (including application guidelines).
Application Information: Only those organizations invited to submit a proposal will receive an Applicant Information Form to be submitted with proposal.
Officers and Directors:* Howard B. Keck,* Chair., Pres., and C.E.O.; Gregory R. Ryan, V.P. and Secy.; Robert A. Day,* V.P.; Walter B. Gerken,* V.P.; W.M. Keck II,* V.P.; Julian O. von Kalinowski,* V.P.; Dorothy A. Harris, Treas.; Lew Allen, Jr., Norman Barker, Jr., Marsh A. Cooper, Naurice G. Cummings, Howard M. Day, Tammis M. Day, Theodore J. Day, Bob Rawls Dorsey, Thomas P. Ford, Erin A. Keck, Howard B. Keck, Jr., John E. Kolb, Max R. Lents, James P. Lower, Kerry K. Mott, Simon Ramo, Arthur M. Smith, Jr., David A. Thomas, C. William Verity, Jr.
EIN: 956092354
Codes: FD, FM

753
The David and Lucile Packard Foundation
300 Second St., Suite 200
Los Altos 94022　　　　(415) 948-7658
Contact: Colburn S. Wilbur, Exec. Dir.

Incorporated in 1964 in CA.
Donor(s): David Packard, Lucile Packard.‡
Financial data (yr. ended 12/31/92): Grants paid, $35,113,000; assets, $871,261,000 (M); gifts received, $53,557,000; expenditures, $40,608,000; qualifying distributions, $38,779,000, including $870,000 for program-related investments.
Limitations: Giving for the arts and community development primarily in Santa Clara, San Mateo, Santa Cruz, and Monterey counties, CA, with some support also in the Pueblo area of CO; national giving for child health and education; national and international giving in Latin America for population and the environment.
Publications: Annual report (including application guidelines), grants list, occasional report, informational brochure (including application guidelines), program policy statement.
Application Information: Application form not required.

Officers and Trustees:* David Packard,* Chair.; Susan Packard Orr,* Pres.; David Woodley Packard,* V.P.; Barbara P. Wright, Secy.; Edwin E. Van Bronkhorst,* Treas.; Colburn S. Wilbur, Exec. Dir.; Nancy Packard Burnett, Robin Chandler Duke, Robert Glaser, M.D., Dean O. Morton, Julie E. Packard, Frank Roberts.
EIN: 942278431
Codes: FD, FM

754
The William and Flora Hewlett Foundation
525 Middlefield Rd., Suite 200
Menlo Park 94025　　　　(415) 329-1070
Contact: David P. Gardner, Pres.

Incorporated in 1966 in CA.
Donor(s): Flora Lamson Hewlett,‡ William R. Hewlett.
Financial data (yr. ended 12/31/92): Grants paid, $31,389,000; assets, $819,596,000 (M); expenditures, $38,631,162; qualifying distributions, $35,769,320, including $2,000,000 for program-related investments.
Limitations: Giving limited to the San Francisco Bay Area, CA, for regional grants program; performing arts partially limited to the Bay Area.
Publications: Annual report, program policy statement, application guidelines, informational brochure.
Application Information: Application form not required.
Officers and Directors:* William R. Hewlett,* Chair.; Walter B. Hewlett,* Vice-Chair.; David P. Gardner,* Pres.; Marianne Pallotti, V.P. and Corp. Secy.; William F. Nichols, Treas.; Robert F. Erburu, Eleanor H. Gimon, Roger W. Heyns, Mary H. Jaffe, Herant Katchdourian, M.D., Arjay Miller, Loret M. Ruppe.
EIN: 941655673
Codes: FD, FM

755
Marin Community Foundation
17 East Sir Francis Drake Blvd., Suite 200
Larkspur 94939　　　　(415) 461-3333
FAX: (415) 461-3386
Contact: Pamela R. Lynch, Corp. Secy.

Incorporated in 1986 in CA; the Buck Foundation Trust, its original donor, was established in 1973 and administered by the San Francisco Foundation through 1986.
Financial data (yr. ended 06/30/93): Grants paid, $25,627,000; assets, $590,055,000 (M); gifts received, $3,182,000; expenditures, $28,518,000, including $923,000 for loans.
Limitations: Giving from the Buck Trust is limited to Marin County, CA.
Publications: Annual report, application guidelines, newsletter, informational brochure.
Application Information: Application form not required.
Officers: Stephen Mark Dobbs, Pres. and C.E.O.; Barbara H. Kehrer, Ph.D., V.P., Progs.; Barbara B. Lawson, V.P., Finance and Administration; Pamela R. Lynch, Corp. Secy.; Michael Groza, Dir., Community Progs.
Trustees: Rev. Douglas K. Huneke, Chair.; Shirley A. Thornton, Vice-Chair.; Peter R. Arrigoni, William L. Hamilton, Grace Hughes, Donald Linker, M.D., David Werderger, M.D.
EIN: 943007979
Codes: CM, FD, FM

756
The San Francisco Foundation
685 Market St., Suite 910
San Francisco 94105-9716　　　　(415) 495-3100

Additional tel.: (510) 436-3100
Contact: Robert M. Fisher, Dir.

Established in 1948 in CA by resolution and declaration of trust.
Financial data (yr. ended 06/30/93): Grants paid, $25,580,243; assets, $286,508,397 (M); gifts received, $34,025,890; expenditures, $28,538,984, including $762,013 for program-related investments.
Limitations: Giving limited to the Bay Area, CA, counties of Alameda, Contra Costa, Marin, San Francisco, and San Mateo.
Publications: Annual report, newsletter, application guidelines, program policy statement, informational brochure.
Application Information: Application form required.
Director: Robert M. Fisher.
Board of Trustees: Mary Lee Widener, Chair.; Lucille S. Abrahamson, Peter E. Haas, Leonard E. Kingsley, Rolland Lowe, M.D., Stephanie C. MacColl, T.J. Saenger, David Sanchez.
EIN: 941101547
Codes: CM, FD, FM

757
The James Irvine Foundation
One Market
Spear Tower, Suite 1715
San Francisco 94105　　　　(415) 777-2244
Southern CA office: 777 South Figueroa St., Suite 740, Los Angeles, CA 90017-5430; Tel: (213) 236-0552
Contact: Luz A. Vega, Dir. of Grants Prog.

Incorporated in 1937 in CA.
Donor(s): James Irvine.‡
Financial data (yr. ended 12/31/92): Grants paid, $25,079,693; assets, $626,228,757 (M); expenditures, $31,424,363; qualifying distributions, $28,931,702, including $1,250,000 for program-related investments.
Limitations: Giving limited to CA.
Publications: Annual report (including application guidelines), informational brochure (including application guidelines), 990-PF.
Application Information: Application form not required.
Officers: Dennis A. Collins, Pres.; Larry R. Fies, Treas. and Corp. Secy.
Directors: Myron Du Bain, Chair.; Samuel H. Armacost, Angela G. Blackwell, Camilla C. Frost, James C. Gaither, Walter B. Gerken, Roger W. Heyns, Joan F. Lane, Donn B. Miller, Forrest N. Shumway, Kathryn L. Wheeler, Edward Zapanta, M.D.
EIN: 941236937
Codes: FD, FM

758
Weingart Foundation
1055 West Seventh St., Suite 3050
Los Angeles 90017-1984　　　　(213) 688-7799
Mailing address: P.O. Box 17982, Los Angeles, CA 90017-0982; FAX: (213) 688-1515
Contact: Charles W. Jacobson, Pres.

Incorporated in 1951 in CA.
Donor(s): Ben Weingart,‡ Stella Weingart.‡
Financial data (yr. ended 06/30/92): Grants paid, $24,594,231; assets, $477,826,421 (M); gifts received, $270,696; expenditures, $28,421,815; qualifying distributions, $25,616,198.
Limitations: Giving limited to Southern CA.
Publications: Annual report (including application guidelines), application guidelines, occasional report.

60　　IN THIS SECTION, WITHIN EACH STATE, FOUNDATIONS ARE
　　　　LISTED IN DESCENDING ORDER BY TOTAL GRANTS PAID

FIGURE 15. Sample Page from the Foundation Name Index in the *Guide to U.S. Foundations*

FOUNDATION NAME INDEX

A & S Foundation, PA, 29241
A. D. Family Foundation, CA, 3512
A.E. Charitable Foundation, CT, 4330
A.G.P.R. Foundation, IL, 8764
A.I.R. Foundation, MI, 36747
A.I.T. Foundation, Inc., CT, 4497
A.L.H. Foundation, Inc., MD, 12549
A.P.S. Foundation, Inc., AZ, 377
A.R.L. Foundation, CA, 2899
A.T.H., Inc., GA, 7193
A-C Trust, NY, 22146
A-P-A Transport Educational Foundation, NJ, 17797
A-T Medical Research Foundation, CA, 35533
AAA Scholarship Fund of the Lehigh Valley Motor Club, PA, 29621
AAASC *see* 35527
Aalfs Family Foundation, IA, 10586
Aaron Foundation, CA, 2853
Aaron Foundation, A. Allen Aaron and Pearle Peltenson, The, NY, 24009
Aaron Foundation, Inc., Bernard J. & Sylvia, NY, 23170
Aaron Memorial Trust Scholarship Fund, Mary M., CA, 1792
Abahac, Inc., AL, 143
Abamo Trust, Daniel, NY, 24868
Abascal Trust, Mary J., CA, 2160
Abbate Foundation, Inc., Grace McLean, The, NY, 37286
Abbey Foundation, Inc., The, FL, 5644
Abbot Home, OH, 37790
Abbot Testamentary Trust, Herbert G., NH, 17514
Abbotsford Story, Inc., WI, 34830
Abbott Charitable Foundation, Ethel S., NE, 17218
Abbott Charitable Trust, Claude A. and Blanche McCubbin, MD, 12651
Abbott Foundation, NE, 17311
Abbott Foundation, Clara, The, IL, 7758
Abbott Foundation, James E. & Rebecca S., NE, 36922
Abbott Laboratories Fund, IL, 7763
Abbott Memorial Scholarship Trust, Clifford, IN, 10436
Abbott Memorial Trust, Inc., Edward J., NH, 17664
Abbott Scholarship Foundation, Inc., Pontiac-Chuck, MA, 13950
ABC Foundation *see* 1453
ABC Foundation, NC, 25186
ABC Mountain Retreat, OR, 37886
Abel Foundation, Ltd., The, NY, 24211
Abel Foundation, The, NE, 17161
Abel Foundation, Ed & Carol, OK, 27619
Abel Trust, Roy, PA, 29582
Abelard Foundation, ME, 36370
Abelard Foundation, Inc., The, CA, 1228
Abele Memorial Fund, Edward and Marie, MI, 15086
Abeles Foundation, Inc., Joseph & Sophia, NY, 20010
Abeles Scholarship Fund, Inc., Nancy Jo, NY, 20823
Abell Education Trust, Jennie G. and Pearl, KS, 11069
Abell Foundation, Inc., The, MD, 12142
Abell Foundation, Inc., Charles S., MD, 12197
Abell Foundation, Mary Hatheway & Robert James, TX, 32059
Abell Trust, Jabez M., NY, 21360
Abell-Hanger Foundation, TX, 30931
Abelson Charitable Foundation, Stanley E. and Dorothy Y., PA, 29272
Abelson Foundation, Lester S., IL, 8119

Abelson Foundation, Morton S., IL, 9120
Abelson Foundation Trust, Lester & Hope, IL, 8658
Abercrombie Foundation, The, TX, 31042
Abernathy Black Community Development & Educational Fund, PA, 38063
Abernathy Charitable Trust, Taylor and Patti, MO, 16466
Abernethy Charitable Education Fund, Sally, FL, 6397
Abernethy Testamentary Charitable Trust, Maye Morrison, NC, 25362
Abess Foundation, Inc., Leonard L. and Bertha U., FL, 6468
Abilene, Community Foundation of, TX, 30980
Abilene Foundation, The, TX, 38336
Abington Foundation, OH, 26185
Able Trust, NY, 23554
Ablett Trust, Eliza Lillian, NY, 24096
ABM Charitable Trust, IL, 8913
Abney Foundation, The, SC, 30217
Aboly Foundation, Inc., FL, 6821
Aborn Foundation, Inc., Louis H., CT, 4228
Abounding Grace Ministries, Inc., NY, 24577
Abraham Ben Israel Memorial Fund, Inc., NY, 23112
Abraham Family Foundation, Ida and Irving, IL, 8272
Abraham Foundation, Inc., The, NY, 19905
Abraham Foundation, Inc., Anthony R., FL, 5529
Abraham Foundation, S. Daniel, The, FL, 5475
Abraham Fund, The, NY, 21309
Abrahamian Foundation, George, RI, 30188
Abrahams Charitable Trust, NE, 17208
Abrahams Family Foundation, Inc., The, MD, 12464
Abrahamson Foundation, ND, 25821
Abramowitz Family Foundation, MA, 13412
Abrams Charitable Trust, Carry & Rudolf, PA, 29860
Abrams Charitable Trust, Maurice I. & Shirley Z., MA, 14126
Abrams Family Foundation, Seymour J., IL, 8428
Abrams Foundation, NJ, 17937
Abrams Foundation, Inc., GA, 7024
Abrams Foundation, Inc., Benjamin and Elizabeth, NY, 20791
Abrams Foundation, Howard and Terri, PA, 29144
Abrams Foundation, Inc., Max & Helen, NY, 20716
Abrams Foundation, Inc., Ruth, NY, 23656
Abrams Foundation, Samuel L., PA, 28733
Abrams Foundation, Saul *see* 30170
Abrams Foundation, Shuree, The, OH, 26792
Abrams Foundation, Talbert & Leota, MI, 14775
Abrams Gemileth Chesed Association, Inc., Rose L., NY, 23140
Abrams-Bell Foundation, RI, 30170
Abramson Family Foundation, Inc., MD, 12189
Abramson Family Foundation, Joseph & Lena, PA, 28530
Abramson Foundation, Inc. *see* 12189
Abramson Foundation, Jacob, CA, 3125
Abramson Foundation, Wayne M. *see* 32300
Abramson-Clayman Foundation, Inc., NJ, 17878
Abreu Charitable Trust u/w of May P. Abreu, Francis L., GA, 7005
Abroms Charitable Foundation, Inc., AL, 35
Abrons Foundation, Inc., Louis and Anne, NY, 18929
Abrons Foundation, Inc., Richard & Mimi, The, NY, 20622
Abt Family Charitable Foundation, IL, 9155

Abundance Foundation, The, MD, 12790
Abundant Life Ministries, OH, 37753
Abundant Life Seed Foundation, WA, 38563
Academy for Myotherapy & Physical Fitness, Inc., MA, 36704
Academy of Art College Library Fund, Inc., CA, 35319
Academy of Columbia, Trustees for the, SC, 30288
Academy of General Dentistry Foundation, IL, 9673
Accountants Foundation, Inc., NY, 23831
Aceto and Scott Hamilton Hunziker Memorial Scholarship Fund, Inc., Caterina Esther, MO, 16901
ACF Foundation, Inc., NY, 21147
Acheatel Family Foundation, Sydell and Clifford, The, CA, 3196
Achelis Foundation, The, NY, 19146
Achelis Foundation, The, UT, 32556
Achenbach Family Foundation, Inc., GA, 7452
Achenbach Trust, Hazel J. & Moore S., CA, 1682
Ackerman Memorial Fund Trust, Joseph & Alice Beller, WI, 34776
Achtentuch Foundation, Inc., The, NY, 23487
Acker Foundation, Inc., The, NY, 22898
Acker Memorial Foundation, Sam, NY, 21906
Ackerberg Foundation, Norman & Lisette, MN, 16064
Ackerman Education Fund, Emmett T. & Louise M., WI, 34721
Ackerman Foundation, Inc., A. Bernard, NY, 21508
Ackerman Foundation, Jerome & Barbara, NY, 37386
Ackerman Foundation, Martin S., NY, 23825
Ackerman Foundation, Inc., Myron H., FL, 6047
Ackerman Foundation, Thomas C., The, CA, 1211
Ackerman Trust, Anna Keesling, CO, 3679
Ackerman Foundation, The, NC, 25400
Acklie Charitable Foundation, NE, 17231
Ackmann Family Foundation, IL, 8535
Acme Cleveland Foundation, OH, 26305
Acme Foundation, MI, 15240
Acme United Foundation, Inc., CT, 4431
Acme-McCrary and Sapona Foundation, Inc., NC, 25295
ACNA Foundation, DC, 35747
Acomb Foundation, The, NJ, 18196
Acorn Alcinda Foundation, Inc., VA, 32868
Acorn Corrugated Box Company Foundation, IL, 8214
Acorn Foundation, CA, 2050
Acorn Foundation, Inc., WI, 34957
Acorn Foundation, The, NY, 19694
ACP Foundation, IL, 8122
Acree Foundation, KY, 11562
Action Industries Charitable Foundation, PA, 28932
Action 81, Inc., VA, 38503
Acts of Barnabus, Inc., TN, 30689
Acushnet Foundation, The, MA, 12968
Ad Astra Foundation, OK, 27668
Ada Foundation, Inc., Julius, The, NY, 21331
Ada Scholarship Foundation, Inc., MN, 15754
Adair Foundation, CA, 2340
Adair-Exchange Bank Foundation, KS, 11184
Adair-Turnbull Memorial Trust Fund, TX, 32327
Adalman Charitable Foundation, Inc., MD, 12351
Adam Family Foundation, NY, 23090
Adam Foundation, Frank, MO, 16680
Adam, Jr. Foundation, Nancy & George F. *see* 23090
Adamant Community Cultural Foundation, VT, 32665
Adamma Foundation, The, CA, 2280

FIGURE 16. Trustee, Officer, and Donor Index from the *Guide to U.S. Foundations*

FOUNDATION TRUSTEE, OFFICER, AND DONOR INDEX

This index is arranged alphabetically by each individual or corporate name and also provides the foundation affiliation and state. Numbers following the names refer to the sequence number of entries in Volume 1. If an individual is both a donor and an officer or trustee, his or her name will appear only once. An individual's name, however, will appear for each separate foundation affiliation. The codes in parentheses indicate in what other Foundation Center publications more detailed information can be found. A key to the codes appears across the bottom of facing pages.

A & A Fuel Oil Co., *The Pierson Family Foundation, Inc.*, NJ, 18243
A & B-Hawaii, Inc., *Alexander & Baldwin Foundation*, HI, 7506
A & C Communications, *The Catto Foundation*, TX, 31197 (FD2)
A.D.E. Management Co., *Indianapolis A.D.E. Charities, Inc.*, IN, 9865 (FD)
A.D.E. Memphis, *Indianapolis A.D.E. Charities, Inc.*, IN, 9865 (FD)
A.D.E. of Birmingham, Inc., *Indianapolis A.D.E. Charities, Inc.*, IN, 9865 (FD)
A.T.&G. Co., Inc., *Bonner Foundation*, MI, 15183
A-P-A Transport Corp., *A-P-A Transport Educational Foundation*, NJ, 17797 (FD)
Aakre, Richard, *Fanny S. Gilfillan Memorial, Inc.*, MN, 15753 (FD2)
Aalfs, Barbara, *Outagamie Charitable Foundation, Inc.*, WI, 34309 (FD)
Aalfs, John W., *Aalfs Family Foundation*, IA, 10586 (FD2)
Aalfs, John W., *Siouxland Foundation*, IA, 10653
Aalfs, N. Wilbur, *Aalfs Family Foundation*, IA, 10586 (FD2)
Aall, Sally Sample, *Port Royal Foundation, Inc.*, NY, 20186 (FD2)
Aamot, Brett N., *Adams Educational Fund, Inc.*, MN, 16108
Aamoth, Mary, *The Ripley Memorial Foundation, Inc.*, MN, 15769
Aaron, Bennett, *The Javitch Foundation*, PA, 28517 (FD2)
Aaron, Bennett, *The Joseph & Bessie Levine Fund*, PA, 28967
Aaron, Bennett, *Phyllis & Norman Lipsett Foundation*, PA, 29069
Aaron, D.J., *Aaron Foundation*, CA, 2853
Aaron, Debra M., *Morgan Stanley Scholarship Fund, Inc.*, NY, 21111 (CD)
Aaron, H.E., *Aaron Foundation*, CA, 2853
Aaron, Jeffrey, *Bernard J. & Sylvia Aaron Foundation, Inc.*, NY, 23170
Aaron, Pearle, *The A. Allen Aaron and Pearle Peltenson Aaron Foundation*, NY, 24009
Aaron, Roy H., *Plitt Southern Theatres, Inc. Employees Fund*, CA, 986 (FD, CD)
Aaron, Sylvia, *Bernard J. & Sylvia Aaron Foundation, Inc.*, NY, 23170
Aarons, Karon, *Medical Society of Atlantic County*, NJ, 18674
Aarons, Morris, *Allied Educational Foundation Fund B*, NJ, 17910 (FD)
Aaronson, Edward, *Gary & Bernice Lebbin Foundation*, MD, 12418
Aaronson, Howard J., *Retinal Diagnostic Research Foundation*, CA, 3398
Aars, Hulen C., *Mary Lola Bradstreet Brewer Community Foundation*, TX, 32102
Aarstad, Norman, *Clara Wheeler Trust*, CO, 3726 (FD2)
Abare, Paul, *VARA Educational Foundation, Inc.*, VT, 32676
Abare, Richard, *VARA Educational Foundation, Inc.*, VT, 32676
Abarta, Inc., *Adams Foundation, Inc.*, PA, 28603 (FD2)
Abate, Ernst N., *Senior Services of Stamford, Inc.*, CT, 4171 (FD)
Abbamont, Thomas J., *The Sexauer Foundation*, NY, 20378 (FD)
Abbate, Grace McClean, *The Grace McLean Abbate Foundation, Inc.*, NY, 37286 (FD2)
Abbenhaus, James I., *Yakima Valley Memorial Fund for Medical Science Education*, WA, 33799
Abbett, Alice, *Rebecca Residence for Protestant Ladies*, PA, 37906
Abbett, Doug, *Alvin C. Ruxer Foundation, Inc.*, IN, 10299
Abbey, Donald C., *Goddard Homestead, Inc.*, MA, 36497
Abbey, Fletcher, *Herbert Frank and Bertha Maude Laird Oakland Scottish Rite Memorial Educational Foundation*, CA, 1965
Abbey, Joseph, *Mary Warren Free Institute of the City of Troy*, NY, 23704
Abbey, Robert, *Scripture Truth Foundation*, VA, 32891 (FD2)
Abbey, Ruth L., *Ludington, Inc.*, NY, 21499 (FD)
Abbey, Wally, *Greater Pueblo Chamber Foundation*, CO, 4079
Abbiati, Lawrence B., *Warren Memorial Foundation*, ME, 36351 (FD)
Abbink, Opal D., *Lisa Duke Bates Foundation, Inc.*, GA, 7244
Abbink, Opal Duke, *The Conboy Foundation*, GA, 7038 (FD2)
Abbitt, Carolyn S., *MAIHS Foundation*, VA, 33259
Abbitt, Diane, *The Foundation for Civil Rights*, CA, 3288
Abbitt, Richard F., *MAIHS Foundation*, VA, 33259

Abbotsford State Bank, *Abbotsford Story, Inc.*, WI, 34830
Abbott, Barbara, *The Jamestown Foundation*, DC, 35755
Abbott, Bill, *The Woodward Home, Inc.*, NH, 36971
Abbott, Charles B., *Margaret Burr Trust*, MA, 14091
Abbott, Dave, *Independent Insurance Agents of Evansville Foundation, Inc.*, IN, 10379
Abbott, Dona Lee, *Erwin H. Weder Family Decks Prairie Historical Educational and Research Foundation*, IL, 36068
Abbott, Ethel S., *Ethel S. Abbott Charitable Foundation*, NE, 17218
Abbott, Frances M., *The 1957 Charity Trust*, PA, 28233 (FD)
Abbott, Gordon, Jr., *Bonnell Cove Foundation*, NY, 22509
Abbott, Herman, *The Amy Morgan Sommer Foundation, Inc.*, NY, 22625
Abbott, Herman, *The Abraham & Beverly Sommer Foundation*, NY, 25081 (FD)
Abbott, James, *Mary M. Aaron Memorial Trust Scholarship Fund*, CA, 1792 (FD2)
Abbott, James E., *Abbott Foundation*, NE, 17311
Abbott, James E., *James E. & Rebecca S. Abbott Foundation*, NE, 36922
Abbott, Janet, *The Drum Foundation*, CA, 1137 (FD)
Abbott, Jim, *Research Ranch Foundation*, AZ, 35101
Abbott, John S., *Pritchard Laughlin Center*, OH, 37716
Abbott, Kyle C., *Talbert & Leota Abrams Foundation*, MI, 14775 (FD)
Abbott, Laura, *AT&T Foundation*, NY, 18843 (FD, CD, FM)
Abbott, LeRoy II, *Abbott Foundation*, NE, 17311
Abbott, Margot, *The Woodward Home, Inc.*, NH, 36971
Abbott, Mary J., *Edward J. Abbott Memorial Trust, Inc.*, NH, 17664
Abbott, Patricia J., *Abbott Foundation*, NE, 17311
Abbott, Rebecca S., *Abbott Foundation*, NE, 17311
Abbott, Rebecca S., *James E. & Rebecca S. Abbott Foundation*, NE, 36922
Abbott, Robin B., *Joseph C. and Esther Foster Foundation, Inc.*, NY, 21445 (FD)
Abbott, Sharon S., *Unicare Foundation*, CA, 3638
Abbott, Wallace, *The Clara Abbott Foundation*, IL, 7758 (FD)
Abbott, Wallace, Mrs., *The Clara Abbott Foundation*, IL, 7758 (FD)
Abbott, William S., *Prospect Hill Home*, NH, 36964
Abbott Bank, The, *Mitchell-Gantz Educational & Charitable Trust*, NE, 17264
Abbott Bank, The, *Edna & Ira Leavitt Foundation Trust*, NE, 17330
Abbott Bank, The, *Henry A. Fricke & John E. Nolan Scholarship Trust*, NE, 17343
Abbott Laboratories, *Abbott Laboratories Fund*, IL, 7763 (FD, CD)
Abbott/Wendermere, *Epilepsy Research Foundation of Florida, Inc.*, FL, 6327
Abboy, Rajamannar, *Indo-American Foundation, Inc.*, CA, 35373
Abboy, Ramadas, *Indo-American Foundation, Inc.*, CA, 35373
Abbuhl, David, *Christian BusinessCares Foundation*, OH, 37808
ABC Capital Cities, *Illinois Broadcasters Association Minority Intern Program, Inc.*, IL, 36132
ABC Market Corp., *The Paul Kodimer Foundation*, CA, 1798
Abdalla, Gerald M., *Joseph C. Bancroft Educational & Charitable Foundation*, MS, 16185
Abdalla, Gerald M., *Croft Metal Products Educational Trust Fund*, MS, 16235 (CD)
Abdela, Angelo S., *CPC Educational Foundation*, NJ, 17858 (FD, CD)
Abdoo, Mary, *Kerri Ann Kattar Memorial Fund, Inc.*, DC, 5312
Abdoo, Richard A., *Wisconsin Energy Corporation Foundation, Inc.*, WI, 34172 (FD, CD, FM)
Abdu, Rashid A., *Department of Surgery Research & Education Fund of Youngstown, Ohio*, OH, 26944
Abegg, Edward, *Woodward Governor Company Charitable Trust*, IL, 7901 (FD, CD)
Abel, Alice, *The Abel Foundation*, NE, 17161 (FD, CD)
Abel, Brent M., *Vailima Foundation*, CA, 35235
Abel, Carol C., *Ed & Carol Abel Foundation*, OK, 27619 (FD2)
Abel, Clinton N., *Luther A. Sizemore Foundation, Inc.*, NM, 18776

FM = *Foundation 1000*   CD = *National Directory of Corporate Giving*   3

FIGURE 17. Foundation Locator from the *Guide to U.S Foundations*

FOUNDATION LOCATOR

The codes in parentheses following the foundation names and states indicate in what other Foundation Center publications additional information appears. A key to the codes appears across the bottom of facing pages. If there is no code after a foundation's name, it is only listed in the *Guide to U.S. Foundations, Their Trustees, Officers, and Donors*. To find a particular foundation's entry in this book, see the "Foundation Name Index", in Volume 1.

A & S Foundation, PA
A. D. Family Foundation, CA
A.E. Charitable Foundation, CT (FD2)
A.G.P.R. Foundation, IL
A.I.R. Foundation, MI
A.I.T. Foundation, Inc., CT
A.L.H. Foundation, Inc., MD
A.P.S. Foundation, Inc., AZ (FD, CD)
A.R.L. Foundation, CA
A.T.H., Inc., GA
A-C Trust, NY
A-P-A Transport Educational Foundation, NJ (FD)
A-T Medical Research Foundation, CA (FD2)
AAA Scholarship Fund of the Lehigh Valley Motor Club, PA
AAASC *see* AIESEC Alumni Association of Southern California
Aalfs Family Foundation, IA (FD2)
Aaron Foundation, CA
Aaron Foundation, A. Allen Aaron and Pearle Peltenson, The, NY
Aaron Foundation, Inc., Bernard J. & Sylvia, NY
Aaron Memorial Trust Scholarship Fund, Mary M., CA (FD2)
Abahac, Inc., AL
Abamo Trust, Daniel, NY
Abascal Trust, Mary J., CA
Abbate Foundation, Inc., Grace McLean, The, NY (FD2)
Abbey Foundation, Inc., The, FL (FD)
Abbot Home, OH
Abbot Testamentary Trust, Herbert G., NH
Abbotsford Story, Inc., WI
Abbott Charitable Foundation, Ethel S., NE
Abbott Charitable Trust, Claude A. and Blanche McCubbin, MD
Abbott Foundation, NE
Abbott Foundation, Clara, The, IL (FD)
Abbott Foundation, James E. & Rebecca S., NE
Abbott Laboratories Fund, IL (FD, CD)
Abbott Memorial Scholarship Trust, Clifford, IN
Abbott Memorial Trust, Inc., Edward J., NH
Abbott Scholarship Foundation, Inc., Pontiac-Chuck, MA
ABC Foundation *see* Ramsay Family Foundation
ABC Foundation, NC (FD, CD)
ABC Mountain Retreat, OR
Abel Foundation, Ltd., The, NY
Abel Foundation, The, NE (FD, CD)
Abel Foundation, Ed & Carol, OK (FD2)
Abel Trust, Roy, PA
Abelard Foundation, ME
Abelard Foundation, Inc., The, CA (FD)
Abele Memorial Fund, Edward and Marie, MI

Abeles Foundation, Inc., Joseph & Sophia, NY (FD)
Abeles Scholarship Fund, Inc., Nancy Jo, NY
Abell Education Trust, Jennie G. and Pearl, KS (FD2)
Abell Foundation, Inc., The, MD (FD, FM)
Abell Foundation, Inc., Charles S., MD (FD)
Abell Foundation, Mary Hatheway & Robert James, TX
Abell Trust, Jabez M., NY
Abell-Hanger Foundation, TX (FD, FM)
Abelson Charitable Foundation, Stanley E. and Dorothy Y., PA
Abelson Foundation, Lester S., IL (FD2)
Abelson Foundation, Morton S., IL
Abelson Foundation Trust, Lester & Hope, IL
Abercrombie Foundation, The, TX (FD)
Abernathy Black Community Development & Educational Fund, PA
Abernathy Charitable Trust, Taylor and Patti, MO (FD2)
Abernethy Charitable Education Fund, Sally, FL
Abernethy Testamentary Charitable Trust, Maye Morrison, NC (FD)
Abess Foundation, Inc., Leonard L. and Bertha U., FL
Abilene, Community Foundation of, TX (FD)
Abilene Foundation, The, TX (FD2)
Abington Foundation, OH (FD)
Able Trust, NY
Ablett Trust, Eliza Lillian, NY
ABM Charitable Trust, NY
Abney Foundation, The, SC (FD)
Aboly Foundation, Inc., FL
Aborn Foundation, Inc., Louis H., CT (FD2)
Abounding Grace Ministries, Inc., NY
Abraham Ben Israel Memorial Fund, Inc., NY
Abraham Family Foundation, Ida and Irving, IL (FD2)
Abraham Foundation, Inc., The, NY (FD)
Abraham Foundation, Inc., Anthony R., FL (FD)
Abraham Foundation, S. Daniel, The, FL (FD)
Abraham Fund, The, NY
Abrahamian Foundation, George, RI
Abrahams Charitable Trust, NE (FD2)
Abrahams Family Foundation, Inc., The, MD
Abrahamson Foundation, ND
Abramowitz Family Foundation, MA
Abrams Charitable Trust, Carry & Rudolf, PA
Abrams Charitable Trust, Maurice I. & Shirley Z., MA
Abrams Family Foundation, Seymour J., IL (FD2)
Abrams Foundation, NJ (FD)
Abrams Foundation, Inc., GA (FD2, CD)
Abrams Foundation, Inc., Benjamin and Elizabeth, NY (FD)
Abrams Foundation, Howard and Terri, PA
Abrams Foundation, Inc., Max & Helen, NY (FD2)
Abrams Foundation, Inc, Ruth, NY
Abrams Foundation, Samuel L., PA

Abrams Foundation, Saul *see* Abrams-Bell Foundation
Abrams Foundation, Shuree, The, OH
Abrams Foundation, Talbert & Leota, MI (FD)
Abrams Gemileth Chesed Association, Inc., Rose L., NY
Abrams-Bell Foundation, RI
Abramson Family Foundation, Inc., MD (FD)
Abramson Family Foundation, Joseph & Lena, PA (FD2)
Abramson Foundation, Inc. *see* Abramson Family Foundation, Inc.
Abramson Foundation, Jacob, CA
Abramson Foundation, Wayne M. *see* Warm Foundation
Abramson-Clayman Foundation, Inc., NJ (FD2)
Abreu Charitable Trust u/w of May P. Abreu, Francis L., GA (FD)
Abroms Charitable Foundation, Inc., AL (FD)
Abrons Foundation, Inc., Louis and Anne, NY (FD, FM)
Abrons Foundation, Inc., Richard & Mimi, The, NY (FD2)
Abt Family Charitable Foundation, IL
Abundance Foundation, The, MD
Abundant Life Ministries, OH
Abundant Life Seed Foundation, WA
Academy for Myotherapy & Physical Fitness, Inc., MA
Academy of Art College Library Fund, Inc., CA
Academy of Columbia, Trustees for the, SC
Academy of General Dentistry Foundation, IL
Accountants Foundation, Inc., NY
Aceto and Scott Hamilton Hunziker Memorial Scholarship Fund, Inc., Caterina Esther, MO
ACF Foundation, Inc., NY (CD)
Acheatel Family Foundation, Sydell and Clifford, The, CA
Achelis Foundation, The, NY (FD)
Achelis Foundation, The, UT
Achenbach Family Foundation, Inc., GA
Achenbach Trust, Hazel J. & Moore S., CA
Acherman Memorial Fund Trust, Joseph & Alice Beller, WI
Achtentuch Foundation, Inc., The, NY
Acker Foundation, Inc., The, NY
Acker Memorial Foundation, Sam, NY
Ackerberg Foundation, Norman & Lisette, MN
Ackerman Education Fund, Emmett T. & Louise M., WI
Ackerman Foundation, Inc., A. Bernard, NY
Ackerman Foundation, Jerome & Barbara, NY
Ackerman Foundation, Martin S., NY
Ackerman Foundation, Inc., Myron H., FL
Ackerman Foundation, Thomas C., The, CA
Ackerman Trust, Anna Keesling, CO (FD)
Ackermann Foundation, The, NC
Acklie Charitable Foundation, NE
Ackmann Family Foundation, IL

expenditures, qualifying distributions and total grants, scholarships, matching gifts, loans or program-related investments, and program amounts; purpose and activities; fields of interest; types of support awarded; application procedures; officers, trustees, and staff; a list of sample grants (when available); and the foundations' IRS employer identification number (see Figure 18). The volume is arranged by state, then alphabetically by foundation name. The sixteenth edition includes the following indexes to help you identify foundations of interest:

- an index of donors, officers, and trustees;

- a geographic index to foundation locations by state and city, including cross-references to foundations located in one state that focus their giving in another state;

- an index to types of support offered by foundations, broken down by the states where the foundations are headquartered;

- an index to giving interests in more than 180 subject categories, each of which is also broken down by the states where the foundations are located;

- an index listing foundations new to the current edition; and

- an index by foundation name.

In the geographic, subject, and types of support indexes, foundations with national or regional giving patterns are indicated in bold type, while foundations restricted to local giving are listed in regular type. As you define the limits of your funding search, these indexes can help you to focus on locally oriented foundations in your community as well as on national foundations that have an interest in your field of activity.

The Foundation Directory Part 2 provides similar information, and sample grants when available, for some 4,000 of the next-largest U.S. foundations—those with assets of less than $2 million and annual giving between $50,000 and $200,000. For a sample entry from this publication, see Figure 19.

The Foundation Directory Supplement provides the latest information on *Foundation Directory* and *Foundation Directory Part 2* grantmakers six months after those volumes are published. The *Supplement* provides complete revised entries for foundations reporting substantial changes in personnel, name, address, program interests, limitations, application procedures, or other areas by the midpoint of the yearly *Directory* cycle.

The 1993 edition of the *Supplement* contains more than 2,400 updated entries. The portions of an entry that have changed are highlighted in bold type to aid you in

FIGURE 18. Sample Entry from *The Foundation Directory*

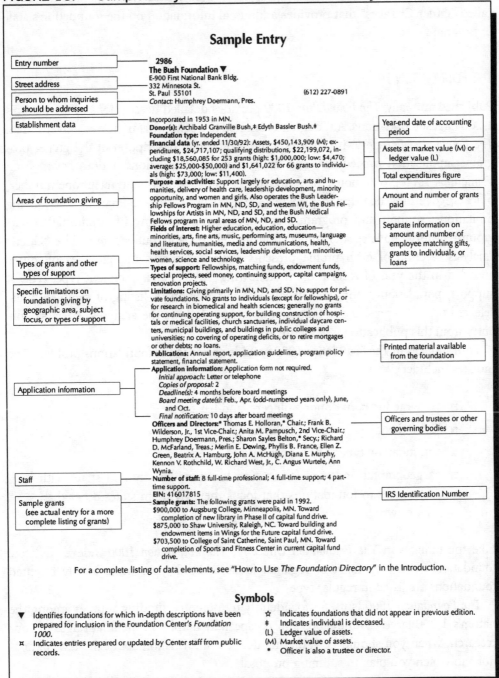

Sample Entry

Entry number

2986
The Bush Foundation ▼
E-900 First National Bank Bldg.

Street address
332 Minnesota St.
St. Paul 55101   (612) 227-0891

Person to whom inquiries should be addressed
Contact: Humphrey Doermann, Pres.

Establishment data
Incorporated in 1953 in MN.
Donor(s): Archibald Granville Bush,‡ Edyth Bassler Bush.‡
Foundation type: Independent
Financial data (yr. ended 11/30/92): Assets, $450,143,909 (M); expenditures, $24,717,107; qualifying distributions, $22,199,072, including $18,560,085 for 253 grants (high: $1,000,000; low: $4,470; average: $25,000-$50,000) and $1,641,022 for 66 grants to individuals (high: $73,000; low: $11,400).

Year-end date of accounting period

Assets at market value (M) or ledger value (L)

Total expenditures figure

Amount and number of grants paid

Separate information on amount and number of employee matching gifts, grants to individuals, or loans

Areas of foundation giving
Purpose and activities: Support largely for education, arts and humanities, delivery of health care, leadership development, minority opportunity, and women and girls. Also operates the Bush Leadership Fellows Program in MN, ND, SD, and western WI, the Bush Fellowships for Artists in MN, ND, and SD, and the Bush Medical Fellows program in rural areas of MN, ND, and SD.
Fields of interest: Higher education, education, education—minorities, arts, fine arts, music, performing arts, museums, language and literature, humanities, media and communications, health, health services, social services, leadership development, minorities, women, science and technology.

Types of grants and other types of support
Types of support: Fellowships, matching funds, endowment funds, special projects, seed money, continuing support, capital campaigns, renovation projects.

Specific limitations on foundation giving by geographic area, subject focus, or types of support
Limitations: Giving primarily in MN, ND, and SD. No support for private foundations. No grants to individuals (except for fellowships), or for research in biomedical and health sciences; generally no grants for continuing operating support, for building construction of hospitals or medical facilities, church sanctuaries, individual daycare centers, municipal buildings, and buildings in public colleges and universities; no covering of operating deficits, or to retire mortgages or other debts; no loans.
Publications: Annual report, application guidelines, program policy statement, financial statement.

Printed material available from the foundation

Application information
Application information: Application form not required.
Initial approach: Letter or telephone
Copies of proposal: 2
Deadline(s): 4 months before board meetings
Board meeting date(s): Feb., Apr. (odd-numbered years only), June, and Oct.
Final notification: 10 days after board meetings

Officers and Directors:* Thomas E. Holloran,* Chair.; Frank B. Wilderson, Jr., 1st Vice-Chair.; Anita M. Pampusch, 2nd Vice-Chair.; Humphrey Doermann, Pres.; Sharon Sayles Belton,* Secy.; Richard D. McFarland, Treas.; Merlin E. Dewing, Phyllis B. France, Ellen Z. Green, Beatrix A. Hamburg, John A. McHugh, Diana E. Murphy, Kennon V. Rothchild, W. Richard West, Jr., C. Angus Wurtele, Ann Wynia.

Officers and trustees or other governing bodies

Staff
Number of staff: 8 full-time professional; 4 full-time support; 4 part-time support.
EIN: 416017815

IRS Identification Number

Sample grants
(see actual entry for a more complete listing of grants)
Sample grants: The following grants were paid in 1992.
$900,000 to Augsburg College, Minneapolis, MN. Toward completion of new library in Phase II of capital fund drive.
$875,000 to Shaw University, Raleigh, NC. Toward building and endowment items in Wings for the Future capital fund drive.
$703,500 to College of Saint Catherine, Saint Paul, MN. Toward completion of Sports and Fitness Center in current capital fund drive.

For a complete listing of data elements, see "How to Use *The Foundation Directory*" in the Introduction.

Symbols

▼ Identifies foundations for which in-depth descriptions have been prepared for inclusion in the Foundation Center's *Foundation 1000.*

¤ Indicates entries prepared or updated by Center staff from public records.

☆ Indicates foundations that did not appear in previous edition.
‡ Indicates individual is deceased.
(L) Ledger value of assets.
(M) Market value of assets.
* Officer is also a trustee or director.

identifying new information quickly. *Supplement* entries may also include a section called "Other Changes" that provides additional information on the foundation's staff or program.

THE FOUNDATION 1000

Published annually, *The Foundation 1000* provides detailed descriptions of the nation's 1,000 largest foundations. Although it's confined to a somewhat narrower universe than *The Foundation Directory*, it provides a more thorough description of the giving programs, application procedures, and history of the foundations it does cover. Each *Foundation 1000* profile notes the foundation's name, address, and telephone number; officers, governing board, and principal staff; purpose; current financial data; giving limitations; support and program areas; sponsoring company (if applicable); background history; policies and application guidelines; and publications. The "Grants Analysis" section of each profile presents statistical charts and analyses of grants awarded in the year of record for the following: subject area, recipient type, type of support, population group, and geographic distribution. A listing of sample grants, selected to best represent the foundation's giving, follows the analyses. For a sample entry from this publication, see Figure 20.

Four indexes in *The Foundation 1000* provide access to the foundations profiled. The indexes include:

- a name index of donors, officers, and trustees;
- an index by subject/giving interests;
- an index by types of support; and
- a geographic index of foundation locations by city and state, with references to foundations that focus their giving in states other than their own.

Like the indexes in *The Foundation Directory*, *The Foundation 1000* indexes indicate foundations with a national or regional focus in bold type, while locally oriented foundations are listed in regular type.

The Foundation 1000 is useful for identifying potential funding sources among the nation's 1,000 largest foundations and is especially helpful in the final stages of your research, when you should be gathering detailed information about the few foundations to which you plan to submit a proposal.

FIGURE 19.   Sample Entry from *The Foundation Directory Part 2*

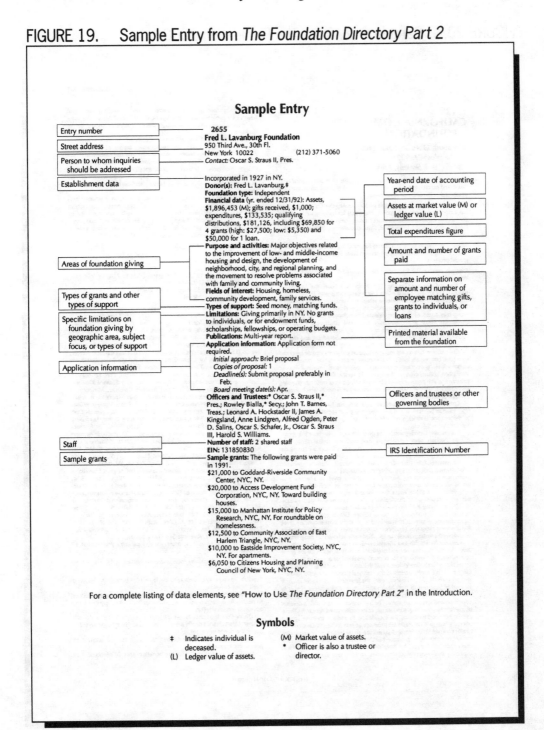

Sample Entry

Entry number	2655
	Fred L. Lavanburg Foundation
Street address	950 Third Ave., 30th Fl.
	New York 10022 (212) 371-5060
Person to whom inquiries should be addressed	*Contact:* Oscar S. Straus II, Pres.

Incorporated in 1927 in NY.

Establishment data — **Donor(s):** Fred L. Lavanburg.‡
Foundation type: Independent
Financial data (yr. ended 12/31/92): Assets, $1,896,453 (M); gifts received, $1,000; expenditures, $133,535; qualifying distributions, $181,126, including $69,850 for 4 grants (high: $27,500; low: $5,350) and $50,000 for 1 loan.

Year-end date of accounting period

Assets at market value (M) or ledger value (L)

Total expenditures figure

Amount and number of grants paid

Areas of foundation giving — **Purpose and activities:** Major objectives related to the improvement of low- and middle-income housing and design, the development of neighborhood, city, and regional planning, and the movement to resolve problems associated with family and community living.
Fields of interest: Housing, homeless, community development, family services.

Types of grants and other types of support — **Types of support:** Seed money, matching funds.

Specific limitations on foundation giving by geographic area, subject focus, or types of support — **Limitations:** Giving primarily in NY. No grants to individuals, or for endowment funds, scholarships, fellowships, or operating budgets.
Publications: Multi-year report.

Separate information on amount and number of employee matching gifts, grants to individuals, or loans

Printed material available from the foundation

Application information — **Application information:** Application form not required.
  Initial approach: Brief proposal
  Copies of proposal: 1
  Deadline(s): Submit proposal preferably in Feb.
  Board meeting date(s): Apr.
Officers and Trustees: * Oscar S. Straus II,* Pres.; Rowley Bialla,* Secy.; John T. Barnes, Treas.; Leonard A. Hockstader II, James A. Kingsland, Anne Lindgren, Alfred Ogden, Peter D. Salins, Oscar S. Schafer, Jr., Oscar S. Straus III, Harold S. Williams.

Officers and trustees or other governing bodies

Staff — **Number of staff:** 2 shared staff
EIN: 131850830

IRS Identification Number

Sample grants — **Sample grants:** The following grants were paid in 1991.
$21,000 to Goddard-Riverside Community Center, NYC, NY.
$20,000 to Access Development Fund Corporation, NYC, NY. Toward building houses.
$15,000 to Manhattan Institute for Policy Research, NYC, NY. For roundtable on homelessness.
$12,500 to Community Association of East Harlem Triangle, NYC, NY.
$10,000 to Eastside Improvement Society, NYC, NY. For apartments.
$6,050 to Citizens Housing and Planning Council of New York, NYC, NY.

For a complete listing of data elements, see "How to Use *The Foundation Directory Part 2*" in the Introduction.

Symbols

‡ Indicates individual is deceased.	(M) Market value of assets.
(L) Ledger value of assets.	* Officer is also a trustee or director.

FIGURE 20.   Sample Entry from *The Foundation 1000*

129
CALIFORNIA COMMUNITY FOUNDATION

606 South Olive St., Suite 2400
Los Angeles, CA 90014   (213) 413-4042
Contact: Jack Shakely, Pres.

Purpose: Giving in the areas of arts and culture, civic affairs, education, health and medicine, and human services, with emphasis on children and youth and community development.

Limitation(s): Giving limited to the greater Los Angeles County, CA, area. No support for sectarian purposes. No grants for building funds, annual campaigns, equipment, endowment funds, debt reduction, operating budgets, scholarships, fellowships, films, conferences, dinners, or special events; no loans.

Support area(s): In general, support for matching funds, technical assistance, emergency funds, program-related investments, seed money, and special projects.

Program area(s): The foundation has identified the following field(s) of interest:

Arts and Culture–Through the Brody Arts Fund, the foundation supports community-based artists and organizations who give voice and expression to Los Angeles' diverse ethnic and minority cultural traditions. Through the J. Paul Getty Trust Fund for the Visual Arts, the foundation recognizes some of the most talented contributors to our lively and challenging visual arts community. Individual artists receive support through the fellowship programs of the Brody Arts Fund and the Getty Fund for the Visual Arts. Prospective applicants should call and request guidelines and application forms for the arts programs that interest them.

Civic Affairs–Grants are made to support programs that develop and train adult community leadership, encourage cooperation among ethnic communities, encourage citizen participation and responsibility, or strengthen philanthropy or the nonprofit sector. Grants are made for programs which prepare residents to participate in community planning and problem solving. Grants are not made for projects which support partisan political activities.

Children, Youth, and Families–This program has been separated from Human Services, and is intended to support social service delivery to children and families, especially where youth are at risk. (This includes recreational activities).

Community Development–This program aims to improve living conditions through community-based neighborhood revitalization, economic development, community organizing, and affordable housing development, especially in low-income communities.

Community Education–Grants will be made to community-based adult literacy programs and other opportunities for life-long learning; promote educational opportunity, with priority given to effective programs that assist and encourage low-income or high-risk youth to achieve at levels that prepare them for college, or that help them over barriers to applying and matriculating; and programs that model strategies for improving the effectiveness of public schools, especially at the level of the classroom or the local school. Grants are not made for curriculum development or implementation at the post-secondary level, the academic programs of colleges or universities, scholarship programs of endowed private schools, or for third-party scholarship programs.

Community Health and Medicine–Grants will be made to support programs that help assure good physical and mental health for the entire community, but particularly for populations with less access to adequate medical care, including children and the poor. Since 1988, the foundation has been a senior partner in the National Community AIDS Partnership program (NCAP). In that capacity, the foundation advocates for local support of programs to meet health and human service needs of people with HIV, and administers a special annual cycle of funding for HIV education and service programs. The foundation also adopted a new set of guidelines governing support for community-based research. These can be obtained by calling the foundation. In addition to these special efforts, grants will be made to: promote access to health care, mental health care, rehabilitation, and substance abuse treatment programs for the entire community; promote health through education and disease prevention; encourage the early detection and treatment of disease, especially in low-income communities; and improve the health of chil-

dren through perinatal care, nutrition education, immunization, and health care programs for school-aged children. Deadlines are the same for community-based research but specific guidelines should be requested.

Environment and Animal Welfare–Grants will be made to promote environmental appreciation and responsibility among all residents, but especially children and youth; involve low-income and minority communities in achieving balance between environmental protection and community development; preserve opportunities for our urban population to enjoy and appreciate the natural world; and promote the welfare of birds and animals, which will be reviewed separately from other environmental requests.

Human Services–Grants will be made to support innovative programs designed to meet a wide variety of social needs, especially in underserved communities. The foundation is particularly interested in: employment development and job training for people with disabilities; day care and other services for the elderly; programs which provide services to the homeless; and combatting family violence.

Financial data (yr. ended 6/30/92):
Assets: $107,906,602 (M)
Gifts received: $7,583,573
Expenditures: $14,121,738
Grants paid: $9,463,593 for 1,114 grants (high: $1,238,519; low: $50; general range: $5,000-$25,000)
Grants to individuals: $248,794 for 81 grants
Loans: $165,000 for 2 loans

Officers: Jack Shakely, Pres.; Linda Shestock, V.P., Finance and Administration; Terri Jones, V.P., Progs.; Joe Lumarda, V.P., Development.
Board of Governors: Stephen D. Gavin, Chair. (Dir. and Member, Exec. Committee, United Way of Los Angeles; Chair., Gavin Associates, Inc.; Dir., United Way of California; Dir., Central City Association); Caroline L. Ahmanson (Vice-Chair., Music Center of Los Angeles, National Committee on U.S.-China Relations, Los Angeles World Affairs Council; Trustee, American Women for International Understanding); Bruce C. Corwin (Pres., Metropolitan Theaters Corporation; Trustee, UCLA and UCSB Foundations; Member, National Board of Governors, Coro Foundation; Founding Pres., Los Angeles Children's Museum); Susanne Donnelly (Pres., Marlborough School Board of Trustees; Co-Chair., Marlborough Centennial Campaign); Claudia H. Hampton, Nini Moore Horn, Arturo Madrid (Pres., Tomas Rivera Center for Hispanic Policy Studies); William G. Ouchi (Professor, Anderson Graduate School of Management Doctoral Program at UCLA; Chair. and Dir., Advisory Board, Leadership Education for Asian Pacific (LEAP); David Peters (Pres., The Regency Group); William F. Podlich (Managing Dir. and C.E.O., Pacific Investment Management Company; Board Member, Art Institute of Southern California); Bruce M. Ramer (Partner, Gang, Tyre, Ramer and Brown, Inc.; Exec. Dir., Entertainment Law Institute; Exec. Dir., USC Law Center; Chair., National Board of Trustees); Virgil Roberts (Member, Board of Governors, Coro Foundation; Board Member, Los Angeles Educational Alliance for Restructuring Now (LEARN), NAACP); Ann Shaw (Dir., United Way of Los Angeles); Jean French Smith, Robert H. Smith (Director, KCET; Member, Board of Governors, Music Center of Los Angeles); Daniel Villanueva (Director, Los Angeles Educational Partnership; Trustee, Tomas Rivera Center for Hispanic Policy Studies); Esther Wachtell (Dir., Central City Association, American Center for the Arts; Pres., Music Center of Los Angeles); Ruth K. Watanabe (Pres., RDW Enterprises); Peggy Fouke Wortz (Trustee, University of California Riverside Foundation; Dir., Riverside Symphony Society).
Number of staff: 14 full-time professional, 1 part-time professional, 10 full-time support.

Background: A community foundation; established in 1915 in CA by bank resolution.

Fund(s): Donors may contribute to the foundation through the following basic types of funds:
Donor-Advised Fund–A testamentary bequest that allows the donor to participate in the process on a continuous basis with suggestions and advice to the foundation.
Donor-Directed Fund–Allows total donor control during the donor's lifetime. Upon donor's death, a field-of-interest fund will be generated to honor the donor in perpetuity.
Field-of-Interest Fund–Established to benefit specific activities or geographic areas.
Restricted Fund–Created for the benefit of specific agencies.

THE FOUNDATION 1000   363

FIGURE 20. Sample Entry from *The Foundation 1000* (continued)

129–California

Scholarship Fund–For gifts to outstanding or needy students.
Unrestricted Fund–Established to be used by the foundation to meet what it determined to be the most critical needs of the community.

Policies and application guidelines: Application form required. Applicants should submit the following:

1) name, address and phone number of organization
2) detailed description of project and amount of funding requested
3) statement of problem project will address
4) population served
5) results expected from proposed grant
6) how project's results will be evaluated or measured
7) how project will be sustained once foundation support is completed
8) contact person
9) copy of current year's organizational budget and/or project budget
10) copy of most recent annual report/audited financial statement/ 990
11) listing of board of directors, trustees, officers and other key people and their affiliations
12) copy of IRS Determination Letter

Art related programs such as the Brody Arts Fund, the J. Paul Getty Trust Fund for the Visual Arts, The Arts Funding Program, a well as the AIDS project, and the Community Bridges Initiative have their own schedules and application forms.

Initial approach: Proposal
Copies of proposal: 1
Board meeting date(s): Quarterly
Deadline(s): Sept. 1, 1993 or Mar. 1, 1994 for Community Development and Human Services; Dec. 1, 1993 and June 1, 1994 for most other programs
Final notification: 5 months after application is received

Foundation publications: Annual report (including application guidelines), application guidelines, informational brochure, newsletter

GRANTS ANALYSIS

Contributions paid during the fiscal year ended June 30, 1992 totaled $9,712,387. This figure represents a 24 percent decrease from funding in fiscal 1991. The following analyses and the list of sample grants reflect only grants reported in the 1992 annual report.

Subject Analysis:

Subject Areas Distribution of Grant Numbers and Grant Dollars Paid in 1992

Subject area	No. of grants	Dollar value	Pct.	General range of grants
Other	197	1,836,177	28	
Education				
Library programs	1	933,684	14	
Other	21	550,817	8	
Grants under $10,000	68	181,167	3	
SUBTOTAL:	90	1,665,668	25	$5,000-30,000
Arts & culture				
Other	35	661,187	10	
Grants under $10,000	60	186,351	3	
SUBTOTAL:	95	847,538	13	5,000-25,000
Human services-- multipurpose				
Other	24	604,678	9	
Grants under $10,000	38	110,462	2	
SUBTOTAL:	62	715,140	11	3,131-20,000
Medicine--mental health				
Alcohol and substance abuse	2	520,000	8	
Other	3	75,000	1	
Grants under $10,000	4	6,500	<1	
SUBTOTAL:	9	601,500	9	2,000-30,000
Medicine--specific diseases				

Subject area	No. of grants	Dollar value	Pct.	General range of grants
Specific named diseases	13	395,350	6	
Grants under $10,000	14	45,500	1	
Medical specialties/ Other	2	25,000	<1	
SUBTOTAL:	29	465,850	7	3,000-15,000
Community improvement & development				
Other	14	319,750	5	
Grants under $10,000	9	19,995	<1	
SUBTOTAL:	23	339,745	5	5,000-25,000
Special Support Categories				
Grants to individuals		112,086	2	
Research fellowships-- to individuals		75,000	<1	
TOTAL:	505	$6,658,704	100%	

High award of the year: $933,684, Los Angeles Public Library, Los Angeles, CA.

Top subject area by dollars: Other (also, largest by grant numbers)
Largest award in field: $50,000, Institute for Twenty-First Century Studies, Arlington, VA.
Second largest award: $48,200, California Health Decisions, Orange, CA.
Largest single recipient: Public Counsel, Los Angeles, CA (2 awards, totaling $70,000).

Second largest subject area by dollars: Education
Largest award in field: $933,684, Los Angeles Public Library.
Second largest award: $112,500, Whittier College, Whittier, CA.

Third largest subject area by dollars: Arts & culture
Largest award in field: $72,602, Los Angeles Childrens Museum, Los Angeles, CA.
Second largest award: $50,000, Los Angeles Philharmonic, Los Angeles, CA.

Recipient Type Analysis:
Analysis of Grants of $10,000 or More Awarded in 1992*

Recipient type	Dollar value	No. of grants
Human service agencies	$1,276,497	54
Libraries	933,684	1
Mental health agencies	575,000	4
Performing arts groups	335,235	19
Colleges & universities	240,252	10
Disease-specific health associations	239,250	3
Community improvement organizations	193,000	7
Public/general health organizations	169,200	6
Arts/humanities organizations	152,800	10
Museums/historical societies	150,652	5
Hospitals/medical care facilities	146,300	8
Churches/temples	135,000	9
Educational support agencies	117,230	5
Environmental agencies	103,921	6
Professional societies & associations	102,518	5
International organizations	95,882	3
Junior/community colleges	85,000	4
Youth development organizations	85,000	4
Graduate schools	80,000	1
Research institutes	75,000	2
Federated funds	71,750	3

FIGURE 20. Sample Entry from *The Foundation 1000* (continued)

California—129

Recipient type	Dollar value	No. of grants
Technical assistance centers	58,130	3
Schools	52,500	3
Media organizations	52,500	4
Civil rights groups	52,500	2
Philanthropy organizations	49,000	3
Recreation organizations	36,500	2
Information/public education centers	30,000	2
Public administration agencies	30,000	1
Government agencies	16,000	1
Medical research institutes	10,000	1
Social science organizations	10,000	1

*Awards may support multiple recipient types, i.e., a university library, and would thereby be counted twice.

Top recipient type by dollars: Human service agencies (also, largest by grant numbers)
   Largest award in field: $125,000, Pestalozzi Childrens Village Trust.
   Second largest award: $100,000, American Red Cross, Los Angeles, CA.

Second largest recipient type by dollars: Libraries
   Largest award in field: $933,684, Los Angeles Public Library.

Third largest recipient type by dollars: Mental health agencies
   Largest award in field: $500,000, Scott Newman Center, Los Angeles, CA.
   Second largest award: $30,000, Mental Health Advocacy Services, Los Angeles, CA.

Type of Support Analysis:
Analysis of Grants of $10,000 or More Awarded in 1992*

Support type	Dollar value	No. of grants
Program support		
Program development	$840,695	37
Faculty/staff development	347,357	12
Seed money	307,028	13
Curriculum development	26,130	1
Film/video/radio	10,000	1
Performance/ production costs	10,000	1
SUBTOTAL:	1,541,210	65
Grants to individuals		
Grants to individuals	112,086	
Fellowships—to individuals	75,000	
SUBTOTAL:	187,086	
Technical assistance	182,100	12
General support		
General operating support	87,129	4
Student aid funds		
Scholarship funds	85,000	4
Capital support		
Endowment funds	20,000	1

*Awards may support multiple support types, i.e., seed money for research, and would thereby be counted twice.

Top support type by dollars: Program support (also, largest by grant numbers)
   Largest award in field: $48,200.
   Second largest award: $45,000.

Second largest support type by dollars: Grants to individuals

Third largest support type by dollars: Technical aid
   Largest award in field: $57,100.
   Second largest award: $15,000.

Multi-year pledges: 2, totaling $78,200
Continuing support: 2 grants, totaling $45,000

Matching support: 3 grants, totaling $67,000

Population Group Analysis:
Analysis of Grants Over $10,000 Designated for Special Populations*

Group	Dollar value	No. of grants
Children & youth	$884,759	33
Economically disadvantaged	575,705	30
Alcohol or drug abusers	500,000	1
Mentally disabled	320,500	6
Women & girls	296,450	14
People with AIDS	266,350	15
Homeless	223,215	9
Minorities, general	146,155	5
Hispanics	85,250	4
Blind & vision impaired	80,500	3
Blacks	80,000	4
Asians & Pacific Islanders	77,000	5
Crime or abuse victims	74,600	3
Men & boys	70,000	3
Offenders or ex-offenders	44,000	1
Immigrants & refugees	35,000	3
Disabled, general	34,503	2
Gays or lesbians	25,000	2
Deaf & hearing impaired	21,250	1
Native Americans	10,000	1
Military & veterans	10,000	1

*Grants which support no specific population are not included; awards may support multiple populations, i.e., an award for minority youth, and would thereby be counted twice.

Top population group by dollars: Children & youth (also, largest by grant numbers)
   Largest award in field: $125,000, Pestalozzi Childrens Village Trust.
   Second largest award: $72,602, Los Angeles Childrens Museum, Los Angeles, CA.

Second largest population group by dollars: Economically disadvantaged
   Largest award in field: $57,100, Kellogg Training Center, Los Angeles, CA (For technical assistance as part of Los Angeles AIDS Partnership. Grant shared with United Way, Inc.).
   Second largest award: $40,000, Blue Cross of California, Burbank, CA (For Caring for Children Initiative, which will provide health insurance to low-income children); $40,000, Public Counsel, Los Angeles, CA (Toward provision of pro bono legal services to nonprofit groups developing low-income housing).

Third largest population group by dollars: Alcohol or drug abusers
   Largest award in field: $500,000, Scott Newman Center, Los Angeles, CA.

Geographic Analysis:
The geographic distribution of institutional awards of $10,000 or more is as follows. (Grants to individuals and with unknown locations are excluded.)

U.S. regional breakdown: Pacific, $4,886,155 (152 awards); Middle Atlantic, $180,000 (7 awards); South Atlantic, $77,850 (3 awards); New England, $54,200 (3 awards); East North Central, $22,000 (2 awards); Mountain, $20,000 (2 awards); West South Central, $10,000 (1 award).

GRANTS: The following is a partial list of grants paid by the foundation in the fiscal year ended 6/30/92. Recipient locations are given when known.

Other

Public Counsel, Los Angeles, CA	$70,000
Toward provision of pro bono legal services to nonprofit groups developing low-income housing, $40,000. For grant in response to riots, $30,000.	
Institute for Twenty-First Century Studies, Arlington, VA	50,000
California Health Decisions, Orange, CA	48,200
2-year grant. Toward pilot project to educate non-English speaking communities about Durable Power of Attorney for Health Care.	

FIGURE 20. Sample Entry from *The Foundation 1000* (continued)

129–California

Blue Cross of California, Burbank, CA	40,000
For Caring for Children Initiative, which will provide health insurance to low-income children.	
Portals House, Los Angeles, CA	30,500
For seed funding of case manager position for second Corporate Cookie store to employ chronically mentally disabled adults.	
Los Angeles Mens Place, Los Angeles, CA	20,000
For salary of part-time development director for Skid Row agency serving homeless mentally ill.	
American Civil Liberties Union Foundation of Southern California, Los Angeles, CA	17,500
Los Angeles Womens Foundation, Los Angeles, CA	17,000
Ethiopian Community Center Outreach Services, Los Angeles, CA	10,000
For grant in response to riots.	
Foundation for Interfaith Research and Ministry, Houston, TX	10,000
House Ear Institute, Los Angeles, CA	5,000
Santa Barbara Cottage Hospital, Santa Barbara, CA	3,000
Championship Auto Racing Auxiliary	2,000
Friends of the Los Angeles River, Los Angeles, CA	2,000
International Center for Development Policy, DC	2,000
Boys and Girls Club of Simi Valley, Simi Valley, CA	995
Fund for Animals, NYC, NY	600

Education

Los Angeles Public Library, Los Angeles, CA	933,684
Whittier College, Whittier, CA	112,500
Los Angeles Educational Alliance for Restructuring Now (LEARN), Los Angeles, CA	30,000
3-year grant. For seed funding for new organization dealing with educational reform in Southern California.	
Cypress College Foundation, Cypress, CA	21,250
To immunize student nurses against Hepatitis B Virus and for nursing scholarship assistance.	
California Polytechnic State University Foundation, San Luis Obispo, CA	14,850
University of California at Riverside Foundation, Riverside, CA	10,000
Park Century School, Los Angeles, CA	8,000
All Saints School, Portland, OR	5,000
Windward School, Los Angeles, CA	2,000
Capistrano Valley Christian Schools, CA	1,000
Pacific Union College, Angwin, CA	600

Arts & culture

Los Angeles Childrens Museum, Los Angeles, CA	72,602
Los Angeles Philharmonic, Los Angeles, CA	50,000
Music Center of Los Angeles County, Los Angeles, CA	25,000
For Artistic Development Project of education program, effort to strengthen participating arts groups' school presentations.	
Los Angeles Center for Photographic Studies, Los Angeles, CA	15,000
Ballet School Foundation, Ketchum, ID	10,000
For Summerdance.	
Boston Ballet, Boston, MA	8,000
John Oliver Chorale, Roslindale, MA	5,000
Santa Barbara Museum of Natural History, Santa Barbara, CA	3,000
Jazz Heritage Foundation	2,000
Los Angeles Mozart Orchestra Association, Sunland, CA	1,000
Professional Dancers Society, Beverly Hills, CA	770

Human services--multipurpose

Pestalozzi Childrens Village Trust	125,000

American Red Cross, Los Angeles, CA	100,000
Family Service Association of Western Riverside County, Riverside, CA	20,000
2 grants: $10,000 each.	
Pets Are Wonderful Support (PAWS), Los Angeles, CA	20,000
To enhance ability of agency to provide long-term and emergency assistance to pets of people with HIV/AIDS and other life-threatening illnesses.	
Los Angeles Youth Programs, Los Angeles, CA	15,000
To expand support and respite services to chronically ill children and their families.	
YMCA, Riverside, CA	8,000
Guide Dogs for the Blind, Los Angeles, CA	3,131
Skid Row Charity Fund, Los Angeles, CA	2,500
A Safe Place, Oakland, CA	1,500

Medicine--mental health

Scott Newman Center, Los Angeles, CA	500,000
Mental Health Advocacy Services, Los Angeles, CA	30,000
Toward implementation of Social Security Income (SSI) Outreach Pilot Project to chronically mentally disabled homeless persons.	
National Alliance for Research on Schizophrenia and Depression (NARSAD), Great Neck, NY	25,000
Threshold Foundation, San Francisco, CA	2,000
Union Rescue Mission, Los Angeles, CA	1,000

Medicine--specific diseases

Autism Society of America, Los Angeles, CA	200,000
Chapter Camp Fund.	
Kellogg Training Center, Los Angeles, CA	57,100
For technical assistance as part of Los Angeles AIDS Partnership. Grant shared with United Way, Inc..	
Aid for AIDS, West Hollywood, CA	24,250
Toward salary of Income Development Director.	
Betty Clooney Foundation for the Brain Injured, Los Angeles, CA	15,000
Clinica Msr. Oscar A. Romero, Los Angeles, CA	15,000
For technical assistance as part of Los Angeles AIDS Partnership.	
Gay and Lesbian Adolescent Social Services (GLASS), West Hollywood, CA	10,000
For technical assistance as part of Los Angeles AIDS Partnership.	
Westside Ecumenical Conference, Santa Monica, CA	10,000
For technical assistance as part of Los Angeles AIDS Partnership.	
Foothill AIDS Project	3,000
Cancer Foundation of Santa Barbara, Santa Barbara, CA	1,000

Community improvement & development

Bid Committee Los Angeles/Pasadena 1994, Los Angeles, CA	70,500
Inland Counties Interfaith Sponsoring Committee, San Bernardino, CA	25,000
Toward start-up costs for two-county community organizing effort to deal with such pressing issues as gang involvement and other social problems in Riverside and San Bernardino counties.	
Jewish Federation Council of Greater Los Angeles, Los Angeles, CA	20,000
Barrio Action Group, Los Angeles, CA	5,000
For development/planning audit.	
United Jewish Federation, San Diego, CA	1,000

Source(s): 05/92 NL, 1992 annual report
Employer Identification Number (EIN): 953510055

STATE AND LOCAL FUNDING DIRECTORIES

State and local funding directories can be extremely useful in identifying foundations that support programs in a particular geographic area. Compiled by commercial publishers, state government groups, libraries, associations of grantmakers, and other nonprofit agencies, there are many such directories available. In general, they vary widely in the type and amount of information they provide. The examples in Figures 21, 22, and 23 will give you an idea of the different formats and types of coverage.

The Foundation Center publishes one such directory, *New York State Foundations: A Comprehensive Directory*. The 1993 edition covers nearly 5,200 foundations located in New York State holding combined assets of $35 billion and awarding $2 billion annually in grants. Arranged by county, *New York State Foundations* includes complete or sample grants lists for 881 foundations (see Figure 24). An additional 786 non-New York grantmakers that fund nonprofits within the state are also covered. Access to this information is facilitated by an index to donors, officers, and trustees; a geographic index that references entries by the county and state in which the foundation maintains its principal office; a types of support index and a subject index, both of which list out-of-state foundations separately; and a foundation name index.

Not all state and regional directories have subject indexes. Where there is a subject index or subject coding, be sure you understand the basis on which the classifications were made. The currency of the information is also a major consideration in using these directories. Be sure to note the fiscal year upon which the information is based as well as the sources (e.g., annual reports, IRS returns, surveys) that were used to compile the information.

State and regional funding directories can be a very good source of information, particularly for smaller foundations not covered in major reference works. Those state and regional directories that do have a subject index may provide the only subject access to the giving patterns of smaller foundations. In addition, many of these directories list sample grants, which give you some indication of a funder's interests. Some directories also include information on corporations that fund giving programs in their geographic area, a very useful complement to foundation information.

Copies of many of these directories are available for public reference in the Center's five libraries (in New York, Washington, D.C., Atlanta, Cleveland, and San Francisco). The Center's Cooperating Collections generally have directories for their own state or region.

FIGURE 21.   Sample Entry from a Regional Directory

NCR Foundation

1700 South Patterson
Boulevard
Dayton, OH 45479
Montgomery County
(513) 445-2577

Contact: R. F. Beach, Vice President

Year ending: December 31, 1989
Fair market value: $ 5,451,882
Total grants: 68
Total grants amount: $ 2,696,040

Samples:

Art Center Foundation, Dayton	$ 800,000
Dayton Museum of Natural History	104,000
American Red Cross, Dayton Chapter	15,000
Montgomery Board of Education	5,000
National Minority Supplier Development Council	5,000
Dayton Fund for Home Rehabilitation	1,000

Types of support: Civic, culture, education, elderly, health, higher education, social service, united funds, youth

Restrictions: None

Solicitation information: Requests for grants should be submitted by letter. There is no deadline.

Officers/Trustees: G. Bassani, President; C. E. Erlley Jr., Chairman; R. F. Beach, Vice President; C. P. Russ, Secretary; N. M. Pao, Treasurer; P. F. Craven, Assistant Secretary; V. H. Hardesty, Jr., H. Holiday, Jr., C. S. Moravetz

---

Noonan Foundation

34 North Main Street
Dayton, OH 45402
Clark County
(513) 399-6358

Contact: Mary Lu Noonan, President

Year ending: June 30, 1990
Fair market value: $ 254,137
Total grants: 8
Total grants amount: $ 17,750

Samples:

Clark State College	$ 7,500
Springfield Arts Council	2,500
Planned Parenthood	2,500
Family Service Agency	1,000
North High Boosters	500
Clark County Special Olympics	250

66

Reprinted with permission from the *Southwest Ohio Foundation Directory.* 1st edition. Cincinnati, OH: MR & Company, 1991.

FIGURE 22.   Sample Entry from a County Directory

John Arrillaga Foundation
2560 Mission College Blvd., Suite 101
Santa Clara, CA 95050
(408) 980-0130

John Arrillaga
Director

Fields of Interest:	Civic, medical, youth and educational activities.
Geographic Preferences:	Grants are made primarily, but not exclusively, in Santa Clara County.
Application Deadlines:	There are no application deadlines.
Application Procedures:	The Foundation makes contributions to preselected charitable organizations and does not accept unsolicited requests for funds.
Total Grants Funded:	$729,510
Grant Range:	$150 - $130,000
Sample Grants:	$1,000 to Palo Alto Adolescent Services $18,800 to Peninsula Center for Blind and Visually Impaired $1,000 to Children's Home Society of California $1,000 to Role Model Program $1,300 to MidPeninsula Hospice Foundation
Total Assets:	$13,194,790
Officers and Directors:	John Arrillaga, President Frances C. Arrillaga, Vice-President John Arrillaga Jr.,Treasurer Richard T. Peery, Director
Source:	Guide to California Foundations IRS Form 990, 1992 Foundation Directory, 1993 Edition
Information Date:	Fiscal year ended September 30, 1992.

13

Reprinted with permission from the *Santa Clara County Foundation Directory.* Santa Clara, CA: Nonprofit Development Center, 1994.

FIGURE 23.   Sample Entry from a State Directory

Ecolab, Inc./Ecolab Foundation

370 Wabasha St.
St. Paul, MN 55102
(612) 293-2259

Contact person: Lois J. West, director, community and
public relations

Type: Corporate giving program and corporate foundation

Program description

Program's purpose: To support programs that support the
health and vitality of communities where Ecolab employees live and work.

Funding priorities: Education, especially secondary; programs that help special-disadvantaged become/remain
self-sufficient; programs that provide services for at-risk
children.

Program limitations/restrictions: No support to fundraisers, individuals, religious organizations, loans or investments, political or lobbying organizations or trade or
professional organizations.

Geographic focus: Twin Cities metro area, Out-of-state,

Geographic limitations: Communities where Ecolab employees live and work.

Types of programs funded:

ARTS, CULTURE, HUMANITIES: Mid-sized arts organizations. *Arts/cultural multipurpose*

EDUCATION: Economic education; institutions that
provide people and services which fit Ecolab's interests
and needs. *Secondary, Vocational/technical, Higher
education*

HEALTH - GENERAL/REHABILITATIVE: Pro-
grams which emphasize cost containment. *Health treatment facilities/outpatient*

HEALTH - MENTAL HEALTH/CRISIS INTERVEN-
TION: *Alcohol and drug abuse prevention/treatment*

CRIME/PUBLIC PROTECTION: *Rehabilitation services for offenders*

EMPLOYMENT/JOBS: *Employment procurement/job
training, Vocational rehabilitation*

HOUSING/SHELTER: *Housing development/construc-
tion/management*

YOUTH DEVELOPMENT: *Youth development programs*

HUMAN SERVICES: *Multipurpose human service organizations, Children/youth services, Emergency assistance (food/clothing/cash), Services promoting the in-
dependence of specific groups*

COMMUNITY IMPROVEMENT: *Community
funds/federated giving programs*

SCIENCE/TECHNOLOGY: *Science - general*

Targeted populations: Youth/adolescents (ages 14-19),
Adults, Ethnic/racial populations - general, Poor/eco-
nomically disadvantaged, Offenders/ex-offenders, Single parents, Disabled - general or unspecified disability

Types of support for organizations: General purpose/op-
erating support, Management/technical assistance

Support for individuals: None

Scholarship program for children of employees: Yes

Employee matching gift program: Higher education, Ele-
mentary/secondary education, Public broadcasting, Vo-
cational/technical

Sample grants: Business Economics Education Founda-
tion (BEEF)/operating/$8,000;
Science Museum of Minnesota/$8,000;
Community Sharing Fund/$2,500;
Children's Hospital of St. Paul/charitable care fund/
$2,000

Financial information

Financial data for year ending: 12/31/91

Assets: $92,193,200

Grants paid: $779,601

Number of grants: 88

Largest/smallest: $100,000/$500

Largest multi-year grant approved: $500,000

Purpose: Capital

Application information

Preferred form of initial contact: Complete proposal, Letter of inquiry

Proposal deadlines: July

Contributions decisions made by: Corporate Contributions Committee

Board meetings: Quarterly - January, April, July, October

Staff/trustees

Staff: Claire Villamor, community relations clerk

Directors/trustees: William Rosengren, chair; Diana
Lewis, John Forsythe, William Mathison, Arthur
Henningsen

Eddy, Edwin H., Family Foundation

230 West Superior St.
Duluth, MN 55803
(218) 723-2773

Contact person: Murray W. George, trustee

Established: 9/08/82

Type: Private foundation

Program description

Program's purpose: Research, rehabilitation, financial assistance, scholarships, projects, assistance in the area of
communicative disorders and related fields of neuro-pa-
thology.

Funding priorities: Research and education work in the
field of communicative disorders

Geographic limitations: Duluth, MN and surrounding
area; Superior, Wisconsin

47

Reprinted with permission from the *Guide to Minnesota Foundations and Corporate Giving Programs, 1993-94.*
Minneapolis, MN: Minnesota Council on Foundations, 1993.

FIGURE 24. Sample Entry from *New York State Foundations: A Comprehensive Directory*

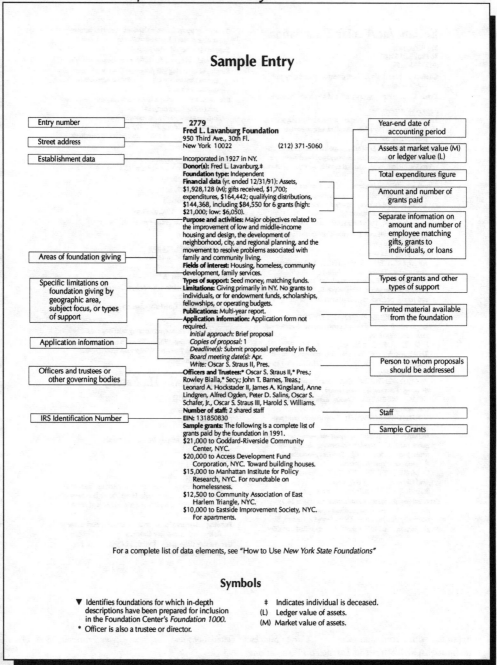

Sample Entry

Entry number
→ **2779**
Fred L. Lavanburg Foundation

Street address
→ 950 Third Ave., 30th Fl.
New York 10022   (212) 371-5060

Establishment data
→ Incorporated in 1927 in NY.
Donor(s): Fred L. Lavanburg,‡
Foundation type: Independent
Financial data (yr. ended 12/31/91): Assets, $1,928,128 (M); gifts received, $1,700; expenditures, $164,442; qualifying distributions, $144,368, including $84,550 for 6 grants (high: $21,000; low: $6,050).
Purpose and activities: Major objectives related to the improvement of low and middle-income housing and design, the development of neighborhood, city, and regional planning, and the movement to resolve problems associated with family and community living.

Areas of foundation giving
→ **Fields of interest:** Housing, homeless, community development, family services.
Types of support: Seed money, matching funds.

Specific limitations on foundation giving by geographic area, subject focus, or types of support
→ **Limitations:** Giving primarily in NY. No grants to individuals, or for endowment funds, scholarships, fellowships, or operating budgets.
Publications: Multi-year report.
Application information: Application form not required.

Application information
→ Initial approach: Brief proposal
Copies of proposal: 1
Deadline(s): Submit proposal preferably in Feb.
Board meeting date(s): Apr.
Write: Oscar S. Straus II, Pres.

Officers and trustees or other governing bodies
→ **Officers and Trustees:*** Oscar S. Straus II,* Pres.; Rowley Bialla,* Secy.; John T. Barnes, Treas.; Leonard A. Hockstader II, James A. Kingsland, Anne Lindgren, Alfred Ogden, Peter D. Salins, Oscar S. Schafer, Jr., Oscar S. Straus III, Harold S. Williams.
Number of staff: 2 shared staff

IRS Identification Number
→ **EIN:** 131850830
Sample grants: The following is a complete list of grants paid by the foundation in 1991.
$21,000 to Goddard-Riverside Community Center, NYC.
$20,000 to Access Development Fund Corporation, NYC. Toward building houses.
$15,000 to Manhattan Institute for Policy Research, NYC. For roundtable on homelessness.
$12,500 to Community Association of East Harlem Triangle, NYC.
$10,000 to Eastside Improvement Society, NYC. For apartments.

Year-end date of accounting period

Assets at market value (M) or ledger value (L)

Total expenditures figure

Amount and number of grants paid

Separate information on amount and number of employee matching gifts, grants to individuals, or loans

Types of grants and other types of support

Printed material available from the foundation

Person to whom proposals should be addressed

Staff

Sample Grants

For a complete list of data elements, see "How to Use *New York State Foundations*"

Symbols

▼ Identifies foundations for which in-depth descriptions have been prepared for inclusion in the Foundation Center's *Foundation 1000*.
* Officer is also a trustee or director.

‡ Indicates individual is deceased.
(L) Ledger value of assets.
(M) Market value of assets.

Specialized Reference Works

The number of specialized reference works available from both commercial and nonprofit publishers covering foundation and corporate grantmaking continues to grow. Given their number, the Foundation Center makes no recommendations as to specific resources beyond our own publications. However, a thorough funding search will most likely encompass a number of pertinent reference sources.

The bibliography in Appendix A provides a listing of some of the titles on philanthropy, fundraising, and the nonprofit sector available from prominent publishers in the field. Copies of the publications listed may be examined at the five Center-operated libraries and, on a selective basis, at many of the Center's Cooperating Collections. Local public and specialized libraries may have copies of some of them as well.

These materials vary widely in scope and format—so much so that it is nearly impossible to generalize about them. When working with a funding guide, for example, you will want to read the introductory material and scan the indexes to determine whether it is an appropriate reference tool for your needs. Funding guides tend to focus on the larger foundations, although some also include information on corporate and government grantmaking. Typically, they provide the grantmaker's address, program interests, some financial data, and deadlines for application.

There are a vast number of subject areas in which organizations seek funding, and a growing number of specialized funding directories available to meet their needs. Specialized funding guides generally cover a range of funding sources within a given subject field, including federal and local government agencies, foundations, corporations, and grantmaking public charities. They may also cover resources for specific population groups, types of support, geographic areas, or a combination of the above. Again, it is essential to study introductory materials and to familiarize yourself with the selection criteria and coverage of a given directory.

The bibliography in Appendix A lists a number of specialized funding guides in such diverse fields as higher education, services to the handicapped, the arts, health, and religion. You should also check with colleagues and your local library to see if a directory or guide exists in a field related to your interests. Trade and professional associations in your field may prove helpful in this regard as well.

Foundation Information Returns

One of the best sources of information on private foundations is the return—Form 990-PF—they are required to file annually with the IRS. Federal law requires that these documents, unlike personal or corporate tax returns, be made available to the public by both the IRS and the foundations themselves. This means that for all foundations, regardless of size, basic facts about their operations and grants are a matter of public record. For many smaller foundations this information return is the only complete record of their operations and grantmaking activities. For larger foundations, 990-PFs supply important information about assets and investments, as well as a complete list of grants awarded. Even when there is an annual report available, it is wise to examine a foundation's most current IRS information return before you decide to approach it for funds.

Generally, community foundations are not classified as private foundations and therefore are not required to file a Form 990-PF with the IRS. They do file Form 990, however. (See "How to Secure a Copy of a Nonprofit Organization's 990 Form" below.) Most community foundations also publish annual reports or otherwise make available information about their activities. See Figure 25 for the kinds of things you can find out by examining a foundation's Form 990-PF.

WHERE TO FIND COPIES OF FOUNDATION IRS RETURNS

To comply with federal law, foundations make copies of their 990-PFs available in their principal office for 180 days after filing. The foundation must announce in a general circulation newspaper that the form is available for inspection; usually these announcements are found in the "public notices" sections.

Free inspection of foundation information returns can be arranged in any IRS district office by writing to the district director ("Attention Taxpayer Service") and requesting the specific returns. You can also order complete sets of foundation returns or copies of individual returns from the IRS for a fee. Further information on this procedure is provided below.

Complete sets of IRS returns for all foundations are available in the Center's New York and Washington, D.C., libraries. The Center's Atlanta, Cleveland, and San Francisco offices have IRS returns for foundations in the southeastern, midwestern, and western states, respectively. Cooperating Collections that keep IRS returns for foundations in their own states are indicated by a bullet in Appendix D.

FIGURE 25. IRS Foundation Annual Return

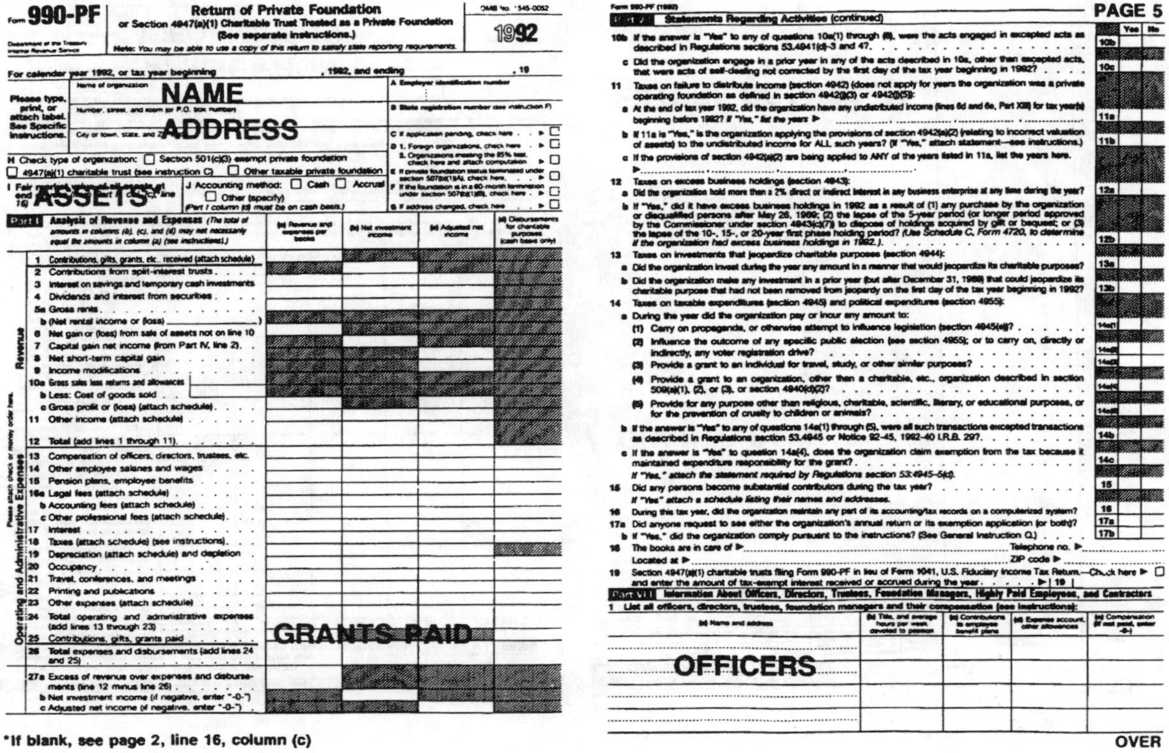

Form **990-PF** Department of the Treasury Internal Revenue Service

Return of Private Foundation
or Section 4947(a)(1) Charitable Trust Treated as a Private Foundation
(See separate instructions.)
Note: *You may be able to use a copy of this return to satisfy state reporting requirements.*

OMB No. 1545-0052
1992

For calendar year 1992, or tax year beginning ...., 1992, and ending ...., 19

Please type, print, or attach label. See Specific Instructions.
Name of organization **NAME**
Number, street, and room (or P.O. box number)
City or town, state, and ZIP **ADDRESS**

A Employer identification number
B State registration number (see instruction F)
C If application pending, check here ▶ ☐
D 1. Foreign organizations, check here ▶ ☐
2. Organizations meeting the 85% test, check here and attach computation ▶ ☐
E If private foundation status terminated under section 507(b)(1)(A), check here ▶ ☐
F If the foundation is in a 60-month termination under section 507(b)(1)(B), check here ▶ ☐
G If address changed, check here ▶ ☐

H Check type of organization: ☐ Section 501(c)(3) exempt private foundation
☐ 4947(a)(1) charitable trust (see instruction C) ☐ Other taxable private foundation
I Fair market value of all assets at end of year **ASSETS**
J Accounting method: ☐ Cash ☐ Accrual
☐ Other (specify)
(Part I column (d) must be on cash basis.)

Part I Analysis of Revenue and Expenses *(The total of amounts in columns (b), (c), and (d) may not necessarily equal the amounts in column (a) (see instructions).)*	(a) Revenue and expenses per books	(b) Net investment income	(c) Adjusted net income	(d) Disbursements for charitable purposes (cash basis only)
Revenue				
1 Contributions, gifts, grants, etc. received (attach schedule)				
2 Contributions from split-interest trusts				
3 Interest on savings and temporary cash investments				
4 Dividends and interest from securities				
5a Gross rents				
b (Net rental income or (loss))				
6 Net gain or (loss) from sale of assets not on line 10				
7 Capital gain net income (from Part IV, line 2)				
8 Net short-term capital gain				
9 Income modifications				
10a Gross sales less returns and allowances				
b Less: Cost of goods sold				
c Gross profit or (loss) (attach schedule)				
11 Other income (attach schedule)				
12 Total (add lines 1 through 11)				
Operating and Administrative Expenses				
13 Compensation of officers, directors, trustees, etc.				
14 Other employee salaries and wages				
15 Pension plans, employee benefits				
16a Legal fees (attach schedule)				
b Accounting fees (attach schedule)				
c Other professional fees (attach schedule)				
17 Interest				
18 Taxes (attach schedule) (see instructions)				
19 Depreciation (attach schedule) and depletion				
20 Occupancy				
21 Travel, conferences, and meetings				
22 Printing and publications				
23 Other expenses (attach schedule)				
24 Total operating and administrative expenses (add lines 13 through 23)				
25 Contributions, gifts, grants paid	**GRANTS PAID**			
26 Total expenses and disbursements (add lines 24 and 25)				
27a Excess of revenue over expenses and disbursements (line 12 minus line 26)				
b Net investment income (if negative, enter "-0-")				
c Adjusted net income (if negative, enter "-0-")				

Please attach check or money order here.

***If blank, see page 2, line 16, column (c)**

Form 990-PF (1992) **PAGE 5**

Part VI Statements Regarding Activities (continued)

		Yes	No
10b If the answer is "Yes" to any of questions 10a(1) through (6), were the acts engaged in excepted acts as described in Regulations sections 53.4941(d)-3 and 4?	10b		
c Did the organization engage in a prior year in any of the acts described in 10a, other than excepted acts, that were acts of self-dealing not corrected by the first day of the tax year beginning in 1992?	10c		
11 Taxes on failure to distribute income (section 4942) (does not apply for years the organization was a private operating foundation as defined in section 4942(j)(3) or 4942(j)(5)):			
a At the end of tax year 1992, did the organization have any undistributed income (lines 6d and 6e, Part XIII) for tax year(s) beginning before 1992? If "Yes," list the years ▶	11a		
b If 11a is "Yes," is the organization applying the provisions of section 4942(a)(2) (relating to incorrect valuation of assets) to the undistributed income for ALL such years? (If "Yes," attach statement—see instructions.)	11b		
c If the provisions of section 4942(a)(2) are being applied to ANY of the years listed in 11a, list the years here. ▶			
12 Taxes on excess business holdings (section 4943):			
a Did the organization hold more than a 2% direct or indirect interest in any business enterprise at any time during the year?	12a		
b If "Yes," did it have excess business holdings in 1992 as a result of (1) any purchase by the organization or disqualified persons after May 26, 1969; (2) the lapse of the 5-year period (or longer period approved by the Commissioner under section 4943(c)(7)) to dispose of holdings acquired by gift or bequest; or (3) the lapse of the 10-, 15-, or 20-year first phase holding period? *(Use Schedule C, Form 4720, to determine if the organization had excess business holdings in 1992.)*	12b		
13 Taxes on investments that jeopardize charitable purposes (section 4944):			
a Did the organization invest during the year any amount in a manner that would jeopardize its charitable purposes?	13a		
b Did the organization make any investment in a prior year (but after December 31, 1969) that could jeopardize its charitable purpose that had not been removed from jeopardy on the first day of the tax year beginning in 1992?	13b		
14 Taxes on taxable expenditures (section 4945) and political expenditures (section 4955):			
a During the year did the organization pay or incur any amount to:			
(1) Carry on propaganda, or otherwise attempt to influence legislation (section 4945(e))?	14a(1)		
(2) Influence the outcome of any specific public election (see section 4955); or to carry on, directly or indirectly, any voter registration drive?	14a(2)		
(3) Provide a grant to an individual for travel, study, or other similar purposes?	14a(3)		
(4) Provide a grant to an organization, other than a charitable, etc., organization described in section 509(a)(1), (2), or (3), or section 4940(d)(2)?	14a(4)		
(5) Provide for any purpose other than religious, charitable, scientific, literary, or educational purposes, or for the prevention of cruelty to children or animals?	14a(5)		
b If the answer is "Yes" to any of questions 14a(1) through (5), were all such transactions excepted transactions as described in Regulations section 53.4945 or Notice 92-45, 1992-40 I.R.B. 29?	14b		
c If the answer is "Yes" to question 14a(4), does the organization claim exemption from the tax because it maintained expenditure responsibility for the grant? *If "Yes," attach the statement required by Regulations section 53.4945-5(d).*	14c		
15 Did any persons become substantial contributors during the tax year? *If "Yes" attach a schedule listing their names and addresses.*	15		
16 During this tax year, did the organization maintain any part of its accounting/tax records on a computerized system?	16		
17a Did anyone request to see either the organization's annual return or its exemption application (or both)?	17a		
b If "Yes," did the organization comply pursuant to the instructions? (See General Instruction Q.)	17b		

18 The books are in care of ▶ .... Telephone no. ▶ ....
Located at ▶ .... ZIP code ▶ ....
19 Section 4947(a)(1) charitable trusts filing Form 990-PF in lieu of Form 1041, U.S. Fiduciary Income Tax Return.—Check here ▶ ☐
and enter the amount of tax-exempt interest received or accrued during the year ▶ | 19 |

Part VII Information About Officers, Directors, Trustees, Foundation Managers, Highly Paid Employees, and Contractors
1 List all officers, directors, trustees, foundation managers and their compensation (see instructions):

(a) Name and address	(b) Title, and average hours per week devoted to position	(c) Contributions to employee benefit plans	(d) Expense account, other allowances	(e) Compensation (If not paid, enter -0-)
OFFICERS				

OVER

FIGURE 25. IRS Foundation Annual Return (continued)

Form 990-PF (1992) **PAGE 9**

Part XIV Private Operating Foundations (see instructions and Part VII, question 9)

1a If the foundation has received a ruling or determination letter that it is a private operating foundation, and the ruling is effective for 1992, enter the date of the ruling . . . . . ▶

b Check box to indicate whether the organization is a private operating foundation described in section ☐ 4942(j)(3) or ☐ 4942(j)(5).

	Tax year	Prior 3 years			
	(a) 1992	(b) 1991	(c) 1990	(d) 1989	(e) Total
2a Enter the lesser of the adjusted net income from Part I or the minimum investment return from Part X (for 1991 and 1992; previously Part IX)					
b 85% of line 2a.					
c Qualifying distributions from Part XII, line 4 (for 1991 and 1992; previously Part XIII, line 6) .					
d Amounts included in line 2c not used directly for active conduct of exempt activities . .					
e Qualifying distributions made directly for active conduct of exempt activities (line 2c minus line 2d)					
3 Complete 3a, b, or c for the alternative test relied upon:					
a "Assets" alternative test—enter:					
(1) Value of all assets					
(2) Value of assets qualifying under section 4942(j)(3)(B)(i) .					
b "Endowment" alternative test—Enter ⅔ of minimum investment return shown in Part X, line 6, (for 1991 and 1992; previously Part IX, line 6) . .					
c "Support" alternative test—enter:					
(1) Total support other than gross investment income (interest, dividends, rents, payments on securities loans (section 512(a)(5)), or royalties) . . .					
(2) Support from general public and 5 or more exempt organizations as provided in section 4942(j)(3)(B)(iii) . . .					
(3) Largest amount of support from an exempt organization.					
(4) Gross investment income . .					

Part XV Supplementary Information (Complete this part only if the organization had $5,000 or more in assets at any time during the year—see instructions.)

1 **Information Regarding Foundation Managers:**

a List any managers of the foundation who have contributed more than 2% of the total contributions received by the foundation before the close of any tax year (but only if they have contributed more than $5,000). (See section 507(d)(2).)

b List any managers of the foundation who own 10% or more of the stock of a corporation (or an equally large portion of the ownership of a partnership or other entity) of which the foundation has a 10% or greater interest.

2 **Information Regarding Contribution, Grant, Gift, Loan, Scholarship, etc., Programs:**

* Check here ▶ ■ if the organization only makes contributions to preselected charitable organizations and does not accept unsolicited requests for funds. If the organization makes gifts, grants, etc., (see instructions) to individuals or organizations under other conditions, complete items 2a, b, c, and d.

a The name, address, and telephone number of the person to whom applications should be addressed:

b The form in which applications s[...] information and materials they should include:

APPLICATION

c Any submission deadlines:

INFORMATION

d Any restrictions or limitations on awards, such as by geographical areas, charitable fields, kinds of institutions, or other factors:

* Foundation does not accept unsolicited applications.

Form 990-PF (1992) **PAGE 10**

Part XV Supplementary Information (continued)

3 **Grants and Contributions Paid During the Year or Approved for Future Payment**

Recipient Name and address (home or business)	If recipient is an individual, show any relationship to any foundation manager or substantial contributor	Foundation status of recipient	Purpose of grant or contribution	Amount
a *Paid during the year*				
GRANTS PAID				
Total . . . . ▶ 3a				
b *Approved for future payment*				
FUTURE GRANTS				
Total . . . . ▶ 3b				

In most states, private foundations are required to file a copy of their 990-PF with the attorney general or charities registration office. You may be able to obtain a copy of a 990-PF by contacting the appropriate office in the state where the foundation is located. For a list of the appropriate offices in all 50 states and Puerto Rico, see Appendix B.

HOW TO SECURE A COPY OF A NONPROFIT ORGANIZATION'S 990 FORM

The annual information return filed by most nonprofits with the IRS is available to the public and can be obtained by writing to the appropriate IRS office. Be sure to enclose as much information about the organization as possible, including its full name, street address and zip code, its employer identification number (if available), and the year or years requested. It generally takes four to six weeks for the IRS to respond, and you will be billed for charges, which can vary depending on the number of pages involved.

If the nonprofit is headquartered in Alabama, Arkansas, Florida, Georgia, Louisiana, Mississippi, North Carolina, South Carolina, or Tennessee, write to:

Public Affairs Officer
Internal Revenue Service Center
P.O. Box 47-421
Doraville, GA 30362

If the nonprofit is headquartered in Arizona, Colorado, Kansas, New Mexico, Oklahoma, Texas, Utah, or Wyoming, write to:

Public Affairs Officer
Internal Revenue Service Center
P.O. Box 934
Austin, TX 78767

If the nonprofit is headquartered in Indiana, Kentucky, Michigan, Ohio, or West Virginia, write to:

Public Affairs Officer
Internal Revenue Service Center
P.O. Box 1699
Cincinnati, OH 45201

If the nonprofit is headquartered in Alaska, California, Hawaii, Idaho, Nevada, Oregon, or Washington, write to:

Public Affairs Officer
Internal Revenue Service Center
P.O. Box 12866
Fresno, CA 93779

If the nonprofit is headquartered in Connecticut, Delaware, Maine, Massachusetts, New Hampshire, New Jersey, New York, Pennsylvania (zip codes beginning with 169-171 and 173-196 only), Rhode Island, or Vermont, write to:

Public Affairs Officer
Internal Revenue Service Center
P.O. Box 400
Brookhaven, NY 11742

If the nonprofit is headquartered in Illinois, Iowa, Minnesota, Missouri, Montana, Nebraska, North Dakota, South Dakota, or Wisconsin, write to:

Public Affairs Officer
Internal Revenue Service Center
P.O. Box 24551
Kansas City, MO 64131

If the nonprofit is headquartered in Maryland, Pennsylvania (zip codes beginning with 150-168 and 172 only), Virginia, the District of Columbia, or any U.S. possession or a foreign country, write to:

Public Affairs Officer
Internal Revenue Service Center
11601 Roosevelt Blvd.
Philadelphia, PA 19154

Other Resources

Beyond the resources described in this chapter, Foundation Center libraries maintain collections of annual reports, information brochures, and newsletters published by foundation and corporate grantmakers in addition to files of news clippings, press releases, and historical materials dealing with philanthropy. Such resources can be particularly helpful in the final stages of your funding search as you try to gather detailed information about the grantmakers you have identified as the most likely funding sources for your program or organization.

In addition to the numerous print, computerized, and library resources covered in this guide and its appendices, there are a number of service organizations that provide assistance, training, and consultation in the areas of nonprofit management, fundraising, and voluntary action. Some of these organizations, such as the Grantsmanship Center in Los Angeles, provide information that complements or supplements information available through the Foundation Center. Others, such as the National Charities Information Bureau or the Philanthropic Advisory Service of the Better Business Bureau, may be able to provide you with information concerning funders that are not private foundations. Additionally, there are many trade and professional associations serving specific nonprofits that publish materials and/or provide training and consultation on fundraising-related matters to their members as part of their broader missions. Nonprofit groups might wish to consult the *Encyclopedia of Associations*, published by the Gale Research Company of Detroit, Michigan, for information about trade and professional associations in their fields.

FOUNDATION ANNUAL REPORTS

Generally, a foundation's annual report will provide the most complete and current information available about that foundation. Annual reports usually include detailed financial statements, a comprehensive list of grants awarded or committed for future payment, the names of officers and staff members, and a definition of program interests. Most annual reports also indicate the application procedures grantseekers should follow, including any application deadlines and particular proposal formats the foundation may prefer. Some annual reports include information on the foundation's donors in addition to essays on the operating philosophy that informs its grantmaking decisions.

Foundations are not required by law to compile a separately printed annual report. Those that do tend to be community foundations and foundations with assets of $1 million or more. Entries in the general reference directories published by the Foundation Center—the *Guide to U.S. Foundations*, *The Foundation Directory*, *The Foundation Directory Part 2*, and *The Foundation 1000*—indicate whether the foundation publishes an annual report. In addition to noting changes at the nation's major foundations in its "Updates on Grantmakers" section, *The Foundation Grants Index Quarterly* includes a listing of annual reports recently received by the Foundation Center along with contact addresses to which you can write to receive a copy of the report. Foundation Center libraries maintain collections of annual reports issued by foundations in their local communities and by national foundations located elsewhere. Because so few foundations publish annual reports, it is wise to check the resources in your local Cooperating Collection before you waste time and money requesting reports from foundations that don't publish them.

OTHER FOUNDATION PUBLICATIONS

Many foundations issue brochures, pamphlets, news releases, or newsletters that provide information on application procedures, specific grant programs or recent grants, and announcements regarding changes in foundation staff and trustees. Although such publications are most frequently issued by larger, staffed foundations, there are any number of smaller foundations that publish descriptive brochures in lieu of a more extensive annual report. These documents are more than a source of facts about the foundation; they are also a good medium for determining its "personality."

The Foundation Center's libraries collect as many foundation pamphlets and news releases as possible. Many of the Center's cooperating libraries also collect publications issued by area grantmakers and make them available to the public. If you have identified grantmakers who are active in your subject field or geographic area, you may even be able to have your name added to their mailing list by writing or calling the foundation directly.

Newspaper and Magazine Articles

From time to time, you may have seen articles about foundations in local newspapers and observed that while a few foundations seem to get all the press, most are never mentioned. The Foundation Center subscribes to a newspaper clipping service that scans hundreds of newspapers from around the country and forwards to the Center any articles dealing with grantmakers and philanthropy.

Occasionally, national magazines print articles on individual grantmakers or on foundations in general. You can look up such articles using major periodical indexes like the *Reader's Guide to Periodical Literature,* the *Business Periodicals Index*, or the *Public Affairs Information Service* (PAIS), most of which are available in your local library. The most comprehensive listing of periodicals and monographs dealing with philanthropy and related fields is *The Literature of the Nonprofit Sector*, a five-volume bibliography with abstracts published by the Foundation Center.

The Center's libraries obtain and catalog copies of relevant articles, studies, and reports. You'll find that the files maintained by the Center's libraries in New York, Washington, D.C., Atlanta, Cleveland, and San Francisco provide the most comprehensive collection of information available on specific grantmakers, philanthropy, and foundation activity in general. While most visitors to its libraries are searching for funding and concentrate on using the materials described in this guide, Center libraries are also used by foundation personnel, journalists, researchers, authors, and students interested in all aspects of philanthropic and nonprofit activity.

People

Published directories, indexes of foundation grants, and materials issued by the grantmakers themselves are an enormous help in sorting out funders who may be interested in providing grant support to your organization from funders who are unlikely to provide such support. But thorough funding research also involves another important resource—people.

Talk to your professional colleagues about funding approaches they have tried as well as about their contacts with grantmakers active in your community or subject field. When you learn about an interesting grant from one of your funding prospects, contact the recipient organization's leaders and ask about their experiences with the funder.

Research the foundation affiliations of board members, volunteers, and other individuals who have an active interest in your work. (Refer to Volume Two of the *Guide to U.S. Foundations, Their Trustees, Officers, and Donors* for help in ascertaining foundation affiliations.) Individuals who are familiar with or have worked with one of your foundation prospects may be able to advise you on preparing your proposal and/or direct you to the person within the foundation who should receive your application.

Sources close to the foundation may be aware of impending changes in funding policies, staff, or application criteria that could affect your grant request.

Your own past and current donors are another resource for learning more about the program interests of potential funding sources. Share your proposal with your current supporters and fill them in on the funders you think will be interested in providing additional support. In addition to providing useful advice, supporters may be willing to tell other people about your programs and about their positive experiences with your organization.

Finally, if a funding prospect has staff, find out if they will meet with you to discuss your idea and the appropriate application procedures. Although most foundations do not have staff, those that do often prefer to discuss proposed projects with applicants prior to the submission of a formal grant request. It is usually best to approach such foundations with a brief letter of introduction describing your organization and program, followed by a phone call to ask for an appointment. For specific recommendations about approaching foundations by letter or phone, consult *The Foundation Center's Guide to Proposal Writing*.

Personal contacts should not be viewed as a substitute for funding research, nor are they a requirement for obtaining grant support. Still, your personal and professional contacts can be a valuable supplement to the published information on funding sources. In the final analysis, a successful fundraising strategy involves intense effort that takes advantage of all the available resources.

To learn all you can about your funding prospects, follow the eight steps outlined in Figure 26.

FIGURE 26.   Learning All You Can About Your Foundation Prospects

Before you apply for a grant, you need to gather as much information as possible about your foundation prospects. Doing so will help you to determine whether your funding needs match their giving interests, whether they are likely to support organizations in your geographic area, whether they are likely to provide the type and amount of support you need, and how and when to submit your grant request. In using the materials below to complete a prospect worksheet for each foundation that might be interested in your proposal, note the date and source of the information gathered to be sure you have the most current and accurate information available.

STEP 1.   FOUNDATION ANNUAL REPORTS are issued by more than 900 foundations. When available, they are generally the most complete source of information on a foundation's current and future interests, restrictions, and application procedures. Check entries in *The Foundation 1000, The Foundation Directory,* and the *Guide to U.S. Foundations, Their Trustees, Officers, and Donors,* as well as the "Grantmakers' Publications" section in *The Foundation Index Quarterly,* to find out if a foundation publishes an annual report.

STEP 2.   OTHER FOUNDATION PUBLICATIONS. More than 700 foundations that do not publish annual reports do issue information brochures, application guidelines, or other materials that describe their giving programs. Check entries in *The Foundation 1000, The Foundation Directory,* and the "Grantmakers' Publications" section in *The Foundation Index Quarterly* to determine if such materials are available.

STEP 3.   *THE FOUNDATION 1000* analyzes the 1,000 largest foundations in depth. In the absence of materials published by the foundation itself, this is the most complete source of information on the largest foundations.

STEP 4.   *THE FOUNDATION DIRECTORY* provides basic descriptions of foundations with $2 million or more in assets or annual giving of at least $200,000. Check *The Foundation Directory Part 2* for descriptions of smaller foundations that make grants totaling $50,000 to $200,000 annually.

STEP 5.   *THE FOUNDATION GRANTS INDEX QUARTERLY* includes "Updates on Grantmakers," which lists changes in name, address, personnel, and/or programs reported by major foundations in the preceding three months.

STEP 6.   FOUNDATION INFORMATION RETURNS (IRS Form 990-PF) are filed annually by all private foundations and include complete lists of grants awarded during the tax year of record in addition to supplemental information on finances, donors, and trustees. These returns are often the only source of information on smaller foundations. Available from the Internal Revenue Service or at Foundation Center libraries.

STEP 7.   NEWSPAPER OR MAGAZINE ARTICLES often provide news or insights on the personnel or program interests of foundations. Check with your local library for foundation files or indexes to relevant articles.

STEP 8.   PEOPLE. Talk to your professional colleagues, board members, volunteers, past and current donors, and anyone else interested in your work for advice on your project proposal and funding prospects.

Chapter 6

Finding the Right Funder:
The Subject Approach

The subject approach to funding research helps a nonprofit organization identify foundations with a common interest in (a) its field of activity, (b) the population group it serves, and/or (c) the type of agency or organization it represents. A church providing services to children with AIDS, for example, would look for funders with some of these same interests.

Identifying a Foundation's Interests

Foundation interests generally are indicated in two ways: by the foundation's own description of its purpose and activities and by the giving priorities reflected in the actual grants it makes. Statements of purpose are often left deliberately broad by foundations to allow for future shifts in emphasis. Although they may provide important information about funders' giving priorities, they should not be taken as gospel. Instead, compare them to actual giving records. Statements such as "general charitable giving" and "to promote human welfare" don't really mean a foundation will support every imaginable type of charitable activity. What a foundation will support is often best determined by what it has supported recently. The directories, annual reports, newsletters, and other resources described in Chapter 5 will help direct you to both statements of purpose and records of actual grants.

Developing a Subject Prospect List

Before you begin to develop your prospect list—that list of funders interested in your subject area—take a few minutes to think about all the fields related to your organization's general mission or to the particular program you're trying to fund. For example, if you're working for a day-care center that is planning a special program for parents on child nutrition, your list of subject terms might include day care, children, food, nutrition, boys, girls, and parental education. Scanning the subject indexes of publications such as *The Foundation Directory* and *The Foundation Grants Index* may suggest other applicable terms.

In developing your initial list, keep the focus broad. This is not the time to concentrate your search too narrowly. Remember, it is rare, and not necessarily desirable, to find a grant that precisely matches your needs: a funder may not want to make a grant for a project that so closely duplicates one it just funded. If you restrict yourself to looking for exact matches, you'll end up overlooking potential funders interested in activities similar, although not identical, to your own.

As you research each foundation, focus on the basic facts outlined in the "Prospect Worksheet" (Figure 8). Check to see that your organization operates in the geographic area where the foundation makes grants and that the foundation gives the type of support your organization needs. Chapters 7 and 8 discuss in greater detail the geographic and types of support approaches to funding research.

Using Reference Sources Effectively

You may well be using several types of reference books to develop your initial prospects list—indexes of foundation grants, national and state directories describing foundation giving interests and guidelines, and specialized funding guides in your subject field. Although all grantseekers develop their own research strategies, the staff of the

Foundation Center recommends the sequence outlined in Figure 27 to those using its publications for the first time.

To avoid duplication of effort with reference sources, take time to read the introductory material explaining the coverage of each directory. Knowing, for instance, that *Grant Guides* are subsets of *The Foundation Grants Index* may prevent you from researching the same grants information twice.

INDEXES TO FOUNDATION GRANTS

Indexes to foundation grants provide listings of actual grants awarded, enabling you to determine the specific subject interests of a foundation, the type and location of organizations it has funded in the past, the size of the grants it has awarded, and the types of support it favors. The three indexes we discuss below are derived from the Foundation Center's database, which was described more fully in Chapter 5. The database tracks grants of $10,000 or more awarded by about 1,000 major foundations. Because many of these foundations make relatively large grants for programs that have a national focus, the indexes will be most helpful to grantseekers whose projects are of a size and scope to attract the interest of national foundations.

You should begin your research by looking at the *Grant Guide* that is most applicable to your program. There are 30 *Grant Guides*; all are arranged alphabetically by foundation state and name. Each *Grant Guide* includes a list of foundations with their addresses and giving limitations, a subject index of keywords, an index of recipients organized by state, and an index of recipients organized by name.

Begin with the alphabetical list of foundations provided in the back of each book. This listing includes the foundation's address and a brief statement of any restrictions on its giving program (see Figure 28). This will help you eliminate foundations that do not award grants in your geographic area. To complete your prospect worksheet—types of grant recipients, types of support awarded, and so on—scan the grants listed under foundations whose restrictions do not seem to prohibit them from funding your proposal.

Once you have developed an initial list of prospects using the *Grant Guides*, you may want to expand your list by checking the references in *The Foundation Grants Index*. The *Grants Index* lists all grants of $10,000 or more reported by foundations in the preceding year, regardless of subject focus. It is particularly useful if your program or organization falls under a variety of subject fields, or if there is no appropriate *Grant Guide* for your subject area.

FIGURE 27. Finding the Right Funder: The Subject Approach

The Subject Approach helps you identify potential funding sources that have expressed an interest in your subject field, the population groups you serve, and the type of organization you represent. Most of the sources listed below cover both national and local funding sources. As you complete your prospect list using these resources, be sure to check for any stated restrictions on the funders' giving programs to eliminate those that do not fund in your geographic area, do not provide the type or amount of support you need, or do not fund your type of organization.

STEP 1. **INDEXES OF FOUNDATION GRANTS** list grants of $10,000 or more awarded by about 1,000 major foundations. By reviewing actual grants, you can identify funders with a demonstrated interest in your subject area.

• *GRANT GUIDES* list grants in 30 broad subject fields. Scan grants lists of foundations located in your state. Use the Recipient Index and list of foundation addresses and limitations to identify foundations in other states that have funded or might fund organizations in your area.

• *THE FOUNDATION GRANTS INDEX* lists all grants reported the previous year. Use if there is no *Grant Guide* for your subject field and to review the broad grant activities of a foundation. Check the Subject Index under all applicable terms, the Type of Support/Geographic Index under your category and state, and the Recipient Category Index under your type of institution, type of support needed, and state.

•*THE FOUNDATION GRANTS INDEX QUARTERLY* lists grants reported during the preceding three months. Use to investigate the most current giving interests of major foundations. Check the Subject Index under all applicable terms and the Grant Recipient Index for organizations similar to your own. Scan grants lists of foundations in your state as well as foundations in other states that are not restricted from giving in your geographic area.

STEP 2. *THE FOUNDATION 1000* analyzes the 1,000 largest foundations in depth. Check the Index of Subjects under all relevant terms for foundations in your own state or national foundations (listed in bold type) in other states.

STEP 3. • *THE FOUNDATION DIRECTORY* describes more than 6,700 foundations with assets of $2 million or more or annual giving of at least $200,000, along with lists of sample grants for approximately 40 percent of the entries.

• *THE FOUNDATION DIRECTORY PART 2* provides similar information on approximately 4,000 foundations with assets of less than $2 million and annual giving between $50,000 and $200,000, along with lists of sample grants for three-quarters of the foundations covered. Check the Subject Index under appropriate terms for foundations in your own state or national foundations (listed in bold type) in other states.

STEP 4. **STATE AND LOCAL FOUNDATION DIRECTORIES.** Coverage and content vary. Check with your local library to find directories that cover your state. Use the subject index, if available, or scan entries to identify possible prospects.

STEP 5. **SPECIALIZED FUNDING GUIDES.** Coverage and content vary. Check the bibliography in Appendix A and your local library to identify relevant guides.

STEP 6. **REVIEW YOUR PROSPECT LIST** to eliminate foundations that are unable or unlikely to provide funding in your geographic area, to provide the type or amount of support you need, or to fund your type of organization. Research your remaining prospects to determine those most likely to consider your request favorably.

FIGURE 28.   Sample List of Foundations in the *Grant Guides* Series

Foundations

The following is an alphabetical list of foundations appearing in this volume, including any geographic restrictions on the foundation's giving program. A full listing of geographic, program, and type of support limitations is provided with the full listing of each foundation's grants in Section 1. Please read these limitations carefully, as well as additional program and application information available in the foundation's report or other Foundation Center publications, before applying for grant assistance. Foundations in bold face are among the 100 largest.

The Abell Foundation, Inc.
1116 Fidelity Bldg.
210 North Charles St.
Baltimore, MD 21201-4013
(301) 547-1300
Limitations: Giving limited to MD,
   with a focus on Baltimore.
Publishes an annual or periodic report.

Abell-Hanger Foundation
P.O. Box 430
Midland, TX 79702
(915) 684-6655
Limitations: Giving limited to TX,
   preferably within the Permian
   Basin.
Publishes an annual or periodic report.

The Ahmanson Foundation
9215 Wilshire Blvd.
Beverly Hills, CA 90210
(310) 278-0770
Limitations: Giving primarily in
   Southern CA, with emphasis on
   the Los Angeles area.
Publishes an annual or periodic report.

The Arcana Foundation, Inc.
901 15th St., N.W., Suite 1000
Washington, DC 20005
(202) 789-7280
Limitations: Giving primarily in
   Washington, DC.

Arizona Community Foundation
2122 East Highland Ave., Suite 400
Phoenix, AZ 85016
(602) 381-1400
Limitations: Giving limited to AZ.
Publishes an annual or periodic report.

The Aspen Foundation
400 East Main St.
Aspen, CO 81611
(303) 925-9300
Limitations: Giving primarily in
   Pitkin, Garfield, and Eagle
   counties, CO.
Publishes an annual or periodic report.

The Beatrice Fox Auerbach Foundation
25 Brookside Blvd.
West Hartford, CT 06107
(203) 232-5854
Limitations: Giving primarily in the
   Hartford, CT, area.

Ball Brothers Foundation
222 South Mulberry St.
P.O. Box 1408
Muncie, IN 47308
(317) 741-5500
Limitations: Giving limited to IN.

George and Frances Ball Foundation
P.O. Box 1408
Muncie, IN 47308
Additional address: 222 South
   Mulberry St., Muncie, IN 47305
(317) 741-5500
Limitations: Giving primarily in
   Muncie, IN.

Baton Rouge Area Foundation
One American Place, Suite 610
Baton Rouge, LA 70825
(504) 387-6126
Limitations: Giving limited to the
   Baton Rouge, LA, area, including
   East Baton Rouge, West Baton
   Rouge, Livingston, Ascension,
   Iberville, Pointe Coupee, East
   Feliciana, and West Feliciana
   parishes.
Publishes an annual or periodic report.

Arnold and Mabel Beckman
   Foundation
Grants Advisory Council
100 Academy Drive
Irvine, CA 92715
(714) 721-2222

Beldon Fund
2000 P St., N.W., Suite 410
Washington, DC 20036
(202) 293-1928
Publishes an annual or periodic report.

BellSouth Foundation
c/o BellSouth Corp.
1155 Peachtree St., N.E., Rm. 7H08
Atlanta, GA 30367-6000
(404) 249-2396
Limitations: Giving primarily in areas
   of company operations in AL, FL,
   GA, KY, LA, MS, NC, SC, and
   TN.
Publishes an annual or periodic report.

Claude Worthington Benedum
   Foundation
1400 Benedum-Trees Bldg.
Pittsburgh, PA 15222
(412) 288-0360
Limitations: Giving limited to WV
   and southwestern PA.

F. R. Bigelow Foundation
1120 Norwest Ctr.
St. Paul, MN 55101
(612) 224-5463
Limitations: Giving limited to the
   greater St. Paul, MN,
   metropolitan area.
Publishes an annual or periodic report.

The *Grants Index* is divided into major subject fields, under which grants are arranged by foundation name and state. It includes indexes to grants listings by recipient name, specific subject focus, type of support categories subdivided by the state location of the grant recipient, type of recipient organization subdivided by the type of support awarded, and an index to grants by foundation.

To add to your prospect list, you should:

1. scan the grants lists of foundations located in your state;
2. check grants in your specific subject field in the Subject Index and the Type of Support/Geographic Index (see Figures 29 and 30);
3. check grants awarded to organizations similar to your own in the Recipient Name Index and the Recipient Category Index (see Figures 31 and 32).

Again, you will want to look at the size and nature of the grants the foundation typically makes in addition to the type and location of the organizations it supports. Note any giving-limitation statement provided immediately under the foundation's name.

To get the most current information on foundation funding interests and to add to your prospect list the names of foundations newly active in your field, check the listings in *The Foundation Grants Index Quarterly*. Each *Quarterly* lists 5,000–7,000 recently reported foundation grants indexed by subject and recipient organization name.

GENERAL REFERENCE DIRECTORIES

At this point you may have developed a fairly long list of prospects. However, because the *Grants Index* publications cover only one thousand or so of the nation's major foundations, you've just gotten started. To expand your prospect list, you should next turn to the general reference directories available to you. Include local foundation directories as well as national ones, and be especially alert to specialized subject directories in your field. Typically, you'll find that indexes to foundation grants provide far more specific subject references than foundation directories, which usually employ a very general terminology to describe foundation program interests; as a result, the terms provided in their subject indexes are equally non-specific.

We usually recommend that you begin with the Foundation Center's *Foundation 1000*, an annual publication that provides detailed analyses of the nation's largest

FIGURE 29. Subject Index in *The Foundation Grants Index*

SUBJECT INDEX

Athletics/sports, blacks 4365, 4394, 53555, 53556, 63810
Athletics/sports, boys & young men 18678, 57887, 57914, 57917, 57918, 57945, 58564, 63431
Athletics/sports, building/renovation 17386, 18628, 19077, 19671, 20160, 20724, 20761, 24213, 24214, 26405, 37471, 38943, 40835, 41463, 41465, 43376, 49571, 49586, 52187, 57729, 57730, 57737, 57749, 57753, 57756, 57759, 57760, 57765, 57771, 57776, 57783, 57786, 57792, 57796, 57802, 57809, 57838, 57860-57862, 57864, 57865, 57876, 57887, 57888, 57899, 57900, 57904, 57906, 57908, 57912, 57914, 57928, 57945, 57969, 57972, 57988, 58016, 58018, 58034, 58039, 58042, 58044-58046, 58049, 58060, 58070, 58073, 58083, 58090, 58106, 58111, 58116, 58122, 58177, 58182, 58195, 58197, 58227-58230, 58247-58251, 58299, 58312, 58318, 58324, 58342, 58352, 58366, 58367, 58369, 58377, 58383, 58385, 58386, 58395, 58414, 58425, 58427, 58430, 58435, 58443, 58487, 58488, 58523, 58525-58527, 58536, 58538, 58539, 58564, 58565, 58569, 58581, 58585, 58587, 58617, 58619, 58624, 58632
Athletics/sports, capital campaigns 57749, 57808, 57859, 57863, 57944, 58082, 58425
Athletics/sports, children & youth 2194, 19077, 19499, 19671, 37888, 37896, 41465, 43376, 47999, 57744, 57758, 57762, 57771, 57813, 57831, 57861, 57864, 57867, 57904, 57915, 57932, 57940, 57969, 57972, 57985, 58040, 58197, 58198, 58226, 58230, 58269, 58294, 58355, 58395, 58417, 58509, 58510, 58512, 58569, 58581, 58617, 60266
Athletics/sports, computer systems/equipment 57905
Athletics/sports, conferences/seminars 19499, 60046
Athletics/sports, deaf 18628, 57932
Athletics/sports, debt reduction 40432
Athletics/sports, disabled 37379, 37774, 37835, 37861, 37888, 37934, 38201, 38435, 38490, 38734, 38943, 39348, 40432, 40835, 41170, 41463, 41465, 41633, 49571, 57756, 57762, 57823, 57830, 57912, 57939, 58305, 58487, 58585
Athletics/sports, economically disadvantaged 38575, 41465, 53555, 53556, 57791, 57857, 57985
Athletics/sports, endowments 58137
Athletics/sports, equestrianism 5900, 9363, 37379, 37774, 37835, 37861, 37888, 37934, 38201, 38435, 38490, 38734, 38943, 39348, 40432, 40719, 40835, 41170, 41546, 41633, 57729, 57762, 57939, 58090, 58096, 58097, 58099-58103, 58192, 58281, 58358, 58487, 58534, 58565, 59316, 59317
Athletics/sports, equipment 17168, 57746, 57768, 57774, 57792, 57861, 57892, 57925, 57935, 58032, 58033, 58040, 58128, 58227, 58228, 58426, 58497, 62345
Athletics/sports, faculty/staff development 19499, 57968, 58041, 58282
Athletics/sports, film/video/radio 58320, 58323, 58480, 58534, 63810
Athletics/sports, football 4718, 37896, 58304, 58523
Athletics/sports, girls & young women 57730, 57809, 57862, 57908, 57914, 57928, 58275, 58276, 63431
Athletics/sports, golf 57921-57923, 58115, 58119, 58249-58251, 58436, 58593, 63892
Athletics/sports, homeless 57914
Athletics/sports, ice sports 57820, 57826, 57828, 57932, 57935, 58098, 58272, 58275, 58276, 58318, 58417, 58531, 58614, 58615, 58632
Athletics/sports, land acquisition 37774
Athletics/sports, mentally disabled 18678, 19077, 19671, 41546, 43376, 57802, 57904, 58230, 58395
Athletics/sports, minorities 19499, 38575, 57857, 57985, 58302
Athletics/sports, Native Americans 58083, 58111
Athletics/sports, Olympics 2194, 57736, 57737, 57749, 57791, 57806, 57840, 57920, 57978, 57979, 57992, 57993, 58089, 58104, 58186, 58252, 58253, 58282, 58325, 58329, 58400, 58402, 58443, 58592, 58608, 58632
Athletics/sports, performance/productions 2194
Athletics/sports, physically disabled 37471, 37896, 40719, 57820, 58565
Athletics/sports, professional leagues 3311, 4365, 4394
Athletics/sports, professorships 58540
Athletics/sports, publication 12481, 57988, 58271
Athletics/sports, racquet sports 57744, 57748, 57867, 57988, 57989, 58198, 58212, 58214, 58269, 58294, 58324, 58349, 58594
Athletics/sports, research 12481, 57825, 57826
Athletics/sports, scholarships 9746, 57845, 58115, 58133, 58610
Athletics/sports, school programs 17168, 17386, 18015, 18678, 19302, 19499, 19671, 20160, 20724, 20761, 24213, 24214, 43376, 57730, 57733, 57751, 57753, 57759, 57765, 57768, 57774, 57841, 57860, 57865, 57876, 57899, 57904, 57908, 57928, 57953, 57972, 58016, 58018, 58032, 58034, 58044-58046, 58049, 58060, 58073, 58083, 58115, 58116, 58133, 58135, 58137, 58177, 58227, 58228, 58230, 58247, 58248, 58271, 58299, 58366, 58383, 58386, 58414, 58418, 58425, 58490, 58523, 58538-58540, 58555, 58581, 58587, 58624, 62345
Athletics/sports, seed money 38734, 41463, 57823, 57918
Athletics/sports, soccer 47999, 57859, 57863, 57946, 58014, 58061, 58404, 58406, 58407, 58611, 58629
Athletics/sports, Special Olympics 57734, 57738, 57739, 57780, 57817, 57821, 57848, 57857, 57869, 57882, 57905, 57915, 57940, 57944, 57964, 57968, 57974, 58035, 58041, 58080-58082, 58084, 58131, 58167, 58285, 58286, 58306, 58307, 58320, 58323, 58399, 58426, 58521, 58609, 58612
Athletics/sports, training 26405, 38575, 49586, 57737, 57749, 57806, 57900, 57914, 57916, 58042, 58187, 58215, 58229, 58352, 58369, 58619
Athletics/sports, water sports 3475, 18628, 19077, 37471, 41463, 41465, 49571, 52187, 57742, 57747, 57756, 57760, 57765, 57783, 57786, 57796, 57800, 57802, 57808, 57838, 57862, 57887, 57892, 57893, 57906, 57912, 57913, 57945, 57985, 58039, 58042, 58044, 58070, 58106, 58111, 58122, 58128, 58174, 58182, 58188, 58195, 58197, 58217, 58226, 58312, 58342, 58385, 58395, 58427, 58430, 58435, 58441, 58488, 58517, 58527, 58545, 58563, 58564, 58569, 58585, 58607, 60266
Athletics/sports, women 57753, 58045, 58073
Athletics/sports, youth 18015, 38575, 57751, 57792, 57857, 57921-57923, 57935, 57995, 58061, 58302, 58346, 58349, 58399, 58406, 58488, 58497, 58525, 58531, 63810, 63892
Australia, arts/culture/humanities 4894, 6939
Australia, community improvement/development 54811, 55984
Australia, education 21324, 21757, 39759, 54812
Australia, food/nutrition/agriculture 61557
Australia, health—general 39759, 40285, 54721
Australia, international affairs/development 40285, 54721, 54811, 54812, 55367, 55606, 55747, 57105, 61557, 63075
Australia, medical research 41931
Australia, philanthropy/voluntarism 55984
Australia, public affairs/government 57105
Australia, religion 59021
Australia, science 61557
Australia, social sciences 54721, 54811, 55367, 63075
Austria, arts/culture/humanities 815, 8481, 62596
Austria, community improvement/development 12368
Austria, education 31237, 54930
Austria, international affairs/development 8481, 54927-54930, 54962, 55059, 55184, 55397, 62597
Austria, public affairs/government 55059
Austria, religion 59900
Austria, science 55184
Austria, social sciences 54927, 54929, 55059, 55397, 62596, 62597, 62604, 63356
Autism, building/renovation 44945, 44946
Autism, children & youth 18458, 19149, 44637, 44945, 53442
Autism, curriculum development 53442
Autism, equipment 44041
Autism, mentally disabled 18458, 19149, 43247, 43474, 44041, 44153, 44530, 44534, 44599, 44637, 44651, 44945, 44946, 53442
Autism, seed money 43474

Ballet 592, 621, 624, 637, 977, 982, 988, 1032, 1072, 1077, 1125, 1191, 1216, 1329, 1454, 1543, 1567, 1818, 1922, 2018, 2019, 2122, 2166, 2237, 2251, 2300, 2340, 2347, 2469, 2508, 2675, 2676, 2911, 2914, 2915, 3042, 3089, 3156, 3157, 3160, 3215, 3273, 3289, 3336, 3358, 3385, 3595, 3811, 4059, 4177, 4190, 4341, 4359, 4399, 4400, 4551, 4618, 4689, 4724, 4772, 4777, 4860, 4879, 4957, 4967, 4991, 5025, 5034, 5045, 5048, 5058, 5067, 5085, 5103-5106, 5177, 5393, 5403, 5415, 5435, 5479, 5515, 5516, 5594, 5817, 5823, 5827, 5828, 5897, 6012, 6389, 6400, 6436, 6441, 6453-6455, 6459, 6472, 6562, 6583, 6601, 6653, 6729, 6731, 6774, 6783, 6976, 7063, 7064, 7125, 7159, 7169, 7196, 7214, 7216, 7218, 7234, 7241, 7263, 7272, 7277, 7298, 7319, 7394, 7438, 7456, 7462, 7517, 7682, 7686, 7800, 7816, 7836, 7877, 7882, 8016, 8027, 8049, 8073, 8086, 8202, 8208, 8261, 8267, 8337, 8374, 8375, 8427, 8443, 8444, 8468, 8504, 8505, 8515, 8529, 8546, 8562, 8565, 8580, 8639, 8654, 8678, 8762, 8820, 8856, 8903, 8921, 8935, 9010, 9015, 9034, 9087, 9144, 9265, 9298, 9311, 9330, 9510, 9553, 9562, 9795, 9824, 9873, 9879, 9930
Ballet, blacks 6771
Ballet, building/renovation 3112, 3650, 3737, 5980, 8109, 8207, 9310
Ballet, capital campaigns 3357, 5980, 8496, 9463
Ballet, children & youth 1896, 2573, 4584, 4836, 4868, 5158, 5374, 5913, 5929, 5956, 6771, 9525
Ballet, computer systems/equipment 1458, 3073
Ballet, curriculum development 6296, 6315, 6318, 6327, 6331, 6334, 6335, 6341, 6344
Ballet, debt reduction 3112, 9463
Ballet, economically disadvantaged 1045, 1896, 4836, 4868, 5385, 5929
Ballet, emergency funds 14929
Ballet, endowments 653, 2204, 5957, 9183, 9257, 9645
Ballet, equipment 1252, 2305, 3073, 4481
Ballet, exhibitions 7150
Ballet, faculty/staff development 1045, 2204, 6296, 6315, 6318, 6327, 6331, 6334, 6335, 6341, 6344, 9463
Ballet, fellowships 2204
Ballet, girls & young women 1045
Ballet, Hispanics 1800, 3123, 4954, 5292, 5794, 5956, 6327, 6391
Ballet, minorities 1045, 1896, 4606, 4836, 5491, 5531
Ballet, performance/productions 1324, 1552, 1676, 1677, 1723, 1741, 2204, 2305, 2573, 2962, 4501, 5354, 5877, 6771, 7789, 7865, 7922, 7965, 8110, 8166, 8283, 8312, 8706, 9016, 9184, 9664
Ballet, professorships 7146
Ballet, research 1045, 14929
Ballet, scholarships 1552, 2365, 4836, 7070, 7416
Ballet, seed money 1039, 2253
Ballet, student aid 4606
Ballet, women 7070
Ballet, youth 5354, 5385
Bangladesh, animals/wildlife 53830
Bangladesh, arts/culture/humanities 5659, 5665, 5689
Bangladesh, civil rights 10669, 62780, 62835
Bangladesh, community improvement/development 13992, 13993, 14039, 14077, 14078, 14082, 36545, 53941, 54932, 62835

1550 FOUNDATION GRANTS INDEX

FIGURE 30.   Type of Support/Geographic Index in *The Foundation Grants Index*

TYPE OF SUPPORT/GEOGRAPHIC INDEX — ANNUAL CAMPAIGNS

Michigan 3588, 3597, 3661, 3710, 3791
Minnesota 3841, 3845
Missouri 4379, 4403, 4475
New York 5142, 5746, 5972, 7114, 7403, 7406, 7494, 9363
Ohio 7786, 8144
Pennsylvania 8511
Texas 9313, 9358, 9527, 9530, 9556, 9572, 53282
Washington 1686
Wisconsin 4321, 9955

Civil rights

Maryland 10501

Community improvement/development

Arizona 11553, 11577, 11581, 13767, 13791, 13792
California 11184, 11202, 11203, 11214-11220, 11295-11300, 11340, 11341, 11343-11351, 11423-11426, 13774, 13775, 13778, 13788, 13789
Colorado 11477, 11562, 11572, 11574, 11576, 11578, 11579, 13790
Connecticut 11609, 11610, 11804
Delaware 11842, 13764
Florida 13760, 13763, 13772
Georgia 12012, 12019, 13478, 13770, 13952
Hawaii 12037, 12042, 12043, 12044, 13787
Idaho 11546
Illinois 11568, 12055, 12058, 12137, 12138, 12366, 13786
Indiana 12450, 12453, 12464, 12468, 12495, 12505, 12511, 13762
Iowa 11549, 11550, 11563, 11575
Kansas 13480, 13481, 13483
Kentucky 13779
Massachusetts 12696, 13769
Michigan 12713, 12714, 12732-12735, 12758, 12783, 12946, 12961, 12965, 12966, 13021, 13040, 13129, 13137, 13139, 13145, 13146, 13758, 15239, 15376
Minnesota 11552, 11558, 11560, 11569, 11570, 13166, 13403
Missouri 13476, 13484, 13766
Montana 11545
Nebraska 11567, 13781
Nevada 11342
New Jersey 13625, 13626
New Mexico 11551
New York 13773, 13784, 13851, 13852, 13961, 14116, 14131, 14186, 14209, 14554, 14559
North Carolina 13761, 13765
North Dakota 11547
Ohio 13785, 14683, 14801, 14803, 14804, 14915, 14922, 14952, 35440
Oklahoma 14966
Oregon 11554, 11556, 11557, 11565
Pennsylvania 13759, 13777, 15015, 15016, 15071, 15081, 15085, 15118, 15126, 15128, 15151, 15166, 15167, 15358
Rhode Island 13776, 15375
South Dakota 11580
Tennessee 15434
Texas 13771, 13783, 15435, 15436, 15443, 15466, 15528, 15564, 15567, 15571, 15621, 15622, 15626, 15629, 15639
Utah 11548, 11566, 13780
Virginia 15734
Washington 11555, 11561, 11564, 11571, 11573, 13768
West Virginia 12513
Wyoming 11559

Crime/courts/legal services

California 15928
Florida 16910

Education, elementary/secondary

Connecticut 20939
Massachusetts 18824
New Jersey 17110

New York 19871, 20482
Oklahoma 20400
Texas 15626, 20938

Education, higher

California 21426, 21427, 21430
Connecticut 25701
Florida 22460
Massachusetts 29093, 29321
Michigan 24329
Minnesota 24683
New York 22384, 22482, 24764, 27213, 27377, 27688
Oregon 21806
Pennsylvania 28439, 28898
Rhode Island 21410
South Carolina 29327
Tennessee 26853, 28896

Education, other

New Jersey 30804
Texas 15626

Environment

New York 35753
Ohio 35440

Health—general/rehabilitative

California 37031, 37033
Florida 39675
New York 41411
Texas 41527

Health—medical research

New York 13851
Virginia 42510

Health—mental health/substance abuse

New York 43782
Texas 44022

Health—specific diseases

Illinois 44493
New York 44509

Human services—multipurpose

California 15928
Delaware 47858
Indiana 12505
Massachusetts 49378
Minnesota 50157
New York 53278
Ohio 52104
Oklahoma 52369
Pennsylvania 15167, 52564
Rhode Island 53027
Texas 53282, 53489
Washington 11555

International affairs/development

New York 54758, 55484

Philanthropy/voluntarism

California 55869
New York 14131, 14186

Recreation/sports/athletics

New York 9363

Religion

Minnesota 59476
New York 59713
Oklahoma 59864

Science/technology

Illinois 2435, 2882

Youth development

Arizona 64877
California 63475
Missouri 64228

BUILDING/RENOVATION

Animals/wildlife

California 20, 78, 120, 942, 3728, 60620
Colorado 66, 67
Connecticut 47778
Delaware 77
Florida 80, 26327
Georgia 83, 85
Idaho 7
Illinois 102, 111
Indiana 148
Louisiana 263
Maryland 152
Massachusetts 163, 293
Minnesota 185, 186, 3963
Nebraska 196, 394
New York 267, 330, 337, 34454, 34951
North Carolina 338
Ohio 109, 342
Oklahoma 1, 358
Oregon 364, 395, 53606
Pennsylvania 378, 379, 382, 390
South Carolina 101
Tennessee 176, 403
Texas 392, 408, 426, 427, 429, 430, 431, 432, 437, 444, 445
Utah 70, 446
Virginia 452
Washington 178, 457, 458, 461
Wisconsin 177

Arts/culture

Alabama 472, 476-478, 480, 483
Arizona 496, 1727, 5940, 7599
Arkansas 8210
Bermuda 7395
California 514, 515, 517, 522, 530, 540, 545, 547, 550, 608, 654, 655, 659, 669-671, 699, 703, 915, 942, 1025, 1027, 1052, 1066, 1071, 1219, 1222, 1228, 1232, 1243, 1256-1258, 1264, 1319, 1337, 1344, 1369, 1372, 1375, 1399, 1435, 1439, 1522-1524, 1546, 2621, 2623, 3728, 5926, 7633, 7931, 8173, 9755, 11439, 17379, 21723, 29971, 33219, 58720, 60532, 60655
Chile 4902
Colorado 1563, 1566, 1574, 1576, 1580, 1581, 1583, 1585, 1592, 1608, 1626, 1628, 1629, 1642, 1646-1648, 1652, 1653, 1655, 1658, 1665, 1666, 3719, 4912, 9179, 9730
Connecticut 1878, 1880, 1882, 1885, 1889, 1894, 1900, 8975
Costa Rica 4883
Delaware 1958, 1959
District of Columbia 1902, 1993, 2062, 2115, 2263, 2373, 2442, 5552, 6255, 8412, 8414, 29989, 31685, 47977
England 1403
Florida 2270, 3735, 4029, 8370, 22634, 60277, 60284, 60285
Georgia 2325, 2330, 2332, 2335-2337, 2341, 2342, 2346, 2363, 2369, 2370, 2372, 8630, 17913, 22396
Hawaii 2376, 2378, 2379, 2382, 2384-2387, 2397, 2401, 2403, 2404, 2408, 3727
Idaho 8963, 9668, 9908, 29584
Illinois 2439, 2479, 2537, 2617, 2784, 2842, 2906, 3007, 3009, 3010, 17985, 48466
Indiana 2264, 3032, 3069, 3079, 3085, 3087, 3091, 3093, 3100, 3112, 3115, 3122, 3127, 3720, 9013
Iowa 1000, 29958
Kansas 2284, 2878, 3165, 8959, 8974
Kentucky 2230, 2261
Louisiana 3225, 3722, 4913
Maine 2138, 3718, 4526

FOUNDATION GRANTS INDEX

FIGURE 31.   Recipient Name Index in *The Foundation Grants Index*

SECTION 2—GRANT RECIPIENTS

Domestic Recipients

A & T University Foundation, NC, 25912, 25913
A Better Chance, MA, 16986, 19009, 19666, 19803, 20093, 20283, 29935, 30447, 30684, 30838, 30889, 30928, 31216, 31267, 31369, 31391, 31424, 31497, 31582
A Better Chance, NJ, 30911
A Better Chance, NY, 19950, 30871, 30987, 31251
A Better Chance, PA, 20572
A Better Chance Foundation, Rochester, MN, 30767
A Central Place, CA, 11261
A Chance to Grow, MN, 18730, 18779, 18791, 47636, 49937, 49966
A Chikls Place, WY, 20425
A Community of Friends, CA, 45516
A Contemporary Theater, WA, 1675, 7225
A Different September Foundation, MA, 19667, 30529
A Plus for Kids Teacher Network, NJ, 19114, 30956
A Safe Place, LA, 15995
A Safe Place, IL, 48475, 48495, 53686
A Territory Resource, WA, 10177
A Very Special Place, NY, 51479
A. A. Cunningham Air Museum Foundation, NC, 3515, 4421, 9064
A. A. White Dispute Resolution Institute, TX, 16931
A. F. Clement Scholarships, NC, 31467
A. G. Rhodes Home, GA, 37914
A. M. McGregor Home, OH, 52072
A. Philip Randolph Educational Fund, NY, 10210
A. T. International, DC, 54775
A.D. 2000 and Beyond, CO, 60017
A-T Medical Research Foundation, CA, 41797
AAA Womens Services, TN, 53105
AAF Rose Bowl Aquatics Center, CA, 57742, 57783, 57800
AAP Education and Research Institute, NY, 31166
Aaron Davis Hall, NY, 5147, 5433, 6559
Aaron Diamond AIDS Research Center for the City of New York, NY, 42276
Abbeville-Greenwood Regional Library, SC, 30805
Abbott House, NY, 51205
Abbott-Northwestern Hospital, MN, 38781, 38818, 44645, 44654, 44659
ABC Club, CA, 32948
ABC Learning Center, IN, 18258
Abilene Center for Nonprofit Management, TX, 15529
Abilene Christian University, TX, 29060, 29440, 31771
Abilene Independent School District, TX, 20909, 53247
Abilene Library Consortium, TX, 31778, 31820
Abilene Preservation League, TX, 9320
Abilene, City of, TX, 15530, 35743, 58553
Abilities of Florida, FL, 37841
Ability Building Center, MN, 32427
Ability Resources, OK, 52396
Abington Art Center, PA, 8702
Abortion Rights Mobilization, NY, 10088
Abraham Joshua Heschel School, NY, 18531, 19581, 20038
Abraham Lincoln Association, VA, 5430
Abraham Lincoln Centre, IL, 43209, 43210, 43215
Abraxas Foundation, PA, 43919
Abrom Kaplan Memorial Hospital, LA, 40109
ABT Associates, MA, 39041, 62775
Abusive Men Exploring New Directions (AMEND), CO, 16042
Abyssinian Development Corporation, NY, 13794, 14269, 14514
Acacia Theater Company, WI, 9984
Academic Decathlon Association of New Jersey, NJ, 19115, 19116

Academic Development Institute, IL, 30327, 30370
Academic Distinction Fund, LA, 18354, 18999
Academy for Educational Development, DC, 19265, 20573, 30626, 31344, 32636, 46465, 64096, 64349
Academy for Educational Development, NY, 20094, 32555, 44849, 44916, 50968, 50969
Academy for Math and Science Teachers of Chicago, IL, 18171
Academy for State and Local Government, DC, 57467
Academy Foundation, CA, 672, 887, 888, 6737, 29877
Academy of American Poets, NY, 5338, 5618, 7497
Academy of Art College, CA, 4368
Academy of Catholic Hispanic Theologians of the United States, TX, 23321
Academy of Childrens Music, PA, 52753
Academy of Holy Angels, LA, 17815
Academy of Hospice Physicians, FL, 37772
Academy of Music of Philadelphia, PA, 8387, 8457, 8621, 8926
Academy of Natural Sciences, DC, 3255
Academy of Natural Sciences of Philadelphia, PA, 2568, 3315, 3386, 5786, 8083, 8388, 8458, 8477, 8500, 8806, 8927, 8955, 9801, 61942
Academy of Notre Dame de Namur, PA, 20479, 20480
Academy of Our Lady High School, IL, 17146
Academy of the New Church, PA, 25537
Academy of the Pacific, HI, 17929, 17935
Academy of the Sacred Heart, LA, 17647
Academy of Vocal Arts, PA, 8703
Academy Research and Development Institute, CO, 21816, 28452, 55289, 55290
ACAP Day Care Association, WA, 53616
Accent on Kids, KS, 49036
ACCEPT, KY, 49057
ACCESS, DC, 54651, 54776, 55742
Access Development Fund Corporation, NY, 46170, 46203, 46212, 46294
Access Living of Metropolitan Chicago, IL, 10227, 10732, 18064, 48639, 48727, 48744, 48822, 53687
Access Theater, CA, 5921, 6269
Access to the Arts, OH, 7827
Access Unlimited-Speech Enterprises, TX, 20929, 20954, 51388, 53199
Access: Networking in the Public Interest, IL, 32766
Access: Networking in the Public Interest, MA, 32387
Accessability, MN, 49967
Accessible Living, OR, 52426, 52452
Accessible Space, MN, 13354, 49741, 49987
Accion Comunal Latino Americano de Montgomery County (ACLAMO), PA, 31634, 52830
ACCION International, DC, 55255
ACCION International, MA, 13044, 13973, 14155, 54353, 54612, 54730
Accord Foundation, MD, 10370
Accountants for the Public Interest, DC, 12970
Accountants for the Public Interest, NJ, 13663
Accountants Hall of Fame, FL, 25214
Accuracy in Media (AIM), DC, 10081, 10119, 10490, 10992, 11001
Achievement Academy, GA, 30262
Achievement Center, VA, 19096
Achievement Center for Children, OH, 40827
Achievement Council, CA, 17349, 20574
Achievement Rewards for College Scientists (ARCS), CA, 60694, 61963
Achievement Rewards for College Scientists (ARCS) Foundation, CA, 60582, 60668
Achilles Track Club, NY, 58187, 58215
Ackerman Institute for Family Therapy, NY, 19424, 43048, 43619, 43707, 47738, 50931

Acom, WI, 43416
Acorn Housing Corporation of Illinois, IL, 45823
ACORN Housing Corporation of Pennsylvania, PA, 45722
Act for Mental Health, CA, 43054
Acting By Children Production, NY, 6065
Acting Company, NY, 4940, 5391, 7035, 7171, 7226, 7498
Action Alliance Research and Education Program, PA, 52831
Action for a Better Community, NY, 20138
Action for Boston Community Development, MA, 10386, 23746, 32337
Action for Children, MN, 17431
Action for Children Council of Franklin County, OH, 20237, 49819, 52208, 52303
Action for Childrens Television, MA, 4805
Action for Corporate Accountability, CT, 37667, 57187
Action Housing, PA, 46415
Action Incorporated, VA, 11301
Action on Smoking and Health, DC, 43280, 43560
Action to Rehabilitate Community Housing (ARCH), DC, 45651
Action Youth Care, WV, 51810, 52537
ActionAIDS, PA, 45282, 45306
Acton Institute for the Study of Religion and Liberty, MI, 10239, 10417, 10854, 11013, 11039, 59639
Actors and Playwrights Initiative, MI, 3644
Actors Fund, NY, 7227, 45133
Actors Playhouse Productions, FL, 60277
Actors Theater of Louisville, KY, 3205, 7228
Actors Theater of Phoenix, AZ, 1083
Ad Hoc Council on Replanting Needs (ACORN), CA, 33265
Ad Hoc Group Against Crime, MO, 16409
Ad House, NJ, 50480, 50530
Ada Christian School, MI, 18679
Ada S. McKinley Community Services, IL, 23142, 48780
Ada S. Niles Senior Center, IL, 48781
Adam Walsh Child Resource Center, CA, 15925
Adam Walsh Child Resource Center, FL, 16157
Adams Memorial Library, PA, 31621
Adare Festival, NJ, 4794
Adat Ari El Temple, CA, 58701
Addison Community Hospital Authority Foundation, MI, 38562
Addison Gilbert Foundation, MA, 38470
Adelphi University, NY, 42145
Adelphoi Village, PA, 46448, 52291, 52486, 52681, 52923
Adhesive and Sealant Council Education Foundation, DC, 13650
Adirondack Council, NY, 34362, 34403, 34525, 34871, 34953, 35122, 35327
Adirondack Historical Association, NY, 6023
Adirondack Lakes Center for the Arts, NY, 6024
Adirondack Land Trust, NY, 34863, 34872
Adirondack Nature Conservancy, NY, 34363, 34428, 34526
Adirondack Scholarship Foundation, NY, 31133
Adirondack Tri-County Nursing Home, NY, 39989
Adirondack Work-Study Program, NY, 35212, 35213
Adler Planetarium, IL, 2418, 2482, 2507, 2625, 2663, 2882
Adolescent Consultation Services, MA, 43311
Adolescent Health Council of Gaston County, NC, 51965
Adolescent Pregnancy Care and Prevention Program (TAPCAPP), NY, 51759
Adolph S. Ochs Elementary School, NY, 19905
Adopt A Beach, WA, 35960
Adoption Centre, CO, 47513, 47610
Adoptive Parent Support Organization, OH, 52053, 52276

FIGURE 32. Recipient Category Index in *The Foundation Grants Index*

RECIPIENT CATEGORY INDEX — ANIMAL-SPECIFIC AGENCIES

ANIMAL-SPECIFIC AGENCIES

Annual campaigns

Illinois 135-137

Building/renovation

California 20, 78, 120, 942, 60620
Colorado 66, 67
Connecticut 47778
Delaware 77
Florida 80
Georgia 83, 85
Idaho 7
Illinois 102, 111
Indiana 148
Louisiana 263
Maryland 152
Massachusetts 293
Minnesota 186, 3963
Nebraska 196, 394, 58109
New York 267, 330, 337, 34454, 34579, 34951
North Carolina 338, 35377
Ohio 109, 342
Oklahoma 1, 358
Oregon 364, 395, 53606
Pennsylvania 378, 379, 382, 390
South Carolina 101
Tennessee 176, 403
Texas 392, 408, 426, 427, 430, 431, 432, 437, 444, 445
Utah 70, 446
Virginia 452
Washington 178, 457, 458, 461
Wisconsin 177

Capital campaigns

Colorado 63
Georgia 453
Maryland 161
Michigan 172, 199
Montana 413
New York 268, 318, 34818
Ohio 346
Pennsylvania 374, 382
Texas 414

Conferences/seminars

California 15
Colorado 201
Illinois 119
New York 33905

Continuing support

New Jersey 34492
New York 216

Endowments

District of Columbia 469
New York 289

Equipment

California 46, 103, 283, 60620
Colorado 65
Delaware 79
Florida 184
Nebraska 6
New Jersey 241
New York 269
Pennsylvania 47854
South Carolina 104
Washington 456

Exhibitions

California 29, 897
Georgia 85
Illinois 144
North Carolina 35399
Pennsylvania 369, 372, 373, 382
Texas 408, 423, 434

1794

Washington 178, 457

Faculty/staff development

Illinois 119, 60880
New York 320
Oregon 33915, 62351
Rhode Island 400
Texas 35729

Fellowships

Florida 164
Illinois 145

Film/video/radio

California 34462
Illinois 93
New York 91
Texas 422

General support

California 3, 4, 9, 46, 58, 62, 107, 110, 362, 33122, 60620
Colorado 47532
District of Columbia 281, 334, 433
Florida 265
Georgia 84, 85, 453
Illinois 100, 123, 126, 127
Indiana 146, 148, 149
Maryland 96, 153
Massachusetts 147
Michigan 173, 180, 182, 34164
Nebraska 5
New York 260, 264, 282, 296, 297, 303, 306, 308, 309, 313, 315, 336, 380, 34650, 34819, 34927, 35234, 63323
Ohio 347, 356, 49017
Oklahoma 359
Oregon 52701
Pennsylvania 371
Philippines 54949
Tennessee 35723
Texas 409, 436, 443, 53125

Land acquisition

Illinois 105
Pennsylvania 35582
Texas 424

Matching or challenge grants

California 62
Colorado 66
Massachusetts 162, 293
New York 337
North Carolina 7698
Tennessee 176
Texas 431
Virginia 247
Washington 178
Wisconsin 177

Other

Arizona 132
California 12, 41, 42-44, 47, 48, 53, 56, 57, 60, 76, 322, 323, 329, 448, 728, 927, 1179, 1295, 6009, 33009, 34852, 46754, 47150, 47412, 47579, 52946
Colorado 54, 133, 141, 192, 302, 328, 34640
Delaware 450
District of Columbia 18, 21, 22, 24, 51, 52, 170, 232, 238, 239, 242, 251, 252, 274, 278, 284, 286, 287, 288, 333, 335, 368, 465, 34851
Florida 50, 272, 33633, 48067
Georgia 33654
Hawaii 87
Idaho 234, 237, 276, 417
Illinois 88, 112, 113, 115, 116, 117, 121, 138, 139, 140, 468, 42153
Indiana 367
Kansas 49039
Louisiana 327, 439

Maryland 154, 155, 156-158, 159, 160, 243
Massachusetts 134, 166, 167, 168, 169, 194, 451, 34094, 50690
Michigan 181
Minnesota 188
Missouri 190, 191, 193, 195, 442, 4472
Montana 236, 273, 58185
Nebraska 197
New Jersey 200, 240, 50424
New York 23, 233, 235, 245, 248-250, 257, 258, 266, 271, 275, 277, 279, 291, 292, 294, 304, 307, 310, 316, 321, 353, 418, 17539, 33319, 34282, 34318, 34641, 35112, 35310, 35412, 35506
North Carolina 246, 339, 340, 341, 7721, 7778
Ohio 348, 349-351, 355, 357
Oklahoma 360, 361, 441
Oregon 365, 366
Pennsylvania 305, 375, 389, 391, 49150
Rhode Island 396-398, 399, 35695
Tennessee 171, 352, 402, 405, 406, 407
Texas 131, 415, 416, 419, 420, 421, 440, 449, 455
Washington 462, 464, 466, 43509
Wisconsin 114, 285, 314, 467, 470, 471

Performance/productions

New Jersey 4583
North Carolina 95

Program development

Alaska 33313
Arizona 2, 46644
California 10, 11, 14, 25, 26, 28, 39, 61, 72, 90, 97, 110, 283, 386, 33015, 33024, 33147, 33231, 34667, 35835, 36015, 46758, 48845, 51012
Colorado 89, 175, 256, 1631, 34864, 35570, 35804, 48139
Connecticut 298
Costa Rica 35195
District of Columbia 13, 37, 106, 128, 150, 215, 259, 261, 325, 326, 332, 385, 393, 33252, 33482, 33771, 33772, 33846, 33911-33914, 34253, 34254, 34813, 35159, 35485, 35578, 35635, 35671-35673, 55653, 62372, 62379, 62382, 63330
Florida 71, 331, 34029, 34039, 34041
Georgia 81
Idaho 377, 412, 460, 35240
Illinois 94, 102, 105, 118, 122, 142, 143, 145, 34622, 60880
Louisiana 438
Maine 34004
Maryland 30, 96, 301
Massachusetts 36, 34055, 34841, 35873, 35932, 36298
Michigan 174, 33749, 33750
Minnesota 183
Montana 295, 33430
Nebraska 69
New Hampshire 34005
New Jersey 204, 205, 207, 211, 217, 222-224, 229, 254
New Mexico 255
New York 270, 312, 317, 33708, 33709, 33780, 33904, 34455, 34614, 34819, 34957, 34958, 35030, 35123, 35376, 35455, 35604, 35775, 35808, 48135, 62377, 63322
North Carolina 14616, 27394, 27406
Ohio 344, 345, 35441, 35466, 35500
Oregon 189, 363, 459, 463, 35807
Pennsylvania 130, 376, 447, 35137
Rhode Island 400, 401, 35694, 35698
South Carolina 101
Texas 410, 411, 425, 35751, 35760
Trinidad & Tobago 129
Utah 70
Virginia 388
Washington 59, 35998, 43650
Wisconsin 68
Wyoming 253, 8234

Publication

California 33084

FIGURE 33. Index of Subjects in *The Foundation 1000*

Accounting
Connecticut: **Deloitte 230**
Illinois: **Scholl 824**
New Jersey: **KPMG 514**
Texas: Shell 837

Adult education
Colorado: El Pomar 277, Gates 337
District of Columbia: Cafritz 125
Florida: Beveridge 75
Illinois: Coleman 181, Polk 735, Sara 812
Indiana: Foellinger 308, Martin 568
Kentucky: Ashland 35
Massachusetts: Boston 91
Michigan: **Kellogg 494,** Whirlpool 973
Minnesota: General 343
New Jersey: Johnson 468, **Newcombe 671**
New York: International 454, Klau 505, McGraw-Hill 592, Price 742
Ohio: GenCorp 341
Pennsylvania: Arcadia 29, Buhl 115, Connelly 191
Rhode Island: **Genesis 346**
Texas: Constantin 193, George 347, Hillcrest 429, Hoblitzelle 434, Meadows 605, Rockwell 786, San Antonio 806, Temple 903
Virginia: Norfolk 676
Washington: Seafirst 829
Wisconsin: Milwaukee 629

Africa
District of Columbia: **Loyola 546**
Michigan: **Kellogg 494**
New Jersey: Johnson 468
New York: **Carnegie 142, Ford 312**
Washington: **Stewardship 876**

Aged
Alabama: Sonat 858
Arkansas: Wal-Mart 948
California: California 129, Doheny 244, Garland 335, Haas 387, Harden 395, Haynes 404, Koret 513, McConnell 582, Mericos 613, Pacific 701, Parsons 709, Roberts 779, San Diego 807, Sierra 842, Taper 896, Valley 938
Colorado: El Pomar 277, Gates 337
Connecticut: Hartford 400, ITT 457, Travelers 921
Delaware: Crystal 207
District of Columbia: Cafritz 125, **Kennedy 496,** Meyer 620, **Public 750**
Florida: Beveridge 75, Bush 122, Dade 213, Davis 222, Selby 833
Georgia: Callaway 130, Georgia 348, Whitehead 977, Whitehead 978, Woodruff 992
Illinois: **Brach 96,** Chicago 162, Crown 206, Inland 453, Retirement 762, Sara 812, **Scholl 824**
Indiana: Indianapolis 452, Martin 568
Maryland: Baltimore 50, **Weinberg 963**
Massachusetts: Boston 91
Michigan: Gerstacker 352, Grand Rapids 375, **Kellogg 494,** Prince 745, Skillman 849, Steelcase 871
Minnesota: General 343, Honeywell 439, Medtronic 607, Minnesota 631
Missouri: Hall 390, Union 928
Nevada: Lincy 535, Wiegand 982
New Jersey: AlliedSignal 11, Hyde 447, Johnson 468, **Johnson 473,** Merck 611, **Nabisco 653,** Union 927
New Mexico: Maddox 559
New York: Abrons 3, Altman 12, Bodman 84, Clark 173, **Commonwealth 185,** Cummings 211, **Dreyfus 254,** Goldsmith 366, Guttman 385, Hagedorn 388, **Hartford 399,** Hatch 402, **Hearst 408, Hearst 409,** Julia 484, **Monell 635,** Morgan 641, Morgan 642, New York 666, New York 667, Pfizer 722, Price 742, Rhodebeck 769, Silverman 843, **Skadden 847,** Wendt 968
North Carolina: Reynolds 765, Winston-Salem 989
Ohio: Bruening 107, Cleveland 176, Nationwide 658, Reinberger 759, Schmidlapp 822
Oregon: Meyer 622, Oregon 696
Pennsylvania: Arcadia 29, Connelly 191, Massey 570, Penn 715, **Pew 720,** Smith 852, Trexler 923
Rhode Island: Champlin 155
Texas: Abell-Hanger 2, Amarillo 13, Anderson 21, Carter 145, Hillcrest 429, Hoblitzelle 434, Meadows 605, San Antonio 806
Utah: Eccles 269
Virginia: Norfolk 676
Washington: Burlington 118, Cheney 161
West Virginia: Clay 175
Wisconsin: **Johnson 469,** McBeath 578, Milwaukee 629, Siebert 841

Agriculture
Arkansas: Rockefeller 784, Rockefeller 785
California: Boswell 93, **Foundation 317,** Harden 395
Colorado: **Needmor 661**
District of Columbia: **Public 750**
Illinois: Deere 228
Michigan: Gerber 349, **Kellogg 494, Mott 649**
Minnesota: Bremer 99, Northwest 681
New York: **Ford 312,** Kaplan 489, **Noyes 683, Rockefeller 782, Wallace 949**
Oklahoma: **Noble 674**
Pennsylvania: Heinz 413
Texas: Meadows 605

AIDS
Alabama: Sonat 858
California: **Beckman 62,** California 129, **Compton 188,** Gap 333, Geffen 340, Haas 387, Hewlett 428, Irvine 455, **Kaiser 487,** Koret 513, Levi 529, MCA 576, Milken 626, Norris 679, Pacific 701, Parsons 709, Rigler-Lawrence 773, San Diego 807, San Francisco 808, Santa Clara 811, Sierra 842, Swig 894, Transamerica 920, Zellerbach 998
Colorado: Denver 233, US 934
Connecticut: **Aetna 4, Casey 149,** Connecticut 190, **General 342,** Hartford 400, ITT 457, New Haven 663, Travelers 921
District of Columbia: Cafritz 125, **Fannie 292, Kennedy 496, MCI 594,** Meyer 620, **Public 750**
Florida: Dade 213, Davis 222, Lowe 544
Georgia: Atlanta 39
Hawaii: McInerny 595
Illinois: Chicago 162, Fry 329, **MacArthur 555,** Payne 712, Polk 735, Sara 812, **Scholl 824**
Indiana: Foellinger 308, Indianapolis 452
Iowa: **Bohen 86**
Massachusetts: Bank 51, Boston 91, Polaroid 734
Michigan: Ford 315, Grand Rapids 375, **Kresge 516,** Steelcase 871
Minnesota: General 343, Grand 374, Honeywell 439, Howe 443, Jostens 481
Missouri: Hallmark 392, Kansas 488
New Jersey: Hyde 447, Johnson 468, **Johnson 473,** Kirby 504, Prudential 749, Victoria 944
New York: Altman 12, **American 15, AT&T 37,** Bodman 84, Bristol-Myers 102, **Bronfman 103,** Buffalo 113, **Chase 158,** Claiborne 170, Clark 171, Cummings 211, **DeCamp 227,** Diamond 238, **Edouard 273, Equitable 286, Ford 312,** Gilman 357, Goldsmith 366, Hagedorn 388, **Hasbro 401, Hearst 408, Hearst 409,** Heckscher 411, Johnson 475, Klau 505, **Merrill 616, Mertz-Gilmore 617, Metropolitan 618, Monell 635,** Morgan 641, Morgan 642, New York 666, **New York 668,** Price 742, **Revlon 763,** Revson 764, **Rockefeller 782,** Scherman 819, **Skadden 847,** Wallach 952, Wendt 968
North Carolina: Bryan 108, Reynolds 765
Ohio: Cleveland 176, Gund 384
Pennsylvania: Connelly 191, Fels 295, Heinz 415, **Pew 720,** Philadelphia 724, Pittsburgh 730, Smith 852
South Carolina: Springs 865
Texas: Burnett-Tandy 119, Cain 127, Fikes 298, Hoblitzelle 434, Meadows 605, Moody 638, Rockwell 786, San Antonio 806
Virginia: **Freedom 323,** Norfolk 676
Washington: Seafirst 829
Wisconsin: **Johnson 469,** McBeath 578, Milwaukee 629

Alcoholism
Alabama: Sonat 858
Arkansas: Wal-Mart 948
California: Cowell 199, Crean 203, **M.E.G. 552,** Montgomery 637, Norris 679, San Diego 807, San Francisco 808, Sierra 842, Transamerica 920
Connecticut: ITT 457
Florida: Lowe 544
Illinois: Illinois 450, **Scholl 824**
Indiana: Foellinger 308
Michigan: Grand Rapids 375
Minnesota: General 343, Minnesota 631
Missouri: Kauffman 490
New Jersey: Johnson 468, **Johnson 473,** Victoria 944
New York: **DeCamp 227,** International 454, **JM 467, Metropolitan 618, Monell 635,** Wendt 968
North Carolina: Reynolds 765
Pennsylvania: Connelly 191, **Pew 720, Scaife 815**
South Carolina: Springs 865
Texas: Cain 127, Fikes 298, Hoblitzelle 434, McGovern 589, McGovern 590, Meadows 605, San Antonio 806
Utah: Eccles 269
Virginia: **Freedom 323**
Wisconsin: McBeath 578, Milwaukee 629

Animal welfare
Arizona: Morris 644
California: California 129, Harden 395, San Diego 807, W.W.W. 945
Florida: Beveridge 75, Dade 213
Illinois: **Archer-Daniels-Midland 31, Brach 96,** Payne 712, **Scholl 824**
Indiana: Martin 568
New Jersey: Dodge 242
New York: Bass 55, Gilman 357, **Monell 635,** Price 742, Schiff 821
North Carolina: Bryan 108
Ohio: Rupp 798
Pennsylvania: Arcadia 29, Heinz 416, McCune 584
Rhode Island: Champlin 155
Texas: Rockwell 786, San Antonio 806, Temple 903
Virginia: Norfolk 676

Anthropology
California: Getty 353
Indiana: **Plumsock 733**

Archaeology
California: **Packard 703,** Skaggs 848
Illinois: **Scholl 824**
New York: Kaplan 489, **Kress 517**
Texas: Meadows 605

Architecture
Colorado: Buell 112
Indiana: Cummins 212
New York: Kaplan 489, **Warhol 954**
Pennsylvania: Heinz 416
Texas: Meadows 605

Arms control
California: Columbia 184, **Compton 188,** Cowell 199, Hewlett 428
District of Columbia: **Public 750**
Illinois: **MacArthur 555**
Maryland: **Town 918**
Massachusetts: **Merck 612**
Michigan: **Mott 649**
New York: **Carnegie 142, Ford 312, Mertz-Gilmore 617, New-Land 670,** Prospect 748, **Rockefeller 782,** Scherman 819
Virginia: **Jones 480**

Arts
Alabama: Alabama 7, Sonat 858

FIGURE 34.   Subject Index in *The Foundation Directory*

Accounting
California: Brenner 189
Connecticut: **Deloitte 902**
Illinois: Hughes 1797, **Kemper 1817,** Scholl 1933
Indiana: Lincoln 2066
New Jersey: **KPMG 3500**
New York: National 4377
Texas: Shell 6272

Adult education
Alabama: Vulcan 51
Arizona: First 67, Wallace 94
California: Sonoma 681
Colorado: El Pomar 801, Gates 806, Hunt 813,
  O'Fallon 836, Saccomanno 844, Weckbaugh 862
Connecticut: Bodenwein 881, Long 964, Macmillan
  967, Palmer 986, Southeastern 1011, Topsfield
  1018, Waterbury 1028
District of Columbia: Cafritz 1099, Strong 1163
Florida: Beveridge 1193, Schultz 1380
Georgia: **Coca-Cola 1461,** Gwinnett 1496, **UPS 1560**
Hawaii: Hawaii 1589
Illinois: Coleman 1696, Forest 1739, Harris 1777,
  Hughes 1797, Kelly 1814, Levie 1831, OMRON
  1882, Peoria 1887, Polk 1898, Sara Lee 1929,
  Siragusa 1946, Sulzer 1969, White 1993
Indiana: Arvin 2006, Dekko 2027, Foellinger 2034,
  Martin 2068
Kentucky: Ashland 2206, Bank 2207
Maine: Maine 2303
Maryland: Knott 2376
Massachusetts: Bayrd 2462, Boston 2473, Cabot 2480,
  Cowan 2502, Hyams 2585, Lowell 2607,
  Ratshesky 2666
Michigan: **Kellogg 2846,** Miller 2873, Whirlpool 2951
Minnesota: American 2969, General 3019
Missouri: Fox 3179, Green 3190, Kauffman 3204,
  Oppenstein 3241
Montana: Washington 3304
New Hampshire: Kingsbury 3384
New Jersey: AlliedSignal 3399, Johnson 3484,
  Newcombe 3529
New Mexico: **Frost 3604,** McCune 3608
New York: **Beck 3690,** Capital 3765, Cowles 3840,
  Initial 4126, International 4128, **Kazanjian 4176,**
  Klau 4195, McGraw-Hill 4326, Price 4483, **Soros
  4648,** United 4731, Western 4784
North Carolina: CP&L 4855, Cumberland 4856, First
  4877, Ginter 4884, Glaxo 4885, Harris 4891,
  Rogers 4944, Triangle 4961
Ohio: Forest 5067, GenCorp 5080, Nordson 5194,
  Rice 5226, Richland 5227, **Women's 5320**
Oklahoma: Taubman 5377
Oregon: Carpenter 5392, Johnson 5412
Pennsylvania: Arcadia 5446, Buhl 5474, Connelly
  5496, Dolfinger-McMahon 5510, Lehigh 5632,
  Stackpole-Hall 5766
Puerto Rico: Puerto Rico 5819
Rhode Island: **Genesis 5831**
South Carolina: Spartanburg 5885
Tennessee: Durham 5917
Texas: Constantin 6040, Edwards 6071, George 6101,
  Haas 6111, Hillcrest 6131, Hoblitzelle 6133,
  Littauer 6171, Meadows 6196, Rockwell 6254, San
  Antonio 6259, Straus 6289, Swalm 6295, Temple
  6300, Wright 6343
Vermont: Vermont 6384
Virginia: Appleby 6389, Norfolk 6463, Olsson 6468
Washington: Horizons 6538, Seafirst 6573, Tacoma
  6584, Wenatchee 6591
Wisconsin: Alexander 6629, Clark 6651, Cudahy 6656,
  Milwaukee 6707
Wyoming: Whitney 6784

Africa
California: **G.A.G. 318,** Margoes 492
District of Columbia: **International 1132, Loyola 1145**
Georgia: Global 1494
Michigan: Besser 2757, **Kellogg 2846**
New Jersey: **Danellie 3436,** Johnson 3484

New York: **Carnegie 3768, Ford 3956,** McConnell
  4321, Normandie 4402, **Open 4423, Rubin 4554**
Texas: Dougherty 6061
Virginia: Little 6449
Washington: **Kongsgaard-Goldman 6546,** Stewardship
  6582
Wisconsin: **Young 6770**

Aged
Alabama: Hill 31, Sonat 49
Arizona: First 67, Marshall 77
Arkansas: Wal-Mart 115
California: ARCO 138, **Atkinson 146,** Benbough 167,
  Bothin 184, Bradford 186, California 209, Callison
  214, Copley 239, Doelger 266, Doheny 267, East
  Bay 276, Elks 282, Factor 288, Fairfield 289,
  Fireman's 297, French 311, Fresno 312, Garland
  325, Gellert 329, Gellert 330, Gellert 331, Gilmore
  340, **Glenn 344,** Goldman 350, Green 360, Gross
  364, Haas 371, Hale 374, Harden 380, Haynes
  383, Irvine 414, Jewish 426, Joslyn 432,
  Kirchgessner 443, Komes 446, Koret 448,
  Langendorf 457, Lytel 486, McConnell 509,
  Mericos 517, Oakland 558, Pacific 573, Parsons
  578, Pasadena 581, Patron 582, Peninsula 584,
  Peppers 585, Pickford 594, Roberts 617,
  Sacramento 626, San Diego 628, Segal 650, Sierra
  667, Smith 676, Soda 679, Sonoma 681, Taper
  708, Valley 731, Welk 753
Colorado: Anschutz 777, Comprecare 796, El Pomar
  801, Gates 806, Hill 811, Hunter 814,
  Kitzmiller-Bales 821, O'Fallon 836, Presbyterian/St.
  Luke's 841, Summit 855
Connecticut: **Adler 867,** Bodenwein 881, EIS 911,
  Fisher 918, Hartford 937, Hartford 938, ITT 945,
  Long 964, Martin 971, New Britain 979, Palmer
  986, Robinson 997, Senior 1005, Southeastern
  1011, Travelers 1020, Waterbury 1028
Delaware: Borkee-Hagley 1043, Crystal 1049, Palmer
  1074
District of Columbia: Cafritz 1099, **Delmar 1104,**
  Fowler 1115, Himmelfarb 1130, **Kennedy 1139,**
  Lehrman 1143, Meyer 1151, **Public 1156**
Florida: Bastien 1184, BCR 1188, Beveridge 1193, Bush
  1205, Catlin 1206, Cohen 1214, Dade 1219, Davis
  1224, Doctors 1229, **duPont 1233, Eagles 1235,**
  Falk 1241, FPL 1251, Greenburg-May 1269,
  Howell 1286, Lost 1312, Meyer 1323,
  NationsBank 1331, Nias 1333, Phillips 1346, Selby
  1381, Stevens 1394, Tampa 1402, Volen 1409,
  Wilson 1423
Georgia: Callaway 1449, English 1475, Georgia 1487,
  Gwinnett 1496, Marshall 1524, Marshall 1525,
  Patterson-Barclay 1535, Pitts 1537, Senior 1550,
  Shallenberger 1552, Trust 1557, **UPS 1560,**
  Whitehead 1568, Woodruff 1572
Hawaii: Cooke 1586, Hawaii 1589, Hughes 1591,
  Wilcox 1603
Illinois: **Abbott 1617, Allen-Heath 1621,** Beidler 1641,
  Brach 1661, Chicago 1688, Crown 1707, Field
  1732, Frank 1742, Green-Field 1767, Inland 1801,
  Levie 1831, Morton 1870, OMRON 1882, Peoria
  1887, Polk 1897, Retirement 1913, Rothschild
  1923, Sara Lee 1929, Scholl 1933, Simms 1944,
  Siragusa 1946, Stern 1963, Sulzer 1969, Willett
  1997
Indiana: Elkhart 2030, Health 2043, Hook 2049,
  Indianapolis 2052, Martin 2068, Smock 2094,
  Willennar 2104
Iowa: Des Moines 2118, Hall 2125, Mid-Iowa 2144,
  Principal 2148, Van Buren 2153, Vermeer 2154,
  Wahlert 2157
Kansas: Beech 2164, Dreiling 2171, Mingenback 2188
Louisiana: Baton Rouge 2251, Shreveport-Bossier 2286
Maine: Maine 2303, UNUM 2309
Maryland: Baltimore 2317, Baltimore 2318, Columbia
  2334, Knott 2376, Shapiro 2419, Warfield 2438,
  Weinberg 2439
Massachusetts: Ashton 2453, Bacon 2459, Bayrd 2462,
  Boston 2473, Boynton 2476, Campbell 2485,
  Clipper 2496, Cowan 2502, Everett 2532,
  Farnsworth 2534, Gorin 2556, Home 2574, Home

  2580, Kelley 2593, Peabody 2641, Ribakoff 2672,
  Sailors' 2684, Stearns 2700, TJX 2717, Wadleigh
  2722, Widows' 2730
Michigan: Ann Arbor 2743, Berrien 2756, Four 2806,
  Fremont 2808, Gerstacker 2815, Grand Rapids
  2818, Granger 2819, Hannan 2821, Holden 2827,
  Kellogg 2846, Pagel 2888, Prince 2894, Skillman
  2912, Steelcase 2919, Thompson 2931, Upjohn
  2939
Minnesota: American 2969, General 3019, Honeywell
  3037, Mardag 3051, Medtronic 3057, Minnesota
  3060, Northwestern 3069, Ordean 3077, Rivers
  3086, Rochester 3088, Thorpe 3101, Wedum 3110
Missouri: Bohm 3150, Community 3161, Gietner 3187,
  Green 3190, Hall 3193, Leader 3215, McGee
  3229, Oppenstein 3241, Slusher 3266, Speas 3270,
  Speas 3271, St. Louis 3272, Union 3287
Montana: Washington 3304
Nebraska: Keene 3320, Lincoln 3327
Nevada: Hall 3353, Lincy 3360, Redfield 3362,
  Wiegand 3368
New Hampshire: Foundation 3378, Kingsbury 3384
New Jersey: AlliedSignal 3399, Duke 3443, Elizabeth
  3445, Hackett 3464, Hyde 3476, **Innovating 3477,**
  Johnson 3484, **Johnson 3486,** Laurie 3507, Merck
  3522, Nabisco 3525, Ohl 3531, **Perkins 3534,**
  Schamach 3552, Schwartz 3561, Union 3582, Van
  Houten 3585, Wallerstein 3592
New Mexico: **Frost 3604,** Maddox 3607, McCune 3608
New York: Abrons 3615, Achelis 3616, **Ada 3618,**
  Adams 3619, Albany's 3626, Alexander 3627,
  Altman 3632, **Beck 3690,** Bennett 3700, Bodman
  3723, **Brookdale 3739, Burden 3753,** Capital
  3765, Clark 3802, Clark 3806, **Commonwealth
  3828,** Consumer 3830, Cowles 3840, Cummings
  3845, Cummings 3847, Davenport-Hatch 3856, de
  Kay 3862, Dreyfus 3898, Eckman 3907, **Einer
  3918,** Faith 3932, Frank 3961, Gifford 3987,
  Goldsmith 4009, Goldstein 4011, Green 4033,
  Greene 4035, Guttman 4056, Hagedom 4057,
  Hartford 4070, Hatch 4075, **Hearst 4081, Hearst
  4082,** Hoyt 4108, **Ittleson 4134,** Jones 4150, Joy
  4154, Julia 4157, Kaufmann 4172, **Kaufmann
  4173,** Killough 4189, Klosk 4202, Krumholz 4219,
  Leibovitz 4244, Lindner 4261, **MacDonald 4285,**
  McConnell 4321, **McDonald 4322,** Monell 4355,
  Morgan 4358, Moses 4366, Mutual 4372, New
  York 4385, New York 4386, Noble 4397, Northern
  4404, **Open 4423,** Parshelsky 4441, Pfizer 4458,
  Price 4483, Ramapo 4494, Rhodebeck 4514,
  Samuels 4568, Schaffer 4575, Schweckendieck
  4597, Silverman 4618, **Skadden 4624,** St. George's
  4659, Utica 4738, Vidda 4747, Vogler 4748,
  Wendt 4779, Western 4784
North Carolina: American 4827, Davis 4860, First
  4877, Henderson 4894, Lane 4906, North Carolina
  4924, Reynolds 4938, Richardson 4941, Triangle
  4961, Winston-Salem 4967
North Dakota: Myra 4972, North Dakota 4973, Stern
  4974
Ohio: Bruening 5008, Cincinnati 5019, Cleveland
  5021, Emsthausen 5051, Fairfield 5054, Finnegan
  5058, Ford 5066, Frohman 5073, Hillier 5105,
  Iddings 5116, Kilcawley 5132, Mayerson 5160,
  Monarch 5177, Moores 5180, Nationwide 5191,
  Nordson 5194, Reinberger 5220, Rice 5226,
  Richland 5227, Rosenthal 5231, Schlink 5242,
  Schmidlapp 5244, Sheadle 5259, Sisler 5265, Stark
  5279, Stocker 5281, Toledo 5293, Wuliger 5321
Oklahoma: Kirkpatrick 5352, Zarrow 5387
Oregon: Collins 5397, **Fohs 5402,** Jackson 5410,
  Johnson 5412, Meyer 5418, Oregon 5420
Pennsylvania: Allegheny 5439, Arcadia 5446, Bard
  5453, Berkman 5461, Buck 5473, Clive 5493,
  Coen 5494, Connelly 5496, Crels 5502,
  Dolfinger-McMahon 5510, Gahagen 5545,
  Greensburg 5566, Huston 5603, Jewish 5612,
  Justus 5614, Kohn 5624, Massey 5646, Morris
  5675, 1957 5682, Penn 5688, **Pew 5692,** Smith
  5751, Smith 5752, Snee-Reinhardt 5757, Teleflex
  5785, Trexler 5789, Wurts 5817
Puerto Rico: Puerto Rico 5819

foundations. *The Foundation 1000* includes a subject index that lists foundations under the subject fields expressed in the "Purpose" section of their entries (see Figure 33). Once you have noted foundation names from the appropriate index categories, you should examine the actual foundation profiles to complete your prospect worksheet. Note especially the giving restrictions printed in bold type under each foundation entry.

Your next stop should be *The Foundation Directory*. The *Directory* covers more than 6,700 foundations with at least $2 million in assets or grant programs totaling $200,000 or more annually, and includes a subject index subdivided by state to help you identify foundations that have expressed an interest in your subject field (see Figure 34). Foundations with national or regional giving patterns appear in bold type under the state in which they are located; foundations that are restricted to local giving appear in regular type. As you check the references in your subject category, you should add to your prospect list foundations in your own state as well as those foundations in other states indicated in bold type. Make a note of the foundation's state and entry number so that you can refer back to the full entry later. Again, the full entry will provide the additional information you need to complete your prospect work-sheet—that is, program interests, giving limitations, and the grant amounts typically awarded.

As we noted in Chapter 5, state and local foundation directories are another good resource, although they do vary in content and coverage. When using them, you should examine the most current edition of each relevant directory and identify potential funding sources through the subject index, where provided, or by scanning the entries themselves.

SUBJECT GUIDES

Over the last several years the Foundation Center has published a number of directories focusing on the major funders and giving trends in a specific subject area. Drawing on information gathered in *The Foundation Directory* (Parts 1 and 2), *The Foundation Grants Index*, and the *National Directory of Corporate Giving*, subject guides combine descriptive financial information with grant records for foundations operating in selected fields. They also include introductions, indexes, and specialized bibliographies prepared from the Center's bibliographic database. They are often referred to as "spin-off" products of the database because they bring together in one convenient format information from various other Center publications. (For a sample subject guide entry, see Figure 35.) The following subject guides are currently available:

- *AIDS Funding: A Guide to Giving by Foundations and Charitable Organizations*, 3rd edition, 1993.
  Includes entries for 453 grantmaking foundations (including 55 community foundations), 58 public charities, and 71 direct corporate giving programs. Grants are listed for 235 private foundations and 34 other organizations, representing approximately $47 million in support for a variety of AIDS/HIV-related programs.

- *Guide to Funding for International and Foreign Programs*, 2nd edition, 1994.
  Includes entries for 622 foundations and 35 corporate giving programs, along with 5,669 sample grants representing $566 million awarded by 234 foundations that have shown a substantial interest in international and foreign programs. Covers public policy groups, legal agencies, educational institutions, and international exchange organizations, among others.

- *National Guide to Funding in Aging*, 3rd edition, 1992.
  Covers 795 foundations, 140 federally administered programs, 68 state bureaus, and 74 additional nonprofit organizations, along with more than 1,600 foundation grants.

- *National Guide to Funding in Arts and Culture*, 3rd edition, 1994.
  Includes entries for 3,840 foundations and 302 corporate giving programs, along with 9,400 sample grants representing $707 million awarded by 545 foundations. Covers film and video, fine arts, historic preservation, humanities, language and literature, media and communications, museums, music, archaeology, architecture, dance, performing arts, and theater.

- *National Guide to Funding for Children, Youth and Families*, 2nd edition, 1993.
  Includes entries for 3,439 foundations and 210 corporate giving programs, along with 9,399 sample grants representing $678 million awarded by 523 foundations. Covers child welfare, family services, family planning, child development, child abuse prevention, delinquency, and youth.

- *National Guide to Funding for the Economically Disadvantaged*, 1st edition, 1993.

Includes entries for 1,238 foundations and 205 corporate giving programs, along with 4,161 sample grants representing $318 million awarded by 307 foundations. Covers employment programs, shelters for the homeless, hunger relief, and welfare initiatives, among others.

- *National Guide to Funding for Elementary and Secondary Education*, 2nd edition, 1993.

  Includes entries for 1,936 foundations and 103 corporate giving programs, along with 4,757 sample grants representing $358 million awarded by 475 foundations. Covers elementary and secondary education, including vocational, bilingual, and special education; early childhood education; religious schools; and grants for academic programs, curriculum development, programs for gifted or minority students, scholarship funds, and school libraries.

- *National Guide to Funding for the Environment and Animal Welfare*, 2nd edition, 1994.

  Includes entries for 1,240 foundations and 89 corporate giving programs, along with 4,078 sample grants representing $356 million awarded by 379 foundations. Covers projects and organizations involved in international conservation, ecological research, litigation and advocacy, waste reduction, animal welfare, and much more.

- *National Guide to Funding in Health*, 3rd edition, 1993.

  Includes entries for 3,019 foundations and 324 corporate giving programs, along with 9,315 sample grants representing $1 billion awarded by 614 foundations. Covers AIDS, alcoholism, cancer, dentistry, dermatology, drug abuse, family planning, health associations, heart disease, hospices, hospitals, leprosy, medical education, medical research, medical sciences, mental health, nursing, ophthalmology, pharmacy, psychiatry, psychology, rehabilitation, schistosomiasis, and speech pathology.

- *National Guide to Funding in Higher Education*, 3rd edition, 1994.

  Includes entries for 3,473 foundations and 184 corporate giving programs that have expressed substantial interest in higher education, either as part of their stated purpose or through the actual grants they reported to the Center. Nearly 10,700 sample grants representing $1.29 billion awarded by 566 foundations are listed. Covers business, nursing, medical, law, and theological schools, among others.

FIGURE 35.   Sample Entry from the *National Guide to Funding for Children, Youth and Families*

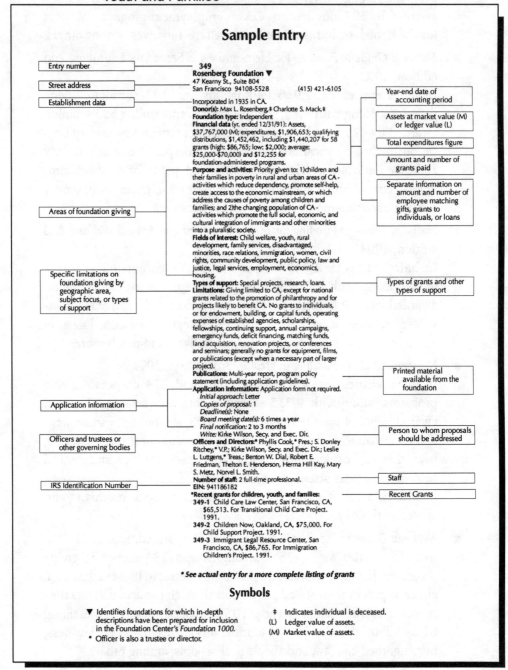

Sample Entry

Entry number → **349**
Rosenberg Foundation ▼
Street address → 47 Kearny St., Suite 804
San Francisco 94108-5528   (415) 421-6105

Establishment data → Incorporated in 1935 in CA.
Donor(s): Max L. Rosenberg,‡ Charlotte S. Mack.‡
Foundation type: Independent
Financial data (yr. ended 12/31/91): Assets, $37,767,000 (M); expenditures, $1,906,653; qualifying distributions, $1,452,462, including $1,440,207 for 58 grants (high: $86,765; low: $2,000; average: $25,000-$70,000) and $12,255 for foundation-administered programs.

Year-end date of accounting period
Assets at market value (M) or ledger value (L)
Total expenditures figure
Amount and number of grants paid
Separate information on amount and number of employee matching gifts, grants to individuals, or loans

Areas of foundation giving →
Purpose and activities: Priority given to: 1)children and their families in poverty in rural and urban areas of CA - activities which reduce dependency, promote self-help, create access to the economic mainstream, or which address the causes of poverty among children and families; and 2)the changing population of CA - activities which promote the full social, economic, and cultural integration of immigrants and other minorities into a pluralistic society.
Fields of interest: Child welfare, youth, rural development, family services, disadvantaged, minorities, race relations, immigration, women, civil rights, community development, public policy, law and justice, legal services, employment, economics, housing.

Specific limitations on foundation giving by geographic area, subject focus, or types of support →
Types of support: Special projects, research, loans.
Limitations: Giving limited to CA, except for national grants related to the promotion of philanthropy and for projects likely to benefit CA. No grants to individuals, or for endowment, building, or capital funds, operating expenses of established agencies, scholarships, fellowships, continuing support, annual campaigns, emergency funds, deficit financing, matching funds, land acquisition, renovation projects, or conferences and seminars; generally no grants for equipment, films, or publications (except when a necessary part of larger project).
Publications: Multi-year report, program policy statement (including application guidelines).
Application Information: Application form not required.

Types of grants and other types of support

Printed material available from the foundation

Application information →
Initial approach: Letter
Copies of proposal: 1
Deadline(s): None
Board meeting date(s): 6 times a year
Final notification: 2 to 3 months
Write: Kirke Wilson, Secy. and Exec. Dir.

Officers and trustees or other governing bodies →
Officers and Directors: Phyllis Cook,* Pres.; S. Donley Ritchey,* V.P.; Kirke Wilson, Secy. and Exec. Dir.; Leslie L. Luttgens,* Treas.; Benton W. Dial, Robert E. Friedman, Thelton E. Henderson, Herma Hill Kay, Mary S. Metz, Norvel L. Smith.
Number of staff: 2 full-time professional.

Person to whom proposals should be addressed

IRS Identification Number → EIN: 941186182
Recent grants for children, youth, and families:
349-1 Child Care Law Center, San Francisco, CA, $65,513. For Transitional Child Care Project. 1991.
349-2 Children Now, Oakland, CA, $75,000. For Child Support Project. 1991.
349-3 Immigrant Legal Resource Center, San Francisco, CA, $86,765. For Immigration Children's Project. 1991.

Staff
Recent Grants

* See actual entry for a more complete listing of grants

Symbols

▼ Identifies foundations for which in-depth descriptions have been prepared for inclusion in the Foundation Center's *Foundation 1000*.
* Officer is also a trustee or director.

‡   Indicates individual is deceased.
(L) Ledger value of assets.
(M) Market value of assets.

- *National Guide to Funding for Libraries and Information Services,* 2nd edition, 1993.
  Includes entries for 574 foundations and 28 corporate giving programs, along with 871 sample grants representing $103 million awarded by 274 foundations. Covers public, academic, research, and special libraries; information clearinghouses, services, programs, and databases; and more.

- *National Guide to Funding in Religion*, 2nd edition, 1993.
  Includes entries for 4,238 foundations and 13 corporate giving programs, along with 3,650 sample grants representing $253 million awarded by 314 foundations to churches, synagogues, missionary programs, theological education, and various religious welfare programs.

- *National Guide to Funding for Women and Girls*, 2nd edition, 1993.
  Includes entries for 946 foundations and 89 corporate giving programs, along with 3,650 sample grants representing $219 million awarded by 314 foundations. Also covers family services and family planning, women's health, victim shelters and services, and teen pregnancy education and prevention.

SPECIALIZED FUNDING GUIDES

The final step in developing your prospect list is to examine any specialized funding guides devoted to your field. A listing of some of the major guides available in Foundation Center libraries is provided in Appendix A. Professional journals in your field may include information about other guides. While these guides vary tremendously in their currency and content, they can be helpful in identifying additional prospects.

Step Two: Refining Your List

At this point, your initial prospect list should be fairly long. Now it's time to narrow it down to those foundations that appear most likely to fund your project or organization. If you've been diligent about filling out your prospect worksheets, you should be able to quickly eliminate foundations:

1. that do not award grants in your geographic area;

2. that do not provide the type of support you need;

3. whose average grant award is too large or too small for your funding needs; and/or

4. that have a different geographic focus (i.e., national, regional, or local) than that of your project.

Once you've done that, you can begin to investigate the remaining foundations on your list to find out whether their funding interests truly match your organization's needs and, if so, how to proceed with your grant application. We'll tell you exactly how to do that in Chapter 10, but first let's look at other approaches you might take to identify potential funding sources.

Chapter 7

Finding the Right Funder:
The Geographic Approach

The phrase "Charity begins at home" sums up the typical pattern of foundation funding: Philanthropy focused on the funder's home base has been a reality since its earliest days. Of the nearly 11,000 foundations tracked by the Foundation Center in the 1994 editions of *The Foundation Directory* and *The Foundation Directory Part 2*, approximately 80 percent restrict their giving to a specific state or multistate region. Although some of the better known foundations tend to break out of this pattern, most have a strong commitment to funding local nonprofits that serve their communities.

Nonprofits interested in attracting foundation funding should learn as much as possible about the funders in their own backyard, both large and small. This is particularly important if you are seeking relatively small grants or funds for projects with purely local impact. Often, it will be possible to build a funding structure using a variety of components. For example, you might approach local foundations for small grants in the $100 to $5,000 range for continuing general support, while approaching larger foundations working in your field when introducing a special project.

Smaller local foundations should be investigated for grants according to their interests and assets. You're likely to discover that many small foundations give to the same organizations year after year and rarely make grants to new recipients. Don't let this fact discourage you from investigating all local sources. Some of your work with potential funders—what professional fundraisers call "cultivation"—can and should be viewed as a learning experience. Make local grantmakers aware of the services you are providing and the ways in which your organization enhances life in their home community.

Step One: Developing a Geographic Prospect List

Developing a list of foundations that are either located in or fund projects in your city or state is relatively easy. The resources available include both general reference directories and indexes of foundation grants. Remember, however, that simply sharing the same area code is not reason enough to request funds from a foundation. Once identified, each foundation must be fully researched to see if its grantmaking activities match up in other ways to your program or proposal. Figure 39 outlines the sequence recommended by Foundation Center staff to identify foundation prospects using the geographic approach. Whether you are focusing on large or small foundations, you'll want to begin your search with local or state directories. (See the bibliography of state and local directories in the most recent edition of the *Guide to U.S. Foundations, Their Trustees, Officers, and Donors*.) If there is more than one directory for your area, use them all until you are able to verify through your research which are more accurate and/or comprehensive.

As you add foundation names from state or local directories to your prospect list, be sure to fill in the appropriate information on your prospect worksheet. Note, in particular, any restrictions on a foundation's giving program that would prevent it from funding your project. Some of the smaller foundations are restricted by will or charter to giving to only a few designated or "preselected" organizations. Others may not fund projects in your subject area or may not be able to offer the type or amount of support you need.

Once you have investigated relevant state or local directories, examine the geographic indexes in *The Foundation 1000*, *The Foundation Directory*, and *The Foundation Directory Part 2*. These indexes group foundations by the state and city in which they maintain their principal offices. The names and entry numbers of foundations that make grants on a regional, national, or international basis appear in boldface. For these funders you can adopt an approach based on subject interest rather than geography. Those foundations that give locally or in a few specified states are listed in regular type. Users interested in local giving within their state should check the series of "see also" references at the end of each state section. These cross-references identify foundations that may be located elsewhere but have a history of grantmaking in your state (see Figures 36 and 37).

If your search is focusing on smaller foundations in your local area, your next stop should be the *Guide to U.S. Foundations, Their Trustees, Officers, and Donors,* the only Center directory that offers access to the more than 35,000 active grantmaking foundations in the United States. The *Guide to U.S. Foundations* is arranged by state and, in descending order within states, by annual grant totals. Although the information presented in the *Guide to U.S. Foundations* is abbreviated, it does allow you to make some preliminary observations about each foundation based on its size, location, and principal officer.

When you identify foundation prospects from the *Guide to U.S. Foundations,* be sure to note the employer identification number. This number will help you locate the foundation's annual IRS information return (Form 990-PF), generally the best and sometimes the only source of information about the giving programs of foundations too small to be included in *The Foundation Directory* or *The Foundation Directory Part 2.* The Foundation Center's New York and Washington, D.C., libraries have 990-PFs for every foundation in the country; the Center's libraries in Atlanta, Cleveland, and San Francisco have 990-PFs for foundations located in the Southeast, Midwest, and West, respectively. If you are unable to visit a Center library, any Foundation Center Cooperating Collection supervisor should be able to order the 990-PF you need from the Center's headquarters in New York.

The *Guide to U.S. Foundations* also includes all currently active community foundations, which can be valuable local resources. In addition to financial support, many community foundations provide technical assistance to nonprofit organizations in areas such as budgeting, public relations, fundraising strategies, and management.

Finally, if your organization is located in New York State, consult *New York State Foundations: A Comprehensive Directory* for all foundations currently active in New York. *New York State Foundations* is arranged and indexed by county, providing an additional point of access to foundations headquartered in your immediate area (see Figure 38).

FIGURE 36.   Geographic Index in *The Foundation Directory*

Pueblo: Chamberlain 792, Thatcher 858
Wray: Kitzmiller-Bales 821

see also 47, 987, 1271, 1417, 1466, 1673, 1683, 2001, 2355, 2440, 2779, 2966, 3015, 3037, 3070, 3264, 3308, 3520, 3571, 3651, 3688, 3904, 4326, 5113, 5350, 5369, 5791, 6053, 6099, 6458, 6536, 6774

CONNECTICUT

Bloomfield: Rogow 998
Botsford: Huisking 944
Branford: Freas 924
Bridgeport: Bridgeport 884, Carstensen 886, Community 892, Jones 948, Jost 950
Bristol: Barnes 874, **Barnes 875**
Clinton: EIS 911, **Fischbach 917**
Cos Cob: Sussman 1017
Danbury: Barden 873, **Foundation 921**, Union 1023
Darien: Lapine 959
Fairfield: **General 928, General 929**
Farmington: Goldfarb 932, Heublein 940, Martin 971
Greens Farms: Smilow 1007
Greenwich: Adler 867, Baker 872, Bennett 877, **Casey 888**, Dennett 903, **Ellis 912**, Fairchild 915, Foster-Davis 920, Frantz 923, Macmillan 967, Mazer 973, Mosbacher 978, Panwy 987, RORD 999, Royce 1001, **Smart 1006**, TWS 1022, Young 1035
Guilford: **Angelina 870**
Hartford: Aetna 868, Bissell 880, **Caruso 887**, Connecticut 893, Donaghue 907, Ensworth 914, Fox 922, Fuller 926, **Gimprich 931**, Goldfarb 933, Hartford 937, Hartford 938, ITT 945, Krieble 957, Long 964, Preston 991, **Pryor 993**, Robinson 997, Saunders 1003, **Society 1008**, Stanley 1014, Sullivan 1016, Travelers 1020, **Tremaine 1021**, Widow's 1031
Harwinton: Folsom 919
Kensington: Vance 1025
Killingworth: **Bingham 879**
Madison: Maguire 969
Manchester: **Price 992**
Marlborough: **Krieble 958**
Meriden: Jones 949, Meriden 974
Middletown: **Braitmayer 883**
New Britain: D & L 899, New Britain 979
New Canaan: Denzler 904, **Perkin 989**, Sosnoff 1010, Tow 1019
New Haven: **Belgian 876, Childs 890**, Eder 908, Edgewood 909, Hahn 935, Meserve 975, New Haven 980, Woman's 1032
New London: Anderson-Paffard 869, Bodenwein 881, Kitchings 952, Palmer 986, Southeastern 1011
New Milford: Harcourt 936
Norwalk: **Conway 895**, Culpeper 898, Dell 901, Fairfield 916, Vanderbilt 1026
Old Greenwich: Remmer 994
Old Lyme: MacCurdy-Salisbury 966
Orange: Hubbell 943
Pomfret: Topsfield 1018
Ridgefield: Kearns 951, **Leiash 961**
Rocky Hill: O'Meara 983
Seymour: Matthies 972
Simsbury: Ensign-Bickford 913
Southport: Kreitler 956, Main 970, Pfriem 990, Wheeler 1029
Stamford: Berbecker 878, Brace 882, Crane 896, **Culpeper 897**, Day 900, **Friends 925**, Garden 927, Gimbel 930, GTE 934, Herzog 939, ITT 946, Jaffe 947, Leonhardt 963, Mad 968, Obernauer 984, Olin 985, Patterson 988, Rosenthal 1000, Senior 1005, **Von Rebay 1027**, Whitehead 1030, Xerox 1034, Ziegler 1036
Suffield: Nirenberg 982
Waterbury: **Clark 891**, Connecticut 894, Long 965, Mills 976, Moore 977, Stanley 1012, Waterbury 1028
Watertown: Woodward 1033
West Hartford: Auerbach 871, Fisher 918, **Hoffman 942**, Kohn-Joseloff 953, Koopman 954, Larrabee 960, Roberts 996, Schiro 1004, Sorenson-Pearson 1009, **Valentine 1024**

Weston: Bulkley 885
Westport: **Educational 910, Heyman 941**, Kossak 955, **Newman's 981, Richardson 995**, Salmon 1002, **Stanley 1013, Stone 1015**
Wilton: Chapin 889, **Deloitte 902**, Dibner 906
Windsor Locks: Dexter 905
Woodbridge: Lender 962

see also 49, 125, 185, 1128, 1469, 1630, 1802, 2306, 2366, 2461, 2488, 2503, 2517, 2576, 2590, 2627, 2630, 2631, 2634, 2641, 2686, 2708, 2737, 2992, 3194, 3417, 3429, 3623, 3691, 3693, 3741, 3743, 3823, 3844, 3847, 3862, 3885, 3949, 3967, 4023, 4042, 4057, 4072, 4075, 4091, 4107, 4131, 4133, 4149, 4183, 4184, 4190, 4220, 4226, 4267, 4289, 4292, 4332, 4357, 4362, 4375, 4397, 4410, 4413, 4428, 4432, 4435, 4450, 4492, 4500, 4516, 4527, 4543, 4559, 4572, 4614, 4634, 4653, 4680, 4713, 4739, 4770, 4775, 4852, 5439, 5490, 5539, 5828, 5843, 6064, 6713

DELAWARE

Claymont: Lovett 1068
Dover: Palmer 1074
Greenville: **Glencoe 1058**
Wilmington: Amsterdam 1037, Beneficial 1038, Bernard 1039, Birch 1040, Bishop 1041, Bishop 1042, Borkee-Hagley 1043, Buckner 1044, Chichester 1045, Cohen 1046, **Common 1047**, Crestlea 1048, Crystal 1049, **Curran 1050**, Delaware 1051, Devonwood 1052, Downs 1053, Ederic 1054, Etnier 1055, Fair 1056, **Gerard 1057, Good 1059**, Hamel 1060, Kent 1061, Kent-Lucas 1062, Kingsley 1063, Kutz 1064, Laffey-McHugh 1065, Longwood 1066, Longwood 1067, Lynch 1069, Marmot 1070, Milliken 1071, MLKA 1072, Morania 1073, Pinkerton 1075, **Raskob 1076, Raskob 1077**, Red 1078, Romill 1079, **Schwartz 1080**, Snyder 1081, **Vale 1082**, Weezie 1083, Welfare 1084, Zock 1085

---

see also 1234, 1237, 1630, 2362, 2766, 3623, 3664, 3741, 4220, 4500, 5590, 5688, 5733, 5746, 5785, 6392, 6500

DISTRICT OF COLUMBIA

Washington: AMS 1086, Appleby 1087, **Arca 1088**, Arcana 1089, **Baruch 1090, Bauman 1091, Beldon 1092**, Bender 1093, Bender 1094, Benton 1095, Bernstein 1096, Bloedorn 1097, Brownley 1098, Cafritz 1099, Cohen 1100, Cohen 1101, **Council 1102**, Covington 1103, **Delmar 1104**, Denit 1105, Dimick 1106, District 1107, Dweck 1108, England 1109, **Fannie Mae 1110, FishAmerica 1111**, Folger 1112, Foundation 1113, Foundation 1114, Fowler 1115, Freed 1116, **Friendly 1117, Gauntlett 1118**, GEICO 1119, Gelman 1120, **German 1121**, Giant 1122, Glen 1123, Goldman 1124, Gottesman 1125, Graham 1126, Godelsky 1127, Gund 1128, Healy 1129, Himmelfarb 1130, **Hitachi 1131, International 1132, Japanese/American 1133, Jensen 1134, Jerusalem 1135**, Johnston 1136, Kapiloff 1137, Kaplan 1138, **Kennedy 1139**, Kiplinger 1140, **Koch 1141**, Lea 1142, Lehrman 1143, Loughran 1144, **Loyola 1145**, Marpat 1146, Marriott 1147, **Marriott 1148, MCI 1149**, Mead 1150, Meyer 1151, **Mitsubishi 1152, Patterson 1153, Pettus-Crowe 1154, Post 1155, Public 1156**, Reich 1157, RJR 1158, Ross 1159, Stewart 1160, Stewart 1161, Stone 1162, Strong 1163, Szekely 1164, Usery 1165, Wasserman 1166, Westport 1167, Willard 1168, Zoline 1169

---

see also 539, 957, 999, 1056, 1294, 1466, 1630, 1809, 1902, 1922, 2078, 2312, 2313, 2321, 2329, 2332, 2333, 2336, 2339, 2340, 2346, 2353, 2358, 2362, 2364, 2379, 2386, 2407, 2411, 2418, 2423, 2441, 2550, 2712, 2859, 2926, 3066, 3164, 3269, 3368, 3437, 3443, 3508, 3648, 3778, 3917, 4121, 4184, 4220, 4326, 4500, 4559, 4678, 4741, 4877, 4959, 5043, 5350, 5467, 5536, 5586, 5594, 6083, 6172,

---

6281, 6387, 6389, 6392, 6396, 6422, 6439, 6442, 6487, 6488, 6500

FLORIDA

Alachua: **Crane 1217**
Arcadia: Morgan 1329
Bal Harbour: Ford 1246, Gann 1255
Bartow: Grader 1268, **Stuart 1396**
Bay Harbor Islands: Taylor 1403
Boca Raton: Bay 1187, Beveridge 1193, **Dettman 1227**, Flynn 1245, Grace 1267, Hoernle 1280, Hovnanian 1285, Lynn 1315, MIDA 1325, **Rales 1355, Rosenberg 1364**, Santa 1374, Schmidt 1378, Simon 1387, Sunburst 1398
Boynton Beach: Chingos 1212, **Messing 1321**
Bradenton: Aurora 1180, Bible 1194, **Eagles 1235**
Clearwater: Bickerton 1195, Eckerd 1237, **Hayward 1278**, Metal 1322, Pinellas 1349, **Saint 1371**
Clewiston: United 1407
Coral Gables: Abbey 1170, Cobb 1213, Fowey 1250, Jennings 1292, Rosenberg 1365, Ware 1413
De Land: Fish 1244
Deerfield Beach: Moore 1328
Delray Beach: Brown 1203, Lattner 1306, Waldbaum 1411
Fort Lauderdale: Amaturo 1176, Broward 1202, Friedman 1252, Goodwin 1265, Gore 1266, Horvitz 1284, Huizenga 1287, Katz 1294, Krueger 1304, Law 1308, **Nicol 1334**, Peterson 1344, **Stacy 1392**, Sylvester 1401, Wells 1416
Fort Myers: Foulds 1249, Southwest 1389
Fort Pierce: Fort Pierce 1247, **Link 1309**
Gainesville: **Koch 1301**
Hialeah: Batchelor 1185
Hobe Sound: Bell 1191, **Donnell-Kay 1231**
Holiday: Speer 1390
Hollywood: Chertkof 1210, Einstein 1239, **Schecter 1377**
Howey-in-the-Hills: Griffin 1270
Jacksonville: Barnett 1183, Beaver 1189, Childress 1211, Cohen 1214, Davis 1220, Davis 1221, Davis 1222, **Davis 1223, Davis 1225, duPont 1233**, duPont 1234, Gooding 1263, Groover 1273, Jacksonville 1288, Kirbo 1298, Marco 1317, Parsons 1341, Posnack 1350, Reinhold 1358, River 1362, Riverside 1363, Ruby 1367, Schultz 1380, Semmes 1382, Setzer 1383, Stein 1393, Stevens 1394, Swisher 1400, Vaughn-Jordan 1408, Winn-Dixie 1424, Wolfson 1427
Juno Beach: FPL 1251
Key Biscayne: Wilder 1421
Key West: Dively 1228, Whitney 1419
La Belle: Oak 1336
Lakeland: Foulds 1282, Jenkins 1291, **Watson 1414**
Lighthouse Point: Howell 1286
Longboat Key: Keating 1295, **Long 1311**, Mote 1330
Longwood: Chatlos 1209, Gooding 1264
Manalapan: **Rothman 1366**
Mango: **Believers 1190**
Melbourne: Binz 1196, Harris 1276
Miami: Abraham 1172, Adams 1174, Arison 1179, Blank 1198, Dade 1219, Dunspaugh-Dalton 1232, Garner 1256, Jaharis 1289, Kennedy 1296, **Knight 1299**, Knight-Ridder 1300, Kramer 1303, **Markey 1318**, Miller 1326, Mills 1327, Pearce 1343, Russell 1369, Ryder 1370, Shulevitz 1385, Simkins 1386, Thatcher 1404, Volen 1409, Weintraub 1415, Wertheim 1417, Wiseheart 1426, Wolfson 1428, Wollowick 1429, Yulman 1431
Miami Beach: Broad 1201, Edelstein 1238, Gerson 1258, Greenburg-May 1269, Meyer 1323, Ratner 1356, Yablick 1430
Moore Haven: Wiggins 1420
Naples: Blair 1197, Brennan 1199, Collier 1215, **Samstag 1373**
New Smyrna Beach: **Landegger 1305**
North Fort Myers: Price 1351
North Miami: Applebaum 1177, Griffith 1271
North Palm Beach: Handleman 1274, Lost 1312, Psychists 1352

FIGURE 37. Geographic Index in *The Foundation 1000*

GEOGRAPHIC INDEX

This index lists foundations by the states and cities in which they are located. Foundations listed in bold type make grants on a national or broad regional basis. The other foundations generally limit giving to the city or state in which they are located. 'See also' references at the end of a state listing identify foundations located elsewhere that have made substantial grants in the state.

ALABAMA
Birmingham Alabama 7, Caring 139, Meyer 621, Sonat 858
Mobile Bedsole 63

see also BellSouth 67, Campbell 132, Chrysler 166, International 454, Lyndhurst 549, Monsanto 636, Motorola 647, Scott 828, Steelcase 871, Weyerhaeuser 972, Whitehead 978

ALASKA
see Bullitt 116, Murdock 650, Scott 828

ARIZONA
Phoenix Flinn 306, **Solheim 857**
Prescott Morris 644
Sun City Thoresen 910
Tucson **Research 761**
Wickenburg Webb 961

see also Bush 122, GenCorp 341, Goldsmith 366, Honeywell 439, Medtronic 607, Motorola 647, Norwest 682, Rhodebeck 769, US 934, Wiegand 982

ARKANSAS
Bentonville Wal-Mart 948, Walton 953
Little Rock Rockefeller 784, Rockefeller 785, Wrape 996
Springdale Jones 478

see also Bridgestone/Firestone 101, GenCorp 341, Gerber 349, International 454, Levi 529, Mabee 553, Southwestern 861, Sturgis 889, Union 929, Weyerhaeuser 972, Whirlpool 973

CALIFORNIA
Arcadia Berger 70
Beverly Hills Ahmanson 5, Bettingen 74, Litton 539, Stein 873
Burbank Burns 120, Disney 241, Rigler-Lawrence 773
Calabasas Lockheed 540
Concord Hofmann 436
Culver City Goldrich 364, **Kest 497**
Irvine **Beckman 62**, Fluor 307
La Jolla Powell 739
Laguna Beach **Homeland 438**
Larkspur Marin 564
Livermore Hertz 423
Long Beach Norris 679
Los Altos **Packard 703**
Los Angeles Autry 42, **Banyan 53**, Boswell 93, Braun 98, California 129, Doheny 244, Drown 255, **Eisenberg 275**, First 301, Geffen 340, **Gluck 360**, Gonda 367, Haynes 404, Hoag 433, Jones 479, Keck 492, Lannan 523, Leavey 525, Mann 562, Max 574, Murphy 651, **Nakamichi 654**, Parsons 709, Pauley 711, Pfaffinger 721, **Riordan 776**, Seaver 831, Taper 896, **Teledyne 902**, Unocal 932, Wasserman 957, Weingart 964
Menlo Park Compton 188, Hewlett 428, Johnson 474, **Kaiser 487**
Newport Beach Crean 203, **Lyon 551**, Steele 872

Oakland Clorox 177, Hedco 412, Skaggs 848
Orange **Baker 45**
Orinda Berry 73
Pacific Palisades Stern 875
Pasadena Garland 335, **Hoover 441, Pasadena 710**, Stauffer 870
Redding McConnell 582
Sacramento Sierra 842
Salinas Harden 395
San Diego **Jacobs 461**, San Diego 807
San Francisco **BankAmerica 52, Bechtel 61**, Columbia 184, Cowell 199, **Energy 282, Foundation 317**, Gap 333, Gerbode 350, Getty 353, Haas 386, Haas 387, Herbst 419, Irvine 455, Irwin 456, Koret 513, Levi 529, McBean 577, McKesson 599, Montgomery 637, Osher 697, Pacific 701, **Potlatch 737**, Roberts 779, Rosenberg 792, San Francisco 808, Shorenstein 839, Stuart 887, Stulsaft 888, Swig 894, Transamerica 920, Wells 967, Wollenberg 991, Zellerbach 998
San Jose Santa Clara 811, Valley 938
San Leandro Treadwell 922
San Ramon Valley 939
Santa Barbara Santa Barbara 810
Santa Monica **Capital 138**, Getty 354, Milken 625, Milken 626
Solvang **M.E.G. 552**
South Pasadena **Confidence 189**, Mericos 613, W.W.W. 945, Whittier 981
Universal City MCA 576
Walnut Shea 835

see also Annenberg 25, Bauer 58, Bush 122, Cheney 161, Dayton 225, GenCorp 341, Gerber 349, Gordon/Rousmaniere/Roberts 368, Hellman 418, Hermann 420, Honeywell 439, Kiewit 500, Lincy 535, McGraw-Hill 592, Medtronic 607, Merck 611, Mobil 633, Nalco 655, Price 742, Prudential 749, Salomon 805, Skirball 850, Smith 855, Stanley 866, Steelcase 871, Union 929, Webb 961, Wiegand 982

COLORADO
Aspen **General 345**
Boulder **Needmor 661**
Colorado Springs El Pomar 277
Denver Boettcher 85, Colorado 183, Coors 196, Denver 233, Gates 337, Johnson 471, Taylor 899
Englewood Buell 112, US 934

see also DeVos 236, Eastman 266, First 299, Honeywell 439, McGraw-Hill 592, Mobil 633, Norwest 682, Phillips 728, Union 929

CONNECTICUT
Danbury **Foundation 318**
Fairfield **General 342**
Farmington Heublein 427
Greenwich **Casey 149, Ellis 279, Fairchild 291**
Hartford Aetna 4, Connecticut 190, Hartford 400, ITT 457, Stanley 866, Travelers 921
New Haven **Childs 163**, New Haven 663
Old Greenwich **Bingham 80**
Stamford **Culpeper 209**, GTE 382, Herzog 424, Xerox 997
West Hartford Auerbach 41, **Hoffman 435**
Westport **Educational 274, Richardson 772**
Wilton **Deloitte 230**

Woodbridge Lender 527

see also Bank 51, Beinecke 64, Brooks 104, Carolyn 143, CIGNA 167, Cox 201, Cummings 211, Fleet/Norstar 305, Frese 325, Gordon/Rousmaniere/Roberts 368, Hagedorn 388, Hallmark 392, Hatch 402, Johnson 475, Moore 639, Morris 645, NYNEX 684, Overbrook 698, Peabody 713, Sonat 858

DELAWARE
Wilmington Crystal 207, **Devonwood 235**, Laffey-McHugh 519, Longwood 542, **Raskob 753**, Welfare 966

see also Bell 66, Brooks 104, Chrysler 166, duPont 260, Hechinger 410, Scott 828

DISTRICT OF COLUMBIA
Washington **AMS 19**, Arca 28, Arcana 30, Cafritz 125, **Fannie 292**, German 351, Graham 372, Johnston 477, **Kennedy 496, Loyola 546**, Marriott 567, MCI 594, Meyer 620, **Public 730, RJR 778**, Stewart 877, Stewart 878

see also Bell 66, Clark-Winchcole 174, Eisig 276, Hechinger 410, Heinz 416, McGraw-Hill 592, Prince 744, Smith 853, Southwestern 861, van Ameringen 940, Wiegand 982

FLORIDA
Boca Raton Beveridge 75, **Grace 370**, Lynn 550
Delray Beach Lattner 524
Fort Lauderdale Sylvester 895
Gainesville **Koch 510**
Jacksonville **Davis 224**, duPont 260, Jacksonville 460, Kirbo 503, Winn-Dixie 987
Lakeland Hollis 437
Longwood **Chatlos 160**
Miami Arison 32, Dade 213, **Knight 508, Markey 565**, Russell 799, Ryder 801
Palm Beach Janirve 462, Lowe 544, **Whitehall 975**
Sarasota Selby 833
Tallahassee **Frueauff 328**
Tavernier Storer 880
West Palm Beach Davis 222, **McIntosh 596**, Rinker 775
Winter Park Bush 122

see also Atlantic 40, BellSouth 67, Buehler 111, Camp 131, Campbell 132, Dayton 225, DeVos 236, Disney 241, Enron 285, Flagler 304, Honeywell 439, Monsanto 636, Motorola 647, Prudential 749, Retirement 762, Thoresen 910, Wean 959, Whitehead 978

GEORGIA
Atlanta Atlanta 39, BellSouth 67, Camp 131, Campbell 132, Carlos 140, Davis 220, Evans 288, Georgia 348, Harland 396, McCamish 579, Whitehead 977, Whitehead 978, Woodruff 992, Woodward 994
Columbus Bradley-Turner 97
Decatur Wilson 985
La Grange Callaway 130

see also Hallmark 392, Kirbo 503, Levi 529, Lyndhurst

107

FIGURE 38. Geographic Index in *New York State Foundations*

GEOGRAPHIC INDEX

Foundations in boldface type make grants on a national, regional, or international basis; the others generally limit giving to the city or state in which they are located.

ALBANY

Albany A-C 1, Albany's 2, Appleton 3, Atwood 4, Biegelsen 6, Blaine 7, Bush 8, Christian 10, Cote 11, Faith 13, Hessberg 17, Holiatric 18, Hotel-Motel 19, Iselin 21, Johnston 22, Kermani 23, **Kirby 24,** Kirsch 25, Klock 26, Lasser 27, Mastrangelo 30, McArdle 31, McDonald 32, McDonald 33, Minard 34, Mintzer 35, Mohawk-Hudson 36, Moul 37, Muldoon 38, Murrin 39, Northeastern 41, Peasley 42, Picotte 43, Potter 44, Reynolds 45, Rosenblum 47, Saint 48, Saxe 49, Simon 50, Stern 52, Swyer 53, Tenrab 55, Thayer 56, Trombly 57, Weir 58, White 59, White 60, Yerdon 61
Delmar Lewis 28
Glenmont Robinson 46
Guilderland Barvoets 5
Latham General 14, Hellman 16
Loudonville Nirenberg 40, Smachlo 51, Tekakwitha 54
Newtonville Gerrity 15
Rensselaerville Huyck 20
Slingerlands Elliott 12
South Bethlehem Callanan 9, Marcelle 29

ALLEGANY

Belmont Robertson 65
Wellsville Belovsky 62, Holbrook 63, Holbrook 64, Wellsville 66

BRONX

Bronx Brooks 69, City 70, **Dodge 71,** Edelstein 72, **Elenberg 73,** Equapart 74, Fishman 75, Freeman 76, Gramercy 78, Grotsky 80, Hartman 81, Klosk 82, Liskin 83, Melnick 85, **Open 86,** Pocasset 87, Schur 88, Schwartz-Marrow 90, Shekhter 91, Stanley 92, **Stratton 94, Wilson 95,** Zelmanowicz 96
Riverdale Brachfeld 67, Bravmann 68, Frenkel 77, Gross 79, Marton 84, Schuster 89, Stinchfield 93

BROOME

Binghamton Ahearn 97, Baker 99, Bishop 101, Botnick 102, Briggs 104, Cohen 105, Decker 106, Gaffney 107, Hershaft 108, Hill 109, Horowitch 110, Horowitz 111, Hotchkiss-Stow 112, Howard 113, Hoyt 114, Klee 115, Levene 119, **Maasbach 120,** Mathews 121, Nelson 122, Olum 123, Olum 124, Raymond 125, Sarkisian 126, Schumann 127, Selkowitz 128, **Travaglini 129**
Endicott Kresge 118
Johnson City BGM 100
Maine Bowers 103
Vestal Alekna 98, Koffman 116, Koffman 117

CATTARAUGUS

South Dayton Jachym 130

CAYUGA

Auburn **Bisgrove 132,** Columbian 133, Ellis 134, Emerson 135, French 136, Metcalf 137, Osborne 138, Schwartz 140
Aurora Bellinzoni 131
Cato Schmidt 139

CHAUTAUQUA

Dunkirk Northern 148
Jamestown Carnahan-Jackson 141, Chautauqua 142, Gebbie 143, Hultquist 144, Lenna 145, Mount Moriah 147, Sheldon 149
Westfield MacLeod 146, Thompson 150, Wilson 151

CHEMUNG

Elmira Anderson 153, Baker 154, Bloomer 155, Chemung 156, Cooper 157, Earl 158, Hilliard 159, Lowman-Howell 161, Shulman 162, Tripp 163, Wurtele 164
Horseheads Anderson 152
Pine City Lindau 160

CHENANGO

New Berlin Preferred 178
Norwich Brown 165, Chenango 166, Chenango 167, Cognitive 168, Dickinson 169, Flanagan 170, Gillen 171, Greater Norwich 172, Hale 173, Jacobs 174, Mabey 176, Schenck 179, Scott 180, Thompson 181, Thomson 182, Totman 183, Weinman 184
Oxford Mead 177
South New Berlin Lyons 175

CLINTON

Plattsburgh Emco 185
Rexford Lawrence 186

COLUMBIA

Chatham Backer 187
East Chatham Common 189
Ghent **Levy 192**
Hudson Children's 188, Gerli 190, Kennedy 191, Lobsenz 193, **Potts 194,** Rheinstrom 195

CORTLAND

Cincinnatus Kellogg 197
Cortland King's 198, **McDonald 199,** Smigel 201, Wilkins 202
Homer Brockway 196, Siegle 200

DELAWARE

Delhi Burkett 205, Henderson 209
Hobart American 203, O'Connor 210
Stamford Robinson-Broadhurst 211
Walton Baptist 204, Eckert 206, Hanford 207, Harby 208, Sanford 212

DUTCHESS

Dover Plains Grinnell 221
Fishkill McManus 226, Wolf 233, Wolf 234
Millbrook Millbrook 228, Winslow 232
Millerton Kawaler 223, Kramer 224
Pawling Monahan 229
Pine Plains Bentley 215, Bentley 216, Coach 218
Poughkeepsie Area 213, Boos 217, Freeman 219, Fusco 220, Hoe 222, McCann 225, Nuhn 230
Rhinebeck VonderLinden 231
Stanfordville Baruch 214
Tivoli Milbrandt 227

ERIE

Akron East 275
Amherst Demakos 270, McLain 321, Millonzi 326, Montague 328
Athol Springs Butler 253
Buffalo Amico 235, Babines 238, Baird 241, Block 242, Bookstaver 243, Brady 244, Brownell 245, Buffalo 247, Buffalo 248, Burchfield 250, Burns 251, Burns 252, Children's 256, Christos 257, Clarke 258, Cornell 259, Cummings 262, Curran 263, Curtis 264, D-B 265, Danforth 266, Darling 267, Day 269, Derose 271, DeSpirt 272, Donmarel 273, Earl 274, Elster 276, Evans 278, Federman 279, Ferguson 280, Fierle 281, Friedman 283, Gardner 284, Gartner 285, GH 286, Ginsberg 287, Goldome 288, Goode 289, Goodyear 290, Hahn 291, Hamilton 292, Hayes 293, Herold 294, Hillery 295, Housing 297, Hull 298, Hurwitz 299, Hyde 300, Joffe 301, Julia 302, Kahle 303, Knox 305, Koon 306, Kurtz 307, Larson 308, **LeBrun 309,** Lewis 310, Lipke 311, Lipke 312, Lippes 313, Littlewood 315, M & J 316, Magavern 317, Mark 318, McCarthy 319, McCormick 320, McTaggart 322, Mernan 323, Merritt 324, Messer 325, Mills 327, Moore 329, Oettel 331, **Parker 334, Parker**

NEW YORK STATE FOUNDATIONS: A COMPREHENSIVE DIRECTORY 873

INDEXES TO FOUNDATION GRANTS

By this point, you have probably uncovered a large number of foundation prospects through your geographic search. Before you complete this phase of your research, you should check the various indexes of foundation grants to identify foundations that have actually awarded grants to organizations in your area.

The Foundation Grants Index is arranged alphabetically by state and includes a Type of Support/Geographic Index that helps you identify grants to organizations in your state (see Figure 40) in addition to a Recipient Category Index that helps you identify grants to like-minded organizations (e.g., hospitals, private universities, museums, youth development centers).

As you scan the listings in *The Foundation Grants Index*, try to eliminate foundations that appear to have awarded grants to organizations in your state solely on the basis of their subject focus or because of an affiliation with a specific institution. Note the types of organizations receiving grants, the subject focus of the grant recipients, and the amount and type of support offered by particular foundations. Invariably, you'll find that some foundations limit their giving to specific subject areas or types of institutions. If a foundation's giving pattern does not match your funding needs, it does not belong on your prospect list.

Step Two: Refining Your List

At this point you may have a fairly long list of potential funding sources based on their geographic location and/or field of interest. As you complete your prospect worksheets, you should continue to gather relevant facts that will enable you to eliminate foundations:

1. that do not award grants in your subject field;
2. that do not provide the type of support you need;
3. whose giving is restricted to a city or county other than your own; and
4. whose average grant award is too large or too small for your funding needs.

You are now almost ready to investigate more carefully the remaining foundations on your list. In an earlier chapter we examined some of the resources and procedures you could use to determine whether your organization's needs really fit with a particular foundation's funding interests. But there is one more approach to foundation funding research—the types of support approach—that you would do well to consider first.

FIGURE 39. Finding the Right Funder: The Geographic Approach

The Geographic Approach helps you identify potential funding sources in your state or community as well as those located elsewhere that have provided funding to organizations in your geographic area. As you complete your prospect list using these resources, be sure to check for any stated restrictions on foundations' giving interests as well as their subject interests and the types of support they offer to determine whether they are likely or able to support your organization and its activities with the type and amount of support you need.

STEP 1. STATE AND LOCAL DIRECTORIES vary in coverage and content, but generally are quite useful in identifying local funders. Check your local library to find current editions of relevant directories.

STEP 2. *THE FOUNDATION 1000* analyzes the 1,000 largest foundations in depth and includes both national and local funders. Check the Geographic Index for foundations either located in your state or with a specific interest in your state (indicated with "see also" references).

STEP 3. *THE FOUNDATION DIRECTORY* describes more than 6,700 foundations with assets of $2 million or more or annual giving totaling at least $200,000. *The Foundation Directory Part 2* provides information on approximately 4,000 foundations with assets of less than $2 million and annual giving between $50,000 and $200,000. These volumes are arranged by state, making it easy to scan entries for foundations in your area. Check the geographic indexes as well to identify foundations located elsewhere that have a specific interest in your state or community.

STEP 4. The *GUIDE TO U.S. FOUNDATIONS* lists all active grantmaking foundations in the U.S. alphabetically by state, then in descending order by grant amount. Check for smaller foundations in your state that do not meet the criteria for inclusion in directories of larger foundations. Check community foundations to identify those in your community or region.

STEP 5. INDEXES OF FOUNDATION GRANTS list grants of $10,000 or more awarded by about 1,000 major foundations. Use to identify national foundations that have awarded grants in your area.
   • ***GRANT GUIDES*** list all grants reported in the previous year within broad fields. Check the Geographic Index for grants in your state and the list of foundations at the back to eliminate funders with specific giving limitations, then review the grant records for the remaining funders to determine possible prospects.
   • ***THE FOUNDATION GRANTS INDEX*** lists all grants reported in the previous year, divided into major fields and arranged alphabetically by state. Check the Type of Support/Geographic Index for grants in your subject areas made to organizations in your state; the Recipient Category Index for grants to organizations in your state that have received the type of support you need; and the Recipient Name Index for grants to organizations in your area or state.
   • ***THE FOUNDATION GRANTS INDEX QUARTERLY*** lists grants reported during the preceding three months. Use to investigate the current giving interests of major foundations in your state and check the Grant Recipient Index for recent grants to organizations in your area.

STEP 6. REVIEW YOUR PROSPECT LIST to eliminate foundations that are unlikely to provide funding in your subject area or are unable to provide the type and amount of support your organization needs. Research remaining prospects to determine those most likely to consider your request favorably.

Chapter 8

Finding the Right Funder: The Types of Support Approach

The types of support approach helps you identify grantmakers, including foundations and corporate giving programs, that have expressed an interest in providing the specific types of support your organization needs.

As your research progresses you'll notice that grants from both foundations and corporate givers usually fall into fairly distinct categories. These may include cash assistance for capital support, operating funds, or seed money, and noncash support such as donations of equipment or supplies, technical assistance, use of facilities, and management advice.

In fact, when considering the types of support your organization needs, it is especially important to investigate avenues other than the traditional dollar grant, or what funders call "in-kind" gifts. For example, a nonprofit that needs a photocopier or computer might look for a local company willing to donate the equipment instead of seeking a grant to buy such equipment. Many grantmakers, especially corporate givers, willingly donate office space, computer time, and facilities; some even lend out executive talent. Securing outright cash donations from these same corporations, on the other hand, can be much more difficult. You'll find that many foundations tend to limit their giving to one or, at most, a few types of support. Therefore, in the planning stages that precede a search for funding sources, you should clarify the specific types of support your organization needs and include only those grantmakers on your prospect list that favor those types of support.

Common Support Types

The following are some common support types:

1. *Capital campaigns*: a campaign, usually extending over a period of years, to raise substantial funds for enduring purposes, such as physical plant or endowment.

2. *Conferences and seminars*: a grant to cover the expenses of holding a conference.

3. *Emergency funds*: a one-time grant to cover immediate short-term funding needs on an urgent basis.

4. *General purposes*: a grant made to further the general purposes or work of an organization, rather than for a specific project; also referred to as an "unrestricted" grant or "operating" support.

5. *In-kind gifts*: a contribution of equipment, supplies, or other property, technical or other services, as distinguished from a monetary grant. Some funders may donate space or staff time as in-kind support.

6. *Operating budgets*: a grant to cover the day-to-day personnel, administrative, and miscellaneous expenses of a project or organization.

7. *Seed money*: a grant or contribution used to begin a new project or organization. Seed grants may cover salaries and other operating expenses for a new project. Also referred to as "start-up funds."

8. *Special projects*: a grant to support specific projects or programs as opposed to a general purpose grant.

Step One: Developing a Broad Prospect List

The following strategy allows you to review descriptions of grants that have been awarded to organizations similar to your own, for the type of support you need.

INDEXES TO FOUNDATION GRANTS

Begin with *The Foundation Grants Index*. As we noted earlier, the *Grants Index* offers concise descriptions of grants of $10,000 or more reported to the Foundation Center during the previous year by about 1,000 major U.S. foundations, including the 500 largest.

Turn to the Recipient Category Index of the *Grants Index* (see Figure 32), which shows a breakdown of grants by specific types of support. You can use this index to identify grants of the type you are interested in made to organizations similar to your own. The index shows grants awarded to 36 different types of organizations (e.g., churches/temples, human service agencies, libraries, performing arts groups, schools) arranged by any of the 29 specific types of support that have been awarded to those institutions.

To speed your research, the grants records are then subdivided by the states in which the grant recipients are located. Note the sequence numbers: Each number leads you back to a grant description in the main text of the volume. In addition, each grant record includes the names of the grantmaking foundation and recipient organization, along with details—amount, purpose, and so on—about the grant itself.

Remember to consider individual grant records as "evidence" of a foundation's giving interests. Look for grant records that describe funding for projects or organizations that appear to be similar in several respects to your own.

The Type of Support/Geographic Index (see Figure 40) is another helpful way to access pertinent grants records. This index allows you to cross-index support type within 28 broadly defined subject categories against the state location of the grant recipient.

When working with either index, be sure to note on your prospect worksheet the name of the foundation awarding the grant, its location, and any limitations on its giving program. Then scan the full listing of grants reported by that foundation in the Index to Grants by Foundation section to determine its general subject focus, the types of organizations it awards grants to, and the typical size of its grants.

Next refer to the *Grant Guides*. Remember, the *Grant Guide* series duplicates the information contained in *The Foundation Grants Index* and repackages it into particular focus areas for your convenience.

Among the *Grant Guide* series, two titles provide ready access to grants that have been awarded for specific types of support. They are:

—"Matching and Challenge Support"

—"Scholarships, Student Aid and Loans"

Each *Grant Guide* is arranged alphabetically by state and, within each state, by foundation name, followed by the actual grant records (see Figure 41). At the back of each *Guide* is an alphabetically arranged list of foundations covered in that volume. For each foundation, the address and a brief statement of geographic and subject restrictions on their giving is included. This feature is especially useful when using a *Grant Guide* that focuses on a particular type of support, as it allows you to quickly exclude foundations that are inappropriate in terms of stated geographic or subject limitations, leaving you with a list of foundations that match your requirements in all three categories.

GENERAL REFERENCE DIRECTORIES AND DIRECTORIES OF CORPORATE FUNDERS

Now turn to *The Foundation 1000* and its Types of Support index. This index identifies the top 1,000 foundations by the types of support they have typically provided. Notice that the arrangement is alphabetical by type of support, then by state (see Figure 42).

You will also notice that certain foundation names are in boldface. Boldface indicates a foundation with a national or broad regional focus. Foundations listed in regular type generally limit their giving to the city or state in which they are located. This distinction can speed your research by allowing you to zero in on those foundations whose geographic focus matches that of your organization.

To further expand your prospect list, turn to the Types of Support indexes provided in *The Foundation Directory* and *The Foundation Directory Part 2*. Keep in mind that, as with *The Foundation 1000*, these indexes list the types of support funders *say* they are interested in, rather than the actual grants they award. While it may seem like a trivial distinction, it can be a significant one for the grantseeker.

FIGURE 40. Type of Support/Geographic Index in *The Foundation Grants Index*

PROFESSORSHIPS — TYPE OF SUPPORT/GEOGRAPHIC INDEX

Washington 59978

Youth development

California 63442, 63468, 63477, 63576, 63802, 64090
Canada 64960
Colorado 63600, 64959
District of Columbia 9779
Florida 63703
Georgia 63751
Illinois 63791
Maryland 63917
Massachusetts 64432
Michigan 64006, 64008, 64030
New Jersey 64433
New York 64089, 64430, 64442
North Carolina 20151
Oklahoma 64662
Texas 64832, 64843, 64891
Washington 53671

PERFORMANCE/PRODUCTIONS

Animals/wildlife

New Jersey 4583
North Carolina 95

Arts/culture

Alabama 2983
Arizona 499, 501, 1676, 4495, 5379
Arkansas 9163
California 548, 682, 686, 696, 697, 704, 759, 886, 896, 905, 958, 994, 1004, 1132, 1137, 1143, 1149, 1199, 1205, 1249, 1250, 1315, 1316, 1324, 1361, 1381, 1382, 1388, 1397, 1406, 1412, 1513, 1790, 1791, 2204, 3909, 3924, 3997, 4497, 4498, 6332, 6819, 6838, 6847, 6848, 6875, 6877, 6878, 6883, 6928, 8962, 9784, 9785, 44262
Canada 4880, 4908
Colorado 1552, 1605, 1609, 1610, 1613, 1630, 1643, 1654, 1685, 1691, 1692
Connecticut 1932, 6849, 8474
District of Columbia 1424, 1977, 1990, 1995, 1998, 2012, 2020, 2065, 2066, 2441, 3280, 5736, 6695, 6844, 7085, 7402, 7559, 8759, 8976, 9066, 9426, 9457
England 6939
Florida 2123-2126, 2247, 2305, 2838, 6889, 6940
Georgia 2267, 2349, 6896, 6931, 44288
Hong Kong 4875-4877, 4887
Idaho 612
Illinois 2232, 2422, 2428, 2432, 2434, 2460, 2519, 2573, 2586, 2588, 2593, 2639, 2646, 2680, 2728, 2733, 2747, 2901, 2962, 2969, 2972, 2977, 2981, 2992, 2995, 6873, 9787, 59591
India 5666, 5670, 5707
Indiana 3063, 3065, 3076, 3102, 3110
Kansas 3166
Kentucky 6810, 6884
Louisiana 6851, 7512
Maryland 801, 1991, 8670, 9783
Massachusetts 2225, 3471, 6777, 6812, 6818, 7525, 9782, 9792, 54163
Michigan 2092, 3513, 3540, 3607, 3750, 3787, 3803, 4005, 4535
Minnesota 1695, 1700, 1705, 1732, 3846, 3878, 3883, 3976, 3982, 3995, 4030, 4094, 4115, 4121-4123, 4135, 4136, 4141, 4254, 6956, 18691
Missouri 4363, 4388, 8988, 8991
Montana 21888
Mozambique 5697
Nebraska 542, 1714, 8986
Nevada 4501-4504
New Jersey 2194, 4552, 4558, 4561, 4563, 4564, 4569, 4573, 4578, 4581, 4583, 4585, 4597, 4598, 4604, 4781, 4782, 4789-4791, 4815, 5671, 5694, 9789, 16433
New Mexico 1415, 1416, 1712, 9209
New York 754, 950, 1785, 1788, 1792, 1793, 2187, 2265, 4100, 4105, 4110-4112, 4130, 4131, 4137, 4143, 4579, 4608, 4870, 5136, 5152, 5163,

5212, 5213, 5215, 5228, 5231, 5236, 5254, 5261, 5263, 5265, 5333, 5334, 5354, 5373, 5442, 5501, 5662, 5663, 5688, 5712, 5738, 5781, 5873, 5875, 5877, 5878, 6046, 6047, 6065, 6087, 6088, 6237, 6243, 6271, 6468, 6624, 6771, 6787, 6804, 6806, 6820-6822, 6825, 6833, 6840, 6843, 6845, 6853, 6854, 6902, 6909, 6919, 6925, 6953, 6959, 6977, 7116, 7128, 7129, 7135, 7137, 7140, 7147, 7148, 7152, 7154, 7155, 7160, 7164, 7282, 7283, 7397, 7408, 7412, 7500, 7607, 7670, 7676, 7890, 8707, 8721, 8727, 8797, 9786, 9788, 9790, 44861
North Carolina 95, 7700
Ohio 3604, 4061, 7787, 7789, 7796, 7844, 7846, 7850, 7860, 7865, 7872, 7876, 7887-7889, 7894, 7914, 7920, 7922, 7949, 7952, 7955, 7959, 7965, 7993, 7994, 8059-8061, 8064-8066, 8110, 8119-8121, 8132, 8133, 8166
Oregon 1407, 1720-1722, 1730, 8273, 8283, 8294, 8298, 8312
Pennsylvania 894, 2255, 2877, 5650, 6807, 6817, 6907, 7034, 7575, 8471, 8481, 8498, 8499, 8572, 8577, 8660, 8671, 8680, 8683, 8685-8687, 8706, 8725, 8752, 8763, 8781, 8802, 8805, 8849, 8861, 8892, 8952, 9016, 9791
Rhode Island 9054, 9059
South Carolina 2147
Tennessee 6826, 9086, 9090, 9104
Texas 3502, 3921, 6857, 8440, 8971, 8992, 9154, 9171, 9184, 9188, 9220, 9246, 9292, 9294, 9312, 9368, 9400, 9437, 9452, 9485, 9496, 9497, 9507, 9516, 9523, 9526, 9536, 9540, 9649, 9781
Utah 1677, 1729, 1742, 7419, 8996, 9663, 9664, 9669, 9670, 9673, 9680, 9685, 21057
Virginia 8453, 8454, 9855
Washington 1675, 1693, 1723, 1735-1737, 4904, 9903, 9905
West Virginia 8422, 8434
Wisconsin 7032, 9971, 9979
Wyoming 1680, 1741, 8966

Civil rights

District of Columbia 47937

Crime/courts/legal services

California 44262
New Jersey 16433

Education, elementary/secondary

Arizona 5379
California 548, 886, 994, 1205, 44262
District of Columbia 2012
Georgia 2267
Illinois 2573, 2593, 2977
Minnesota 1695, 18691
Missouri 8991
New Jersey 4561, 4573, 4581, 4598, 4604
New York 4608, 4870, 5152, 6771, 44861
Ohio 7889, 7993, 7994
Rhode Island 9054
Tennessee 9086
Texas 8992, 9154, 9368, 9496
Utah 7419, 21057

Education, higher

California 2204
Montana 21888
New Jersey 4558

Education, other

California 3909
New Jersey 4581
New York 4111, 4112, 4608

Environment

New York 6065
Oregon 33397

Health—general/rehabilitative

Illinois 38721
New York 44861

Pennsylvania 894

Health—specific diseases

California 1315, 44262
District of Columbia 47937
Georgia 44288, 44755, 44756
New Jersey 4791
New York 6853, 44861

Human services—multipurpose

District of Columbia 2012, 47937

International affairs/development

California 6883
Florida 6940
Georgia 6896
Illinois 2428, 6873
Indiana 3102
Kentucky 6810, 6884
Louisiana 6851
Massachusetts 54163
New York 6065, 6804, 6820, 6822
Pennsylvania 7034, 8481
Texas 6857
Wisconsin 7032

Philanthropy/voluntarism

California 697

Recreation/sports/athletics

Colorado 1630
District of Columbia 9426
Illinois 2747
New Jersey 2194
North Carolina 95
Ohio 7796, 8066
Oregon 33397
Pennsylvania 8680
Texas 9246

Religion

Illinois 59591

Science/technology

New Jersey 4583

Youth development

California 548
New York 5354

PROFESSORSHIPS

Animals/wildlife

District of Columbia 60593
Oklahoma 28035

Arts/culture

California 21592
District of Columbia 6169
Georgia 62983
Illinois 3761
Maryland 2084
Massachusetts 6145, 6364, 62980
Michigan 2239, 3794
New York 7146, 22537
North Carolina 27431
Ohio 7919
Pennsylvania 2161, 2208, 8637, 8864
Texas 9376, 9447
Washington 6184, 24687, 24688

Civil rights

Massachusetts 62991

117

FIGURE 41. Sample Page from a *Grant Guide*

Section 1—Grant Listings

ALABAMA

The Sonat Foundation Inc.
Limitations: Giving primarily in AL, CT, and TX. No grants to individuals (except for employee-related scholarships).

1. Samford University, Birmingham, AL. $30,325, 1991. For matching gift for capital campaign.

ARIZONA

Arizona Community Foundation
Limitations: Giving limited to AZ. No support for sectarian religious purposes. No grants to individuals, or for deficit financing, annual campaigns, land acquisition, endowment funds, travel to or support of conferences, consulting services, or capital grants; no loans.

2. Kivel Geriatric Center, Phoenix, AZ. $24,000, 1991. For matching grant.

CALIFORNIA

The Ahmanson Foundation
Limitations: Giving primarily in Southern CA, with emphasis on the Los Angeles area. No grants to individuals, or for continuing support, annual campaigns, deficit financing, professorships, internships, fellowships, film production, underwriting, exchange programs; no loans.

3. Glendale College Foundation, Glendale, CA. $15,000, 1992. Toward U.S. Department of Education endowment challenge grant.
4. University of Southern California, KUSC-FM, Los Angeles, CA. $40,000, 1992. Toward membership subscription renewal challenge grants.

Arnold and Mabel Beckman Foundation
Limitations: No grants to individuals; no loans.

5. California Institute of Technology, Pasadena, CA. $1,000,000, 1991. For matching trustee pledge.
6. California Institute of Technology, Pasadena, CA. $700,000, 1991. For balance of prior matching pledge.

California Community Foundation
Limitations: Giving limited to the greater Los Angeles County, CA, area. No support for sectarian purposes. No grants for building funds, annual campaigns, equipment, endowment funds, debt reduction, operating budgets, scholarships, fellowships, films, conferences, dinners, or special events; no loans.

7. Angels Flight, Los Angeles, CA. $12,000, 1992. For technical assistance as part of Los Angeles Community AIDS Partnership. For grant shared with Catholic Charities.
8. Blue Cross of California, Burbank, CA. $40,000, 1992. For Caring for Children Initiative, which will provide health insurance to low-income children.

9. L.C., Inc., Los Angeles, CA. $15,000, 1992. Toward documenting Liaison Citizen Youth Program, leadership training program geared to high school students from low-income neighborhoods.

Columbia Foundation
Limitations: Giving primarily in San Francisco Bay Area. No support for private foundations, institutions supported by federated campaigns or heavily subsidized by government funds, or projects in medicine or religion. No grants to individuals, or for scholarships, fellowships, or operating budgets of established agencies.

10. Institute for Alternative Agriculture, Greenbelt, MD. $10,000, 1992. Toward matching grant to expand program in public policy, research and public education on sustainable agriculture.

Compton Foundation, Inc.
Limitations: No grants to individuals, or for capital or building funds; no loans.

11. Montalvo Association, Saratoga, CA. $10,000, 1991. For matching grant for earthquake repair of Artist-in-Residence cottages.
12. San Francisco State University Foundation, Romberg Tiburon Center for Environmental Study, San Francisco, CA. $10,000, 1991. For general support.

The Walt Disney Company Foundation
Limitations: Giving primarily in areas where the company's businesses are located, including central FL, and Los Angeles and Orange County, CA. No grants to individuals (except for scholarships to children of company employees), or for endowment funds.

13. California Institute of the Arts, Valencia, CA. $150,000, 1991. To match ticket sales from benefit premier of The Rescuers Down Under.

Joseph Drown Foundation
Limitations: Giving primarily in CA. No support for religious purposes. No grants to individuals, or for endowments, building funds, or seminars or conferences.

14. Arthritis Foundation, Southern California Chapter, Los Angeles, CA. $50,000, 1992. For matching funds for general support.

The Fieldstone Foundation
Limitations: Giving limited to Southern CA. No grants to individuals.

15. Boys and Girls Club of Cypress, Cypress, CA. $15,000, 1991. For matching grant for general operating budget.
16. Living Well, Orange, CA. $10,000, 1991. For matching gift.

Foundation for Deep Ecology
Limitations: Giving on an international basis, including Japan, southeast Asia, Europe, Australia, New Zealand, Malaysia, India,

GRANTS FOR MATCHING & CHALLENGE SUPPORT   1

HELPFUL HINT: While a history of grants actually awarded is generally considered to be a better indication of a foundation's willingness to provide a particular type of support than a mere statement to that effect, you shouldn't take such indications too literally. In other words, just because a prospective funder has failed to offer a particular type of support in the past does not mean it will continue to do so in the future. Funders that specifically restrict the types of support they provide (e.g., "no grants for endowment"), on the other hand, should probably be taken at their word and eliminated from your prospect list.

After checking the relevant *Grant Guide* volumes, your next stop should be the *National Directory of Corporate Giving*, which provides descriptions of more than 2,300 corporate foundations and direct-giving programs. The Types of Support Index is arranged first by support type, then in alphabetical order by company name (see Figure 43).

The steps outlined above will enable you to identify major foundations and corporate giving programs that favor the type of support you are seeking. Of course, you'll want to do as much research on other aspects of these grantmakers as your time and resources permit. Refer to *The Foundation Directory*, *The Foundation 1000*, 990-PF information returns, annual reports, and other sources described in Chapter 5 for details on each prospective funder you identify by the types of support approach.

SPECIALIZED FUNDING GUIDES

Finally, there are a number of specialized guides and handbooks that discuss fundraising techniques geared to a specific type of support. Refer to the bibliography in Appendix A for a select listing of some of these, and be sure to check with your local librarian for the titles of new publications that have been developed specifically for your geographic area. Of particular interest to the grantseeker adopting a types of support approach might be books on conducting capital campaigns as well as those dealing with "bricks and mortar" and equipment grants.

Step Two: Refining Your List

As we noted in the previous chapter, you now need to analyze your prospect list to eliminate foundations whose preferred subject or geographic focus or typical grant award prevents them from supporting your organization and its needs.

FIGURE 42.   Index of Types of Support in *The Foundation 1000*

INDEX OF TYPES OF SUPPORT

Minnesota: **McKnight 600**
New York: **Echoing 270, Ford 312, Open 695, Pollock-Krasner 736, Rockefeller 783, Soros 859**
North Carolina: Duke 256

In-kind gifts
Alabama: Sonat 858
California: Gap 333
Florida: Beveridge 75, Ryder 801
Massachusetts: Reebok 755
Michigan: Gerber 349
Minnesota: Minnesota 631
Missouri: Hallmark 392, Monsanto 636
New York: Morgan 641
Ohio: Centerior 154, Eaton 267, GenCorp 341
Pennsylvania: Miles 624, Westinghouse 969
Texas: Compaq 187
Virginia: Norfolk 677
Washington: Seafirst 829

Internships
California: Haynes 404, **Packard 703,** Parsons 709
Connecticut: Connecticut 190, **Richardson 772,** Stanley 866, **Xerox 997**
District of Columbia: **German 351**
Florida: Dade 213, **Davis 224,** Jacksonville 460
Illinois: Fry 329, Harris 398, Quaker 751
Indiana: Ball 48
Iowa: McElroy 588
Kansas: **Koch 509**
Maryland: Procter 747
Massachusetts: Alden 10, Boston 92, Reebok 755, Stoddard 879
Minnesota: Bremer 99, Minnesota 631
Missouri: Hallmark 392
New Jersey: Buehler 111, Schering-Plough 818
New York: Buffalo 113, **IBM 448, JM 467, Kress 517,** Lang 521, **Luce 548, Mellon 609,** Moore 639, New York 669, New-Land 670, Pfizer 722, **Pforzheimer 723,** Revson 764, **Rockefeller 782,** Rubinstein 795, **Soros 859, Wallace 950**
North Carolina: Duke 256, **Morehead 640**
Ohio: Gund 384
Oklahoma: Phillips 728
Pennsylvania: Fels 295, Heinz 413, **Pew 720**
Texas: Cain 126, Meadows 605

Land acquisition
Alabama: Meyer 621, Sonat 858
Arizona: Morris 644
California: Ahmanson 5, Cowell 199, First 301, Haas 386, Hedco 412, Hewlett 428, Irwin 456, Marin 564, **Packard 703,** Santa Barbara 810, Stern 875
Colorado: Boettcher 85, **Buell 112,** El Pomar 277, Gates 337, Johnson 471
Connecticut: Hartford 400
Delaware: Crystal 207, Laffey-McHugh 519, Longwood 542
Florida: Beveridge 75, Bush 122, **Chatlos 160,** Dade 213, **Davis 224,** Selby 833
Georgia: Atlanta 39, Callaway 130, Campbell 132, Evans 288, Whitehead 977, Wilson 985, Woodruff 992
Hawaii: Castle 152
Illinois: Chicago 162, Dillon 239, Nalco 655, Quaker 751
Indiana: Foellinger 308, **Lilly 533**
Kentucky: Brown 106
Maryland: Abell 1, Procter 747
Massachusetts: Alden 10, Davis 221, Riley 774, State 869, Stoddard 879
Michigan: Dalton 214, General 344, Gerstacker 352, Gilmore 358, Grand Rapids 375, **Kresge 516**
Minnesota: Bigelow 77
Missouri: Union 928
Nebraska: Kiewit 500
New Jersey: Hyde 447, Turrell 925, Victoria 944
New York: Bodman 84, Buffalo 113, Cary 148, Hayden 403, Heckscher 411, Jackson 459, Kaplan 489, Lang 521, McCann 580, Moore 639, **Weeden 962**

Ohio: Gund 384, Procter 746, Schmidlapp 822, Stranahan 882, Timken 913
Oklahoma: McMahon 602, Phillips 728
Oregon: Oregon 696
Pennsylvania: Grundy 381, Hillman 430, J.D.B. 458, Mellon 610, Penn 715, Pittsburgh 731, Smith 852, Trexler 923
Rhode Island: Champlin 155
Tennessee: Benwood 69, HCA 407, Tonya 917
Texas: Amarillo 13, Carter 145, Communities 186, Constantin 193, Cullen 208, Fikes 298, Halsell 393, Hillcrest 429, Hoblitzelle 434, Houston 442, Johnson 472, Kimberly-Clark 501, McDermott 586, Meadows 605, Moody 638, Richardson 771, Rockwell 786, San Antonio 806
Virginia: **Freedom 323,** Norfolk 676
Washington: Weyerhaeuser 972

Lectureships
Alabama: Sonat 858
Connecticut: GTE 382
District of Columbia: **German 351**
Florida: Davis 224
Kansas: **Koch 509**
Minnesota: Phillips 726
Missouri: Kansas 488
New Jersey: KPMG 514
New York: **Alavi 8, Cummings 210,** Dow 251, Littauer 538, Olin 693, Tinker 915
North Carolina: **Burroughs 121**
Pennsylvania: Miles 624
Texas: McDermott 586, McGovern 589, McGovern 590, Meadows 605, Rockwell 786, San Antonio 806, Southwestern 861
Washington: Weyerhaeuser 972
Wisconsin: Helfaer 417

Loans
California: Gerbode 350, Marin 564, **Packard 703,** San Francisco 808, Santa Clara 811, Sierra 842
Connecticut: Connecticut 190, Hartford 400, New Haven 663
Florida: Bush 122, Jacksonville 460
Illinois: Chicago 162, Joyce 483
Maryland: MNC 632, Straus 884
Massachusetts: Polaroid 734
Michigan: Grand Rapids 375, **Mott 648**
Minnesota: Bremer 99, Minneapolis 630
New York: **American 14,** Gebbie 339, **Hartford 399,** New York 666
Ohio: Cincinnati 168, Nord 675

Matching funds
Alabama: Alabama 1, Sonat 858
Arkansas: Rockefeller 784, Wal-Mart 948
California: Ahmanson 5, **BankAmerica 52,** Berry 73, California 129, Clorox 177, **Compton 188, Confidence 189,** Cowell 199, Drown 255, First 301, Getty 354, Haas 386, Harden 395, Hedco 412, Hewlett 428, Hofmann 436, Hoover 441, **Kaiser 487,** Levi 529, **M.E.G. 552,** Marin 564, McKesson 599, Mericos 613, Norris 679, Pacific 701, **Packard 703,** Parsons 709, Powell 739, **Riordan 776,** San Diego 807, Santa Barbara 810, Santa Clara 811, **Seaver 831,** Sierra 842, Stauffer 870, Steele 872, Stern 875, Stulsaft 888, Transamerica 920, Valley 938, Valley 939, W.W.W. 945, Weingart 964, Whittier 981
Colorado: Boettcher 85, Denver 233, Gates 337, Johnson 471, US 934
Connecticut: **Bingham 80,** Connecticut 190, **Educational 274,** Hartford 400, New Haven 663, **Richardson 772,** Stanley 866
Delaware: Laffey-McHugh 519, **Raskob 753,** Welfare 966
District of Columbia: Cafritz 125, **Fannie 292,** Graham 372, **Loyola 546,** Meyer 620, **Public 750,** Stewart 878
Florida: Beveridge 75, Bush 122, **Chatlos 160,** Dade 213, **Davis 224,** duPont 260, **Prueauff 328,** Grace

370, Jacksonville 460, **Knight 508,** Lowe 544, **Markey 565,** Selby 833, Storer 880, Winn-Dixie 987
Georgia: Atlanta 39, Callaway 130, Campbell 132
Hawaii: Atherton 38, McInerny 595
Illinois: Chicago 162, Coleman 181, **Crowell 205,** Crown 206, Dillon 239, Fel-Pro/Mecklenburger 294, Fry 329, Joyce 483, **MacArthur 553,** McCormick 583, McGraw 591, Northern 680, Quaker 751, Retirement 762, Woods 993
Indiana: Ball 48, Cummins 212, Foellinger 308, Lilly 533, **Lilly 534,** Martin 568, **Moriah 643,** Ogle 690
Iowa: Cowles 200, McElroy 588
Kansas: **Koch 509,** Powell 738
Kentucky: Brown 106
Maryland: Abell 1, Goldseker 365, Procter 747, Ryan 800
Massachusetts: Alden 10, Balfour 47, Bank 51, Boston 91, Peabody 714, Polaroid 734, Reebok 755, State 869, Stoddard 879
Michigan: Dalton 214, Ford 315, Gerber 349, Gerstacker 352, **Gilmore 358,** Grand Rapids 375, Hudson-Webber 445, **Kresge 516, Manoogian 563, Mott 648, Mott 649,** Towsley 919, Whirlpool 973, Wilson 986
Minnesota: Bigelow 77, Blandin 81, Bremer 99, Bush 123, Dayton 225, General 343, Grand 374, McKnight 601, Medtronic 607, Minnesota 631, Saint 804
Missouri: Hallmark 392, Kansas 488, Union 928
Nebraska: Kiewit 500
New Hampshire: Lindsay 536
New Jersey: Dodge 242, Hyde 447, Johnson 468, **Johnson 473, KPMG 514,** Prudential 749, **Schumann 826, Simon 845,** Turrell 925, Union 927, Victoria 944, Warner-Lambert 955
New Mexico: Maddox 559
New York: Astor 36, **AT&T 37, Baker 46,** Bodman 84, Booth 88, **Brencanda 100,** Buffalo 113, Cary 148, Claiborne 170, Cummings 211, **Donner 248,** Emerson 281, **Ford 312,** Gebbie 339, Goldsmith 366, Hayden 403, Icahn 449, International 454, Jackson 459, **JM 467, Johnson 470, Joukowsky 482,** Jurzykowski 485, Kimmelman 502, Littauer 538, **Mellon 609,** Moore 639, Morgan 641, New York 667, **New-Land 670,** Noble 673, Pfizer 722, **Pforzheimer 723,** Prospect 748, **Rockefeller 782,** Scherman 819, Sister 846, Sprague 864, **Teagle 900, Tinker 915,** '21' 926, **United States 931,** van Ameringen 940, **Warhol 954**
North Carolina: **Babcock 43,** Cannon 135, Duke 256, Duke 257, Foundation 319, **Kenan 495,** Reynolds 765, Reynolds 768, Winston-Salem 989
Ohio: **Bingham 79,** Borden 89, Bridgestone/Firestone 101, Bruening 107, Centerior 154, Cincinnati 168, Cleveland 176, 1525 297, GAR 334, Gund 384, Jennings 463, Mead 604, Murphy 652, Nationwide 658, Nord 675, Reinberger 759, Second 832, TRW 924
Oklahoma: Bemsen 72, McMahon 602, **Noble 674,** Phillips 728, Williams 984
Oregon: Collins 182, First 302, Meyer 622, Oregon 696
Pennsylvania: Alcoa 9, Barra 54, Benedum 68, CIGNA 167, Consolidated 192, Elf 278, Fels 295, Heinz 414, Hillman 430, J.D.B. 458, Mellon 610, **Oberkotter 688,** Penn 715, **Pew 720,** Philadelphia 724, Pittsburgh 731, **Scaife 816,** Smith 852, Trexler 923, Union 929, USX 937, Westinghouse 969
Rhode Island: Fleet/Norstar 305, **Ford 313, Genesis 346,** Textron 907
South Carolina: Fullerton 331, Springs 865
Tennessee: Benwood 69, HCA 407, Lyndhurst 549, Maclellan 556, Maclellan 557, Plough 732
Texas: Abell-Hanger 2, Amarillo 13, Anderson 21, Brown 105, Cain 126, Carter 145, Cockrell 179, Communities 186, Constantin 193, Cooper 195, Cullen 208, Dunn 259, Enron 285, Fair 290, Fikes 298, George 347, Hillcrest 429, Hoblitzelle 434, Johnson 472, **Kleberg 506,** LTV 547, McGovern 589, McGovern 590, Meadows 605, Moody 638, Richardson 771, San Antonio 806, Southwestern 861, Strake 881, Sturgis 889, Temple 903, Wortham 995
Utah: Eccles 268, Eccles 269
Virginia: **Freedom 323,** Jones 480

FIGURE 43. Types of Support Index in the *National Directory of Corporate Giving*

Principal 1516, Procter 1518, Public 1529, Public 1532, Quaker 1538, Questar 1540, Reebok 1562, Republic 1572, Rhode 1580, Rich 1582, Rochester 1595, Royal 1612, Ryder 1618, Schering-Plough 1632, Schwab 1638, Scrivner 1644, Seafirst 1646, Sears, Roebuck 1652, Security 1653, Shaklee 1666, Signet 1683, Simpson 1686, SNET 1703, Sonat 1712, Springs 1729, Sprint 1730, Sterling 1760, Tandem 1794, Tenneco 1809, Texas 1815, Texas 1817, 3M 1830, Time 1832, Time 1833, Toro 1842, Toyota 1846, Tracor 1847, Transco 1852, TRW 1864, U.S. Bank 1871, Unilever 1879, Union 1882, Union 1883, Union 1886, United Gas 1892, United Illuminating 1893, United Technologies 1899, Unitrode 1903, UNUM 1911, Upjohn 1913, UST 1920, Valspar 1928, Virginia 1939, Washington 1963, Washington 1965, Washington 1967, Waste 1969, Westinghouse 1985, Wiley 2001, Williams 2002, York 2040

Internships

Affiliated 18, Alcan 28, American Honda 64, Ameritech 79, ARCO 105, Blair 229, Bristol-Myers 265, Capital 305, Cargill 308, Carus 317, Coca-Cola 396, Colonial 407, Connecticut 431, Degussa 510, Dow 554, Ensign-Bickford 605, Equifax 608, Exxon 620, Genesco 767, Gibraltar 777, Hallmark 835, Heinz 873, IBM 921, James 974, Kemper 1018, Kennecott 1020, Kohler 1046, Minnegasco 1234, New York 1339, Northwestern 1364, Olin 1395, Omaha 1397, Pfizer 1463, Phillips 1470, Procter 1519, Quaker 1538, Reebok 1562, Rochester 1597, Royal 1612, Schering-Plough 1632, Sears, Roebuck 1652, Sony 1714, Stanley 1744, Sterling 1760, Tenneco 1809, 3M 1830, United Parcel 1896, Universal Leaf 1908, Washington 1967, Xerox 2035

Land acquisition

American Saw 72, ARCO 104, Badger 134, Banta 162, Block 231, Brooks 269, Brown 276, Citizens 376, Colonial 407, Commerce 417, Copley 453, Crestar 477, Cyclops 487, Dana 493, DeKalb 512, Ensign-Bickford 605, Equifax 608, Exchange 617, First Hawaiian 660, First Interstate 664, First Mississippi 672, General Motors 760, Hospital 903, ITT 964, Jeld-Wen 983, Kimberly-Clark 1034, Lilly 1098, Mascoma 1154, Morgan 1266, Nalco 1292, Olin 1395, Phillips 1470, Pittsburgh 1484, Procter 1518, Procter 1519, Quaker 1538, Simpson 1686, Sonat 1712, Sony 1714, Sovereign 1724, St. Paul 1734, Star 1745, State Street 1754, Ukrop's 1876, Union 1883, Vogt 1941, Weyerhaeuser 1989

Lectureships

Agway 19, Alcon 32, Ameritech 79, AUL 129, Burroughs 294, Carus 317, Dow 554, GTE 827, Integon 945, Jaydor 980, KPMG 1049, Lefton 1082, Little 1103, Miles 1225, National Computer 1301, Red 1560, Sonat 1712, Southwestern 1723, Weyerhaeuser 1989, Wiley 2001

Loaned talent

Air 21, ARCO 104, AUL 129, Binney 222, Boeing 241, Boston 250, Burlington 287, Cabot 298, Capital 305, Cargill 308, Carolina 312, Central Fidelity 333, Central Maine 334, Coast 395, Colonial 407, Comdisco 415, Commercial 432, CPI 466, EDS 585, Federal 635, Freeport-McMoRan 728, Georgia 770, Graco 799, Gulf 831, Hallmark 835, Household 904, Hyster 920, IBM 921, IDS 926, Kohler 1046, Mack 1124, Mallinckrodt 1130, McDonnell 1178, Mellon 1192, Metropolitan 1211, Midlantic 1220, Minnegasco 1234, Minnesota 1235, Morgan 1265, Morrison 1271, Murphy 1285, Nalco 1292, National City 1300, National Life 1307, Nationwide 1319, NBD 1321, NCR

1322, Nordson 1347, Northeast 1355, Northern 1361, Northwestern 1364, Oklahoma 1389, Oryx 1408, Pacific Gas 1426, Patagonia 1440, People's 1453, Phoenix 1473, Prudential 1526, Public 1529, Public 1532, Quaker 1538, Questar 1540, Recognition 1556, Seafirst 1646, Searle 1651, Sears, Roebuck 1652, Signet 1683, Signet 1684, Society 1707, 3M 1830, U.S. Bank 1871, Union 1886, Unitrode 1903, Wisconsin 2016

Loans

Connecticut 431, Lincoln 1100, MNC 1247, National City 1300, Northern 1361, People's 1453, Playboy 1487, Plitt 1488, Polaroid 1490, Sumimoto 1773, Washington 1963

Matching funds

Air 21, Alabama 24, Alberto-Culver 27, Alco 30, ALCOA 31, Alliant 39, AMAX 44, American Express 58, American Greetings 63, American Honda 64, AMETEK 80, Andersons 91, Anheuser-Busch 92, ARCO 104, ARCO 105, Arizona 108, Armco 112, AT&T 124, Ball 142, Bank of Boston 152, Bank of Boston 153, BankAmerica 160, Banta 162, Barnett 170, Beech 189, Belk 194, Bell 196, BellSouth 200, Ben 205, Berwind 210, Best Products 212, Betz 214, BHP 216, Binney 222, Block 231, Blount 233, Boeing 241, Borden 246, Bowne 255, Bridgestone/Firestone 261, Brooks 269, Burlington 287, Burnett 290, Burroughs 294, Cabot 298, Capital 305, Carrier 314, Centerior 330, Central Maine 334, Champion 345, Chase 348, Chase 349, Chrysler 364, CIGNA 366, Cincinnati 367, Citizens 374, Citizens 375, Claiborne 382, Clorox 391, CNA 394, Coca-Cola 396, Colonial 409, Congoleum 430, Connecticut 431, Consolidated 433, Consumers 437, Cooper 448, CPI 466, Cray 473, Crestar 477, Cummins 484, CUNA 485, Dana 493, Dayton 501, DeKalb 512, Digital 532, Dow 553, Dravo 558, Duke 565, Elf 594, Engelhard 602, Enron 603, Fairchild 625, Federal 636, Federal-Mogul 638, Fel-Pro 639, Fieldstone 648, First Interstate 664, First Interstate 667, First Interstate 668, First Mississippi 672, First National 677, Fleet 696, Foley 707, Ford 713, FPL 722, Freeport-McMoRan 728, GATX 748, General Mills 759, General Tire 766, Gerber 772, Gibraltar 777, Giddings 778, Grace 798, Graco 799, Grand 801, Grandma 804, Great Western 813, Hallmark 835, Hancock 844, Harcourt 851, Harris 856, Hawaiian 867, Heileman 870, Henley 875, Hewston 879, Hitachi 885, Hoechst 887, Hoffmann-La 889, Hofmann 890, Home 893, Honeywell 899, Hospital 903, Household 904, Huffy 911, Hyster 920, ICI 923, Indiana 939, Interlake 949, International Paper 954, ITT 963, ITT 964, Jantzen 975, Jeld-Wen 983, Jersey 985, Johnson 989, Johnson 992, Kellwood 1015, Kemper 1018, Kennametal 1019, King 1035, Kingsbury 1036, Kohler 1046, KPMG 1049, Laclede 1058, Levi 1090, Lilly 1098, LTV 1117, Lubrizol 1118, Lukens 1120, Mallinckrodt 1130, Maritz 1143, Maxus 1163, Maytag 1165, McCormick 1170, McDonald's 1177, McKesson 1181, McKesson 1182, Mead 1186, Medtronic 1190, Mellon 1192, Meredith 1202, Minnesota 1236, Mississippi 1242, Monsanto 1255, Morgan 1265, Murphy 1285, Mutual 1287, Nabisco 1290, National Computer 1301, National Medical 1309, Nationwide 1319, New England 1331, New England 1332, New York 1338, Nordson 1347, Northern 1358, Northern 1361, Northwestern 1364, Norton 1366, Nutrasweet 1372, NYNEX 1375, Ohio 1385, Old Kent 1392, Olin 1395, Omaha 1397, Ontario 1400, Owens-Illinois 1422, Pacific Enterprises 1425, Pacific Gas 1426, Pacific Telesis 1428, Pfizer 1463, Philip 1469, Phillips 1470, Pittsburgh 1484, Polaroid 1490, Portland 1495, Procter 1519, Provident 1524, Prudential 1526, Public 1529,

Public 1530, Public 1532, Quaker 1537, Quaker 1538, Raymond 1549, Red 1560, Reebok 1562, Rexham 1576, RJR 1591, Royal 1612, Safeco 1620, Saint 1624, Schwab 1638, Sealed 1649, Shaklee 1666, SIFCO 1681, Skinner 1694, Society 1707, Sonat 1712, Southern 1718, Southwestern 1723, SPS 1731, St. Paul 1734, Stanley 1744, State Street 1754, Stein 1758, Sterling 1760, Subaru 1772, Sunbeam-Oster 1776, Syntex 1789, TECO 1800, Teleflex 1804, Teleklew 1805, Tenneco 1809, Texas 1816, Textron 1819, 3M 1830, Time 1832, Times 1834, Toro 1842, Transamerica 1851, TRW 1864, '21' 1867, U.S. Bancorp 1870, U.S. Bank 1871, U.S. Trust 1874, UJB 1875, Union 1881, Union 1883, Union 1885, United Parcel 1896, United States Leasing 1897, United Technologies 1899, UNUM 1911, Upjohn 1913, US West 1914, USG 1917, USX 1921, Varian 1929, Wal-Mart 1952, Warner-Lambert 1960, Washington 1963, Washington 1965, Waste 1969, Wauwatosa 1972, West Company 1978, Westinghouse 1985, Whirlpool 1993, Williams 2002, Winn-Dixie 2010, Wolverine 2021

Operating budgets

Abbott 1, Affiliated 18, Air 21, Airborne 22, Alabama 24, ALCOA 31, Alexander 34, AlliedSignal 40, American Cyanamid 55, American Electric 57, American Fidelity 60, American Financial 61, American General 62, American Greetings 63, American Honda 64, American National 66, American Natural 67, American Saw 72, Ameritech 79, Amoco 82, AMP 83, Amsted 86, Analog 89, Apache 96, Appleton 100, ARCO 104, Aristech 107, Arizona 108, Arvin 117, Asea 119, Associates 123, AT&T 124, AUL 129, Avon 131, Badger 134, Ballet 143, Banc One 146, Bank IV 148, Bank of America 151, Bank of Boston 153, Bank of New York 155, Bankers 161, Banta 162, BayBanks 183, BDM 184, Belden 191, Belk 193, Bell 195, South Central 197, Bemis 204, Ben 205, BHP 215, Blair 229, Block 231, Boatmen's 238, Boise 244, Borden 246, Boston 249, Bowne 255, BP America 256, Briggs 262, Brown 273, Brown 276, Brunswick 277, Bucyrus-Erie 279, Buffalo 282, Cabot 298, Carbon 306, Cargill 308, Carolina 312, Caterpillar 324, CBI 325, CBS 326, Centerior 330, Chase 349, Chatham 350, Chemical 352, Chesebrough-Pond's 354, Chicago 357, Chrysler 364, CIGNA 366, Cincinnati 367, Circuit 370, Citizens 375, Claiborne 382, CLARCOR 383, Clements 387, Clorox 391, Coca-Cola 396, Coleman 402, Colonial 407, Colorado 411, Coltec 412, Comdisco 415, Commerce 417, Commonwealth 421, ConAgra 426, Connecticut 431, Connecticut 432, Consolidated 433, Consolidated 434, Consumers 437, Continental 440, Contran 446, Cooper 448, County 459, CPC 465, CPI 466, Cranston 471, Cray 473, Cummins 484, CUNA 485, Curtice 486, Dain 491, Dana 493, Dayton 501, Dayton 502, Dayton 503, Deere 509, Delmarva 513, Deluxe 516, Deposit 519, Detroit 524, Disney 537, Donnelley 546, Dow 554, Dun 566, Duriron 568, Eastern 575, Eastman 577, Eaton 579, Eckerd 581, Ecolab 582, Elf 594, Enron 603, Exxon 620, Fairchild 625, Federal 635, Federal 636, Fel-Pro 639, Ferro 641, Fieldstone 648, First Bank 653, First Commercial 657, First Hawaiian 660, First Interstate 662, First Interstate 663, First Interstate 664, First Interstate 667, First Interstate 668, First Mississippi 672, First National 677, First Nationwide 681, First of America 683, First Tennessee 687, First Union 688, Fisher-Price 692, Fleming 697, Florida 698, Fluor 703, Freddie 724, Freeport-McMoRan 728, Fuller 733, Gannett 740, Gap 742, GATX 748, GenCorp 754, General Mills 759, General Motors 760, General Public 761, Genesee 768, Georgia 770, Gibbs 776, Giddings 778, Glaxo 782, Gleason 783, Goldome 790, Grace 798, Graco 799, Grand 801, Grandma 804, Great Lakes 811, Great Western 813, GTE 827, Gulf 831, Halliburton 834, Hallmark 835, Hamrick

If you have followed through on each of the three research approaches we've described, you should now have a reasonable number of foundations on your list that are likely to consider your proposal favorably. In the next chapter we'll look at corporate grantmaking, and then we'll conclude with a discussion of the ins and outs of proposal writing.

Chapter 9

Corporate Grantmaking

A ccording to *Giving USA*, published by the AAFRC Trust for Philanthropy, U.S. business contributions to nonprofits came to $6 billion in 1992, or 4.8 percent of total charitable giving, roughly the same as in 1991. There are indications, however, that in the next few years corporate contributions may drop for the first time since 1970. The fact that 10 of the top 20 corporate givers showed declines in their 1992 giving is cause for concern. Likewise, the amount of money contributed by corporations to their foundations has been less than the grants paid out by those foundations for several years running. Preliminary estimates suggest that these trends will continue into the near future.[1]

On a more positive note, corporate dollar allocation in the four basic subject categories should remain at current levels. Education, with a focus on higher education, accounted for roughly 38 percent of corporate giving in 1992; health and human services received almost 28 percent; civic and community affairs received 14 percent; culture and arts contributions held steady at 12 percent; and a variety of other causes

---

1. American Association of Fund-Raising Counsel. *Giving USA*, Ann Kaplan, ed. New York: American Association of Fund-Raising Counsel (annual).

accounted for the remaining 8 percent. Clearly, corporate giving does not represent a limitless pool of funding, although it is a source nonprofits would be wise to consider.

There is no simple answer as to why corporations support nonprofit organizations and their causes. Many, if not most, contribute out of a combination of altruism and self-interest, and it is nearly impossible to determine where one leaves off and the other begins. The attitudes of top management more than any other factor seem to impact the giving philosophies of corporations. CEOs often play a primary role in company giving, with contributions officers usually reporting directly to the CEO. Grantseekers should remember that corporations, unlike foundations and other charitable agencies, do not exist to give money away. Their allegiance, instead, is to their employees, customers, shareholders, and—most of all—to the bottom line. It is fair to assume, therefore, that corporate givers will seek some benefit from their charitable activities.

Corporations give, among other reasons, to guarantee a supply of well-trained potential employees or to attract new ones, to build community relations, to enhance their image in the eyes of customers and shareholders, to return favors, and/or to obtain tax deductions. They may also give for the more general goal of improving the quality of life in the geographic locales in which they operate. Cleaner, safer, better-educated communities are good for business; the people who live in such communities make better customers and more productive, satisfied employees.

At the same time, many corporations are wary of having their charitable activities publicized. They fear being inundated with requests they cannot fill or shareholder ire aroused by the giving away of "their" profits; others want to stay clear of any controversy that might result in their losing the patronage and/or support of the public. As a result, it is often quite difficult to track down information on corporate giving, especially on non-foundation support. In fact, when approaching corporations, the lack of information may be the biggest obstacle the grantseeker faces.

Corporate Direct Giving and Company-Sponsored Foundations

Corporations provide support to nonprofits through direct-giving programs, private foundations, or both. Company-sponsored foundations often maintain close ties with the parent company, and their giving usually reflects company interests. They generally maintain small endowments and rely on regular contributions ("gifts received") from the parent company to support their giving programs. In addition, their managers try to accumulate funds in fat years that can be tapped in leaner years. Company-sponsored foundations must follow the appropriate regulations, including filing a yearly Form 990-PF with the IRS.

In contrast, corporate direct giving—all non-foundation giving—is less regulated. Corporations are not required to publicize direct-giving programs or to sustain prescribed levels of funding. For federal tax purposes they can deduct up to 10 percent of their pretax income for charitable contributions. They can also make other kinds of contributions, sometimes treated as business expenses, which are not necessarily included in giving statistics.

The Conference Board estimates that donations or loans of noncash resources constitute 20 percent of corporate giving. Often omitted from corporate contribution statistics, noncash resources are sometimes overlooked by organizations seeking corporate support. Similarly, nonmonetary support costs are frequently considered operating expenditures rather than charitable contributions. And direct-giving programs and company-sponsored foundations may share the same staff, adding to the confusion.

Noncash Support

The managers of corporate giving programs are becoming more interested in offering nonmonetary, or "in-kind," support along with, or in lieu of, cash grants. Such support includes products, supplies, and equipment; facilities and support services (e.g., meeting space, mailing, computer services); and public relations (e.g., printing and duplicating, graphic arts, advertising). Corporations also provide employee expertise in areas such as legal assistance and tax advice, market research, and strategic planning. In addition, many companies encourage and reward employee voluntarism, and some even permit their employees to take time off with pay to perform volunteer work. Corporations tend to support organizations where their employees are involved as volunteers, and some companies donate funds to these organizations exclusively. Newer forms of corporate activity, including event sponsorship, cause-related marketing, and social investing—none of which can be considered pure "giving"—also have been on the rise in recent years.

How to Find Corporate Funders

Although there are always exceptions, corporate giving tends to be concentrated in fields related to corporate interests or in communities where the company operates.

Therefore, your search for corporate funders should focus on local businesses as well as multinational corporations.

The *National Directory of Corporate Giving*, published by the Foundation Center, indexes companies by their officers, donors, and trustees; location; type of business; subject areas of giving; and types of support provided. The 3rd edition (1993) profiles 2,050 companies making contributions to nonprofits through 1,739 foundations and 621 direct-giving programs. Entries include plant and subsidiary locations, *Forbes* or *Fortune* rankings, descriptions of business activities, financial data, contact persons, giving interests, application guidelines, and types of support awarded. A new feature of the 3rd edition is a listing of the top ten grants made by corporate foundations with assets of more than $2 million and annual giving in excess of $50,000. (See Figure 44 for a sample entry.) The directory was compiled from a variety of sources, including information supplied directly by companies in annual reports, corporate giving reports, newsletters, brochures, and flyers, as well as the 990-PF forms filed by company foundations. All entries are sent to the corporations for verification, and the information becomes part of the Center's database, where it is continually updated.

Company-sponsored foundation information returns (990-PF forms) are available at Foundation Center libraries and Cooperating Collections (see Appendix D for a complete listing of the latter), through IRS district offices (see pages 77–78), at the foundation's own office, or through the attorney general and/or charities registration office in the state in which the foundation is chartered (see Appendix B).

You should also consult your local public library for regional and local business indexes. The Chamber of Commerce or Better Business Bureau in your community may also have such indexes. Last but not least, the local business community is accessible through the business Yellow Pages and your own staff's knowledge of the community. In corporate grantseeking, personal contacts are especially valuable. Staff, board members, and volunteers who have contacts at, or know of, potential corporate funders should be encouraged to investigate the giving policies at these companies.

The Subject, Geographic, and Types of Support Approaches

When looking for corporate funders, the strategic approaches described in Chapters 6, 7, and 8 (e.g., subject, geographic, and types of support) may be adopted sequentially or simultaneously.

FIGURE 44. Sample Entry from the *National Directory of Corporate Giving*

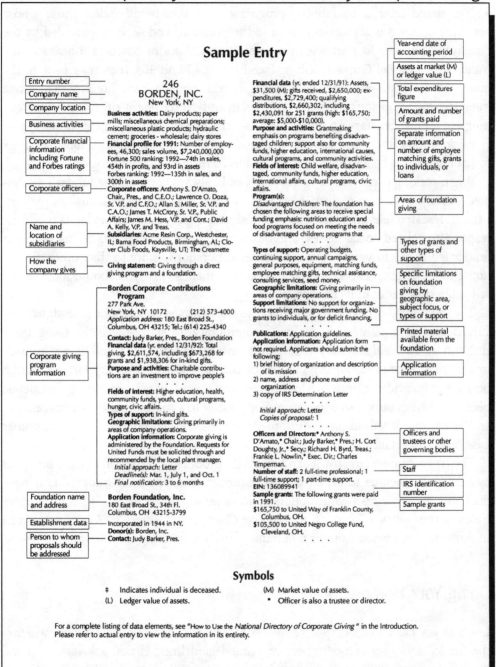

Sample Entry

Entry number

Company name

Company location

Business activities

Corporate financial information including Fortune and Forbes ratings

Corporate officers

Name and location of subsidiaries

How the company gives

Corporate giving program information

Foundation name and address

Establishment data

Person to whom proposals should be addressed

246
BORDEN, INC.
New York, NY

Business activities: Dairy products; paper mills; miscellaneous chemical preparations; miscellaneous plastic products; hydraulic cement; groceries - wholesale; dairy stores

Financial profile for 1991: Number of employees, 46,300; sales volume, $7,240,000,000 Fortune 500 ranking: 1992—74th in sales, 454th in profits, and 93rd in assets Forbes ranking: 1992—135th in sales, and 300th in assets

Corporate officers: Anthony S. D'Amato, Chair., Pres., and C.E.O.; Lawrence O. Doza, Sr. V.P. and C.F.O.; Allan S. Miller, Sr. V.P. and C.A.O.; James T. McCrory, Sr. V.P., Public Affairs; James M. Hess, V.P. and Cont.; David A. Kelly, V.P. and Treas.

Subsidiaries: Acme Resin Corp., Westchester, IL; Bama Food Products, Birmingham, AL; Clover Club Foods, Kaysville, UT; The Creamette

Giving statement: Giving through a direct giving program and a foundation.

Borden Corporate Contributions Program
277 Park Ave.
New York, NY 10172   (212) 573-4000
Application address: 180 East Broad St., Columbus, OH 43215; Tel.: (614) 225-4340

Contact: Judy Barker, Pres., Borden Foundation
Financial data (yr. ended 12/31/92): Total giving, $2,611,574, including $673,268 for grants and $1,938,306 for in-kind gifts.
Purpose and activities: Charitable contributions are an investment to improve people's
. . . .
Fields of interest: Higher education, health, community funds, youth, cultural programs, hunger, civic affairs.
Types of support: In-kind gifts.
Geographic limitations: Giving primarily in areas of company operations.
Application information: Corporate giving is administered by the Foundation. Requests for United Funds must be solicited through and recommended by the local plant manager.
Initial approach: Letter
Deadline(s): Mar. 1, July 1, and Oct. 1
Final notification: 3 to 6 months

Borden Foundation, Inc.
180 East Broad St., 34th Fl.
Columbus, OH 43215-3799

Incorporated in 1944 in NY.
Donor(s): Borden, Inc.
Contact: Judy Barker, Pres.

Financial data (yr. ended 12/31/91): Assets, $31,500 (M); gifts received, $2,650,000; expenditures, $2,729,400; qualifying distributions, $2,660,302, including $2,430,091 for 251 grants (high: $165,750; average: $5,000-$10,000).
Purpose and activities: Grantmaking emphasis on programs benefiting disadvantaged children; support also for community funds, higher education, international causes, cultural programs, and community activities.
Fields of interest: Child welfare, disadvantaged, community funds, higher education, international affairs, cultural programs, civic affairs.
Program(s):
Disadvantaged Children: The foundation has chosen the following areas to receive special funding emphasis: nutrition education and food programs focused on meeting the needs of disadvantaged children; programs that

Types of support: Operating budgets, continuing support, annual campaigns, general purposes, equipment, matching funds, employee matching gifts, technical assistance, consulting services, seed money.
Geographic limitations: Giving primarily in areas of company operations.
Support limitations: No support for organizations receiving major government funding. No grants to individuals, or for deficit financing.

Publications: Application guidelines.
Application information: Application form not required. Applicants should submit the following:
1) brief history of organization and description of its mission
2) name, address and phone number of organization
3) copy of IRS Determination Letter
. . . .
Initial approach: Letter
Copies of proposal: 1
. . . .
Officers and Directors:* Anthony S. D'Amato,* Chair.; Judy Barker,* Pres.; H. Cort Doughty, Jr.,* Secy.; Richard H. Byrd, Treas.; Frankie L. Nowlin,* Exec. Dir.; Charles Timperman.
Number of staff: 2 full-time professional; 1 full-time support; 1 part-time support.
EIN: 136089941
Sample grants: The following grants were paid in 1991.
$165,750 to United Way of Franklin County, Columbus, OH.
$105,500 to United Negro College Fund, Cleveland, OH.
. . . .

Year-end date of accounting period

Assets at market (M) or ledger value (L)

Total expenditures figure

Amount and number of grants paid

Separate information on amount and number of employee matching gifts, grants to individuals, or loans

Areas of foundation giving

Types of grants and other types of support

Specific limitations on foundation giving by geographic area, subject focus, or types of support

Printed material available from the foundation

Application information

Officers and trustees or other governing bodies

Staff

IRS identification number

Sample grants

Symbols

‡ Indicates individual is deceased.
(L) Ledger value of assets.

(M) Market value of assets.
* Officer is also a trustee or director.

For a complete listing of data elements, see "How to Use the *National Directory of Corporate Giving* " in the Introduction. Please refer to actual entry to view the information in its entirety.

The *subject approach* leads grantseekers to national and multinational corporations with a stated interest in funding programs in certain fields and/or those whose principal business is somehow related to the programs and services provided by the nonprofit. You should start with the Subject and Types of Business indexes in the *National Directory of Corporate Giving* (see Figures 45 and 46), then refer back to the main entries in the alphabetically arranged text. Some shared nonprofit/corporate interests will be obvious. A sporting goods manufacturer might subsidize an athletic program for disadvantaged youth; a manufacturer of musical instruments may support a music appreciation program; a pharmaceutical company or alcoholic beverage distributor would be a likely candidate to fund a drug-education program.

When seeking corporate support, you should always consider the funder's *motivation*. Usually, a corporate giver is seeking to develop a pool of potential employees, support research relevant to its principle business, improve the market for its products, respond to related social issues, and/or increase sales. Establishing a link with the funder is the key to your success. Because corporations, more so than other institutional funders, often expect a quid pro quo for their giving, you should focus on its self-interest rather than its benevolence.

The *geographic approach* requires you to concentrate on corporate headquarters, subsidiaries, and plants in your home community. To start, check the Geographic Index in the *National Directory of Corporate Giving* (see Figure 47), and then refer back to the main entries. Company executives can be convinced to support a program because it provides direct service to employees and other community residents, because it brings public recognition and/or prestige to a company and its management, and/or because it will improve customer relations and help build a future customer base in an important market.

The *types of support approach* can be equally productive. Types of support provided by companies include funds for capital improvements, operating budgets, employee matching gifts, noncash contributions, and other aid. Refer to the Types of Support Index in the *National Directory of Corporate Giving* (see Figure 43). Again, some connections will be obvious; others will require creative thinking on your part.

Doing Your Homework

Learn all you can about a corporate giver before submitting a request. Find out whether the funder issues an annual report or printed guidelines. If not, ask for an annual business report. While annual reports usually do not contain actual information on

FIGURE 45. Subject Index in the *National Directory of Corporate Giving*

Literacy—SUBJECT INDEX

446, Coors 452, Copley 453, Cowles 462, CPC 465, CPI 466, Dayton 503, Delmarva 513, Digital 532, Dollar 540, Donnelley 546, Dow 553, East 574, Fifth Third 649, First Fidelity 658, First Interstate 662, First Nationwide 681, Gannett 740, GenCorp 754, Genesco 767, Graco 799, Grede 815, Greene 818, GTE 827, Heublein 880, Honeywell 899, Household 904, ICI 923, Indiana 939, International Multifoods 953, Jostens 997, Kaman 1005, Knight-Ridder 1043, Kohler 1046, Lamco 1063, Landmark 1068, Lockheed 1106, Lubrizol 1118, Mack 1124, Mallinckrodt 1130, McDonald's 1177, McGraw-Hill 1179, McKesson 1182, Mead 1186, Mellon 1192, MidCon 1218, Mutual 1287, Nabisco 1290, NCR 1322, NEC 1323, Nestle 1328, New York 1335, Nordson 1347, Northern 1361, Northwestern 1364, Oceanic 1379, Ohio 1383, Oxford 1423, Penn 1447, Pfizer 1463, PHH 1465, Philip 1469, Portland 1495, Provident 1523, Public 1532, Reader's 1553, Rockefeller 1599, Salomon 1625, SBE&S 1631, Scott 1641, Scripps 1643, Scrivner 1644, Seafirst 1646, Sears, Roebuck 1652, Shawmut 1670, Signet 1683, Southern 1718, Stanley 1744, Subaru 1772, Tenneco 1809, Texas 1817, Third National 1822, Time 1833, Times 1834, Tracor 1847, Transco 1852, Union 1883, Vogt 1941, Volvo 1944, Wal-Mart 1952, Walgreen 1953, Washington 1965, West One 1979, Westinghouse 1985, Whirlpool 1993, Wiley 2001, Woodward 2022

Marine sciences

Leigh 1085, Little 1103, UST 1920

Mathematics

Alliant 39, AT&T 124, Bechtel 188, Cabot 298, Carus 317, Coca-Cola 396, Cray 473, Exxon 621, General Electric 757, General Motors 760, Glaxo 782, GTE 827, Hoffmann-La 889, Hypertronics 919, Little 1103, McDonald's 1177, McDonnell 1178, Minnesota 1236, Motorola 1277, NEC 1324, Nordson 1347, NYNEX 1375, Pacific Telesis 1428, Raytheon 1550, Storage 1766, Texas 1817, Toshiba 1844, TRW 1864, United Technologies 1899, Whirlpool 1993

Media and communications

Affiliated 18, Amdur 48, American Dredging 56, Ameritech 79, Appleton 100, Arkla 110, Atlanta 125, BASF 176, Buchalter 278, Burlington 287, Cablevision 297, Campbell 301, Capital 304, Chicago 360, Cincinnati 367, Coghlin 397, Cooper 448, Cowles 462, CPC 465, Dow 554, Elf 594, Federal 636, Fibre 643, Fisher 691, Fleck 694, Gazette 750, Gibraltar 777, Gray 807, Homecrest 896, Index 937, Jantzen 975, Johnson 989, Journal 998, Knight-Ridder 1043, Kohler 1046, Landmark 1068, Marshall 1149, Menasha 1193, Mid America 1217, Montgomery 1260, National Broadcasting 1296, National City 1300, National Presto 1311, News 1343, Oceanic 1379, Oryx 1408, Page 1430, Panhandle 1434, Pioneer 1480, Scripps 1643, Security 1654, Sharon 1668, Sierra 1680, Stauffer 1756, Tennant 1808, Times 1834, Union 1881, Wachovia 1948, Washington 1965

Medical education

Abbott 1, AEGON 13, Alcon 32, Burroughs 294, Carter-Wallace 316, Consolidated 433, Consolidated 434, Enerpec 601, Gerber 772, Hoechst 887, Hook 900, International Flavors 951, Johnson 989, Marion 1141, Merck 1199, Metropolitan 1211, National Medical 1309, New York 1335, Northern 1359, Oshmans 1417,

Principal 1516, Pro 1517, Sandoz 1626, Schering-Plough 1632, Seagram 1647, SmithKline 1698, Standard Insurance 1738, Upjohn 1913, Warner-Lambert 1960, Witco 2018, Worthington 2029

Medical research

Abbott 1, AEGON 13, Alcon 32, Allegheny 37, Amcast 46, AMETEK 80, Amoco 82, Bard 166, BASF 176, Beneficial 206, Bernstein 208, Boh 242, Boiron-Borneman 243, Bristol-Myers 265, Budweiser 281, Burger 285, Burress 293, Burroughs 294, Campbell 301, Carillon 309, Carter-Wallace 316, CBI 325, Centel 329, Cohn 399, Cole 401, Commercial 420, Contico 438, D&K 489, Dart 497, Doyle 556, Dreyer's 561, Dynamet 571, Eaton 579, Emerson 597, Fairchild 625, FINA 650, First Financial 659, FMR 705, Ford 713, French 729, Gerber 772, Godfrey 786, Grandma 804, Groves 824, GSC 825, Guaranty 828, Harcourt 851, Heileman 870, Heinz 873, Hoffmann-La 889, Hofmann 890, Honda 898, Humana 912, IMT 933, International Flavors 951, Jacobson 971, Johnson 989, Kearney 1010, Kirkhill 1037, Klein 1040, Kowalski 1048, Kuhns 1051, Ladish 1059, Lafarge 1061, Lance 1066, Liberty 1097, Lincoln 1100, Long 1111, Marion 1141, Marshall 1149, Massachusetts 1155, McDonald's 1177, Mercedes-Benz 1196, Merck 1199, Mercury 1201, MISCO 1239, Mrs. Fields 1280, MSI 1281, Multimedia 1284, National City 1300, National Semiconductor 1312, Nelson 1327, O'Connor 1376, Ohio 1385, Ohio 1386, Ormet 1406, Pemco 1444, Pennzoil 1451, Plitt 1488, Porsche 1493, Principal 1516, Puget 1533, Pukall 1534, Reedman 1564, Rockford 1600, Safeco 1620, Sandoz 1626, Schering-Plough 1632, Scrivner 1644, Searle 1651, Seton 1664, SmithKline 1698, Spang 1726, Stroh 1769, Talley 1791, TECO 1800, 3M 1830, Trans 1850, '21' 1867, U.S. Bank 1871, Union Bank 1880, Universal Leaf 1908, Upjohn 1913, USAA 1915, Uslico 1919, Victory 1935, Warner-Lambert 1960, Waste 1969, Weight 1975

Medical sciences

Burroughs 294, Hoechst 887, Hofmann 890, Johnson 989, Louisiana-Pacific 1115, Merck 1199, Miles 1225, OMRON 1398, PepsiCo 1457, SmithKline 1698, Society 1706, Sterling 1760, Upjohn 1913, Varian 1929

Mental health

American Dredging 56, Arkla 110, Bakewell 138, Cabot 298, Colonial 407, Comdisco 415, Community 422, Consumers 437, CPC 465, CPI 466, Delmarva 513, GATX 748, Giant 775, Hallmark 835, Indiana 939, Inland 942, International Flavors 951, Iowa-Illinois 960, Kennecott 1020, Lockheed 1106, Long 1111, Nordson 1347, Northern 1358, Northern 1361, Orange 1401, Oryx 1408, Oscar 1411, Plitt 1488, Recognition 1556, Safeco 1620, 3M 1830, Transco 1852, Trust 1863, USX 1921, Volvo 1944, Walgreen 1953

Mexico

Fuller 733, Hallmark 835, Johnson 990, Levi 1090, Mattel 1159, Merck 1199, Syntex 1789, United Technologies 1899, Woolworth 2023

Middle East

American Express 58, Xerox 2035

Military personnel

Aerospace 15, BDM 184, Coors 452, USAA 1915, Wheelabrator 1991

Minorities

Aetna 16, Alberto-Culver 27, Alcan 28, Allegheny 37, Alliant 39, AlliedSignal 40, Alschuler 42, American Brands 53, American Express 58, American Stock 74, AMR 85, Anheuser-Busch 92, Archer 103, ASARCO 118, Asea 119, AT&T 124, Atlanta 125, Avon 131, Ball 142, Baltimore 145, Bank of America 151, BASF 176, BDM 184, BellSouth 200, Ben 205, Berwind 210, Block 231, BMC 236, Boeing 241, Bowne 255, Bristol-Myers 265, Budd 280, Burlington 287, Burnett 290, Butler 296, Campbell 301, Capital 304, Centel 329, Central Fidelity 333, Champion 345, Chicago 357, Chrysler 364, Clark 384, Coca-Cola 396, Colgate-Palmolive 403, Congoleum 430, Connecticut 431, Connecticut 432, Consolidated 435, Consumers 437, Contran 446, Cooper 448, Coors 452, CPC 465, CPI 466, Cummins 484, Delmarva 513, Dow 554, Dresser 559, Du Pont 562, East 574, Eastman 577, Eaton 579, Ecolab 582, EDS 585, Exxon 620, Exxon 621, Fairchild 625, Fel-Pro 639, Ferro 641, First National 677, Fisher 691, FMC 704, Ford 713, FPL 722, Freeport-McMoRan 728, GATX 748, General Public 761, Georgia 770, Grace 798, GTE 827, Hallmark 835, Hancock 844, Harcourt 851, Hershey 878, Hewlett-Packard 881, Hoechst 887, Hoffmann-La 889, Huntington 915, IBM 921, ICI 923, IDS 926, Indiana 939, Inland 942, Jersey 985, Johnson 989, Johnson 990, Jostens 997, K Mart 1001, Keebler 1012, Kellogg 1014, KFC 1027, Lockheed 1106, Lotus 1113, Maritz 1143, MCA 1167, McDonnell 1178, Medtronic 1190, Mercedes-Benz 1196, Merck 1199, Metropolitan 1211, MidCon 1218, Morgan 1265, Morgan 1267, Nabisco 1290, National City 1300, National Medical 1309, National Service 1313, Nationwide 1319, NCR 1322, Nissan 1345, Nordson 1347, Northwestern 1364, NYNEX 1375, Ohio 1387, Oryx 1408, Oscar 1411, Owens-Coming 1421, Owens-Illinois 1422, Pacific Gas 1426, Pacific Telesis 1428, Panhandle 1434, Penn 1447, Pfizer 1463, Pioneer 1479, Playboy 1487, Polaroid 1490, Portland 1495, Principal 1516, Procter 1518, Prudential 1526, Public 1532, Raytheon 1550, Reebok 1562, Republic 1572, Revlon 1575, Rochester 1597, Rockefeller 1599, Ryder 1618, Salomon 1625, Schering-Plough 1632, Sealed 1649, Sears, Roebuck 1652, Snap-on 1701, SNET 1703, Society 1706, Soft 1709, Sonat 1712, Southern 1718, Sprint 1730, Sumimoto 1773, Supermarkets 1782, Syntex 1789, TECO 1800, Texas 1817, Textron 1819, 3M 1830, Time 1833, TJX 1838, Transamerica 1851, U.S. Bancorp 1870, U.S. Bank 1871, Union Bank 1880, Union 1883, Union 1885, United Airlines 1887, United States Leasing 1897, Upjohn 1913, US West 1914, USF&G 1916, UST 1920, USX 1921, Virginia 1939, Volkswagen 1942, Wal-Mart 1952, Walgreen 1953, Wetterau 1988, Wolverine 2021, Woodward 2022

Museums

Aerospace 15, Affiliated 18, Allegheny 37, American Brands 53, American Express 58, American Paper 69, Amway 87, ARCO 104, AT&T 124, AXIA 132, Baltimore 145, Bank of New York 155, BayBanks 183, BDM 184, Bell 198, Best Products 212, Binswanger 224, Bionetics 225, Boston 249, Bridgestone/Firestone 261, Brown 273, Builder 283, Burns 292, Cantor 303, Carnation 311, CBS 326, Centerior 330, Cessna 343, Champion 345, Chase 349, Chicago 359, Chicago 360, CLARCOR 383, Cleveland-Cliffs

FIGURE 46. Types of Business Index in the *National Directory of Corporate Giving*

Time 1832, Travelers 1856, UJB 1875, Unigard 1878, United Wisconsin 1902, USAA 1915, Washington 1964

Insurance, fire, marine, and casualty, Aetna 16, Allendale 38, American Family 59, American General 62, American Re-Insurance 71, AON 95, Associates 123, Chubb 365, CIGNA 366, Clark 384, CNA 394, Colonial 409, Continental 442, Enron 603, Equitable 609, Farmers 630, Fireman's 651, Fortis 719, GEICO 753, General Accident 755, Grinnell 822, Halliburton 834, Hartford 859, IMT 933, Integon 945, ITT 963, Lebanon 1078, Meridian 1205, Montgomery 1259, MSI 1281, Mutual 1286, Mutual 1287, National Grange 1304, National Life 1307, Nationwide 1319, Northwestern 1365, NWNL 1374, Preferred 1505, Presidential 1511, Royal 1612, Safeco 1620, Safeco 1621, St. Paul 1734, State Farm 1751, Transamerica 1851, Travelers 1856, Unigard 1878, USF&G 1916, Utica 1922, Wausau 1970, Zurich 2048

Insurance, life, Aetna 16, American Brands 53, American Family 59, American Fidelity 60, American General 62, Ameritas 78, AON 95, AUL 129, Capital 305, CIGNA 366, CNA 394, Colonial 407, Colonial 409, Connecticut 431, CUNA 485, Equitable 609, Farmers 630, First Security 685, Fortis 719, Franklin 723, GEICO 753, General American 756, Geneve 769, Gerber 772, Hancock 844, Integon 945, Jefferson-Pilot 982, Kemper 1018, Liberty 1096, Lincoln 1100, Loews 1110, Massachusetts 1155, Metropolitan 1211, Minnesota 1235, Montgomery 1260, MSI 1281, National Life 1307, National Travelers 1316, New York 1335, Northwestern 1364, Northwestern 1365, NWNL 1374, Ohio 1386, Pacific Mutual 1427, Pemco 1444, Penn 1447, Phoenix 1473, Physicians 1475, Presidential 1511, Primerica 1514, Principal 1516, Provident 1523, Provident 1524, Prudential 1526, Safeco 1620, Security 1653, Sentry 1659, Shelter 1675, Standard Insurance 1738, State Mutual 1753, Teledyne 1803, Temple-Inland 1807, Time 1832, Transamerica 1851, Travelers 1856, USAA 1915, Usilco 1919, Utica 1922, Washington 1964, West One 1979, Western 1981

Insurance, miscellaneous, Berwind 210, Geneve 769, Leucadia 1089, MSI 1281, Sears, Roebuck 1652

Insurance, surety, Aexcel 17, Allendale 38, Beneficial 206, Fireman's 651, Mortgage 1272, National Grange 1304, Preferred 1505, Presidential 1511, Royal 1612, Safeco 1621, St. Paul 1734

Insurance, title, Lawyers 1075, Meridian 1205, Presidential 1511, Universal Leaf 1908

Investment offices, Discount 536, FMR 705, Jefferson-Pilot 982, Johnson 990, Jones 994, Paine 1431, U.S. Trust 1874

Investors, miscellaneous, Ben 205, Binswanger 223, Domino's 542, Dunkin' 567, Eastover 578, Equitable 609, Florida 700, Friedland 730, Huna 913, International Multifoods 953, Long 1111, Louisiana 1114, McDonald's 1177, Meredith 1202, Nutri/System 1373, Odyssey 1381, Pacific Mutual 1427, Pearle 1441, Playboy 1487, Sequent 1661, Sizzler 1691, Turner 1866, Weight 1975, Wheat 1990

Iron and steel foundries, Abex 3, Alhambra 35, Allegheny 37, Amcast 46, AMPCO-Pittsburgh 84, Amsted 86, Atlas 126, Betts 213, Brillion 263, Budd 280, Eastern 576, Fansteel 628, Farr 632, Great Lakes 812, Grede 815, Interlake 949, Marley 1145, McWane 1185, Monarch 1251, Morgan 1266, National Forge 1302, Neenah 1325, North American 1352, Oglebay 1382, Osco 1414, Pelton 1443, Sandusky 1627, Stockham 1761, Tyler 1868, Walter 1956, White 1995

Jewelry and notions, costume, Avon 131, Ball 141, Belding 192, Napier 1294, RB&W 1551, Reed 1563

Jewelry, precious metal, Jostens 997, Kilmartin 1031, Reed 1563

Laboratories, medical and dental, Corvallis 458, Hoffmann-La 889, Lancaster 1065, SmithKline 1698

Laboratory apparatus, Abbott 1, AMETEK 80, Analog 89, Badger 134, Ball 142, Barber-Colman 163,

Bausch 180, Betz 214, Boums 254, Brown 270, Chrysler 364, Digital 532, Dover 551, Dresser 559, EG&G 588, Federal-Mogul 638, FMC 704, General Electric 757, General Machine 758, General Signal 764, Gleason 784, Goulds 797, Henley 875, Hewlett-Packard 881, Hitachi 885, Honeywell 899, International Metals 952, Johnson 992, Kaman 1005, Kepco 1021, Leeds 1081, Litton 1104, Mark 1144, McDonnell 1178, Mentor 1194, Millipore 1231, Mine 1233, Monsanto 1255, Robertshaw 1593, Schlumberger 1634, SmithKline 1698, Square 1733, Tektronix 1802, Texas 1817, Thermo 1820, Tokheim 1840, Tracor 1847, Trinova 1859, Varian 1929, Venture 1931, Wallace 1954, Westinghouse 1985, Whirlpool 1993, Woodward 2022, Yarway 2038

Landscape and horticultural services, Davey 499, DWG 570, Ecolab 582, Rollins 1606, ServiceMaster 1663

Laundry, cleaning, and garment services, American Building 54, National Service 1313, ServiceMaster 1663, Steiner 1759

Leather footwear, Ballet 143, Brown 276, Dexter 528, Farley 629, Florsheim 702, Genesco 767, Hanson 849, Interco 948, Myers 1289, New Balance 1329, Phillips-Van Heusen 1472, Red 1560, Reebok 1562, Sara Lee 1628, Stride 1768, Wolverine 2021

Leather goods, miscellaneous, Brizel 266, Page 1430

Leather luggage, Jostens 997

Leather tanning and finishing, Akzo 23, Amdur 48, Brizel 266, Foot 709, Pfister 1462, Seton 1664, Wolverine 2021

Legal services, Alschuler 42, Baker 136, Buchalter 278, Donovan 547, Foley 707, Greenebaum 819, Kaye 1008, Keck 1011, Kirkland 1038, Larkin 1071, Law 1074, Morris 1270, Pope 1492, Ray 1547, SBE&S 1631, Schiff 1633, Shughart 1677, Snow 1704, Sommers 1711, Wachtell 1949, Winthrop 2012

Lighting and wiring equipment, electric, Aladdin 25, AMP 83, Bardes 168, Betts 213, Butler 296, Coleman 402, Continental 444, Cooper 448, Federal-Mogul 638, GTE 827, Guth 832, Johnson 991, Joslyn 996, Lamson 1064, Leviton 1091, Mark 1144, National Service 1313, Teleflex 1804, Thomas 1823, Thomas 1825, Triangle 1858, Westinghouse 1985, Wiremold 2013

Liquor stores, Brodbeck 268

Logging, Boise 244, Halliburton 834, ITT 964, Scott 1641, Weyerhaeuser 1989

Lumber and construction materials - wholesale, Best Distributing 211, Binswanger 224, Bird 226, Builder 283, Central National-Gottesman 336, CertainTeed 342, Doyle 556, Erb 610, Forest 714, Georgia-Pacific 771, Hartzell 862, Hawaii 866, Jeld-Wen 983, Kaibab 1003, Lafarge 1061, Lowe's 1116, McCray 1172, Simpson 1687, Union 1881, Universal Companies 1905, Von Tobel 1945

Lumber and other building materials - retail, Batson-Cook 177, CertainTeed 342, Cleveland 388, Erb 610, Fibreboard 644, Hawaii 866, Hechinger 869, Home 893, Jeld-Wen 983, K Mart 1001, King 1035, Levy's 1093, Lowe's 1116, Pukall 1534, Spahn 1725, Star 1747, Supermarkets 1782

Lumber and wood products, Balfour 140, Canal 302, CertainTeed 342, Contran 446, Doyle 556, Fibreboard 644, Gilman 780, Independent 936, Kaibab 1003, Langdale 1069, Louisiana-Pacific 1115, MacMillan 1126, Masco 1153, Menasha 1193, Nagel 1291, Ochoco 1380, Potlatch 1496, Sonoco 1713, Temple-Inland 1807, Von Tobel 1945

Machinery, construction, mining, and materials handling, AMETEK 80, Armco 112, Ashland 120, AXIA 132, Blount 233, Bucyrus-Erie 279, Budd 280, Case 320, Caterpillar 324, Clark 384, Deere 509, Dover 551, Dresser 559, Fansteel 628, FWD 737, Gehl 752, Halliburton 834, Hamischfeger 853, Hyster 920, Interlake 949, Kennametal 1019, Klein 1041, Koch 1045, Litton 1104, Montgomery 1258, Norton 1366, Oshkosh 1416, PACCAR 1424, Portec 1494, Raymond 1549, Schlumberger 1634, Tomkins 1841, United Conveyor 1890, United Technologies 1899, Venture 1931, Vermeer 1932, White 1995, Wurzburg 2033

Machinery, farm and garden, Brillion 263, Butler 296, Case 320, Clark 384, DEC 508, Deere 509, Ford 713, Fuqua 736, Gehl 752, Hesston 879, International Metals 952, MTD 1282, Sioux 1688, Smith 1697, Specialty 1728, Tenneco 1809, Toro 1842, Universal Cooperatives 1906, Valmont 1927, Vermeer 1932

Machinery, general industry, AMETEK 80, Amsted 86, Avery 130, Barden 167, Barrett 173, Blount 233, Buffalo 282, Burress 293, Caterpillar 324, Clark 384, Dana 493, Dethmers 522, Dover 551, Dresser 559, Duriron 568, Electric 591, Emerson 597, Federal-Mogul 638, FWD 737, Gear 751, General Refractories 763, Gleason 783, Gleason 784, Goulds 797, Graco 799, Great Lakes 812, Greenheck 820, Hammond 841, Hilliard 883, Hitachi 885, Illinois 929, International Metals 952, Koch 1045, Marley 1145, Masco 1153, Maxon 1162, McDonald 1176, Monarch 1251, Monsanto 1255, Morgan 1266, MPB 1279, Mueller 1283, New Hampshire 1333, Nordson 1347, Pennzoil 1451, Premier 1508, Reliance 1570, Rexnord 1577, Rieke 1586, Robbins 1592, Sonoco 1713, SPS 1731, State Industries 1752, Sundstrand 1777, Thomas 1825, Timken 1835, Tokheim 1840, Trinova 1859, Trion 1860, TRW 1864, Vesper 1933, Warner 1959, Wicor 1998, Wurzburg 2033, XTEK 2036

Machinery, industrial and commercial, AlliedSignal 40, Amsted 86, Blount 233, Buffalo 282, Cyclops 487, Dana 493, Donaldson 543, Duriron 568, Dynamet 571, Enerpac 601, Freedom 726, Graco 799, Henley 875, Hilliard 883, Midmark 1221, Parker 1438, Reliance 1570, Remmele 1571, Sandusky 1627, SPX 1732, Stafast 1735, Trinova 1859, Wicor 1998, Witco 2018, XTEK 2036

Machinery, metalworking, Acme-Cleveland 7, American Saw 72, AMPCO-Pittsburgh 84, Baldor 139, Bardes 168, Bodine 240, Brown 270, Buffalo 282, Cincinnati 369, Cone-Blanchard 429, Cooper 448, Crane 470, CTS 483, Dover 551, Fairchild 625, Giddings 778, Gleason 783, Gleason 784, Hammond 841, Ideal 925, Illinois 929, International Metals 952, Johnson 992, JSJ 1000, Kennametal 1019, Kingsbury 1036, Lincoln 1099, Litton 1104, Minster 1238, Monarch 1251, Monarch 1252, Morgan 1266, Motch 1275, National Machinery 1308, Neenah 1325, Norton 1366, Pennstar 1452, R & B 1543, Snap-on 1701, SPS 1731, Stanek 1742, Starrett 1749, Tippins 1836, XTEK 2036

Machinery, refrigeration and service industry, AMETEK 80, AMPCO-Pittsburgh 84, Amsted 86, Brillion 263, Buffalo 282, Carrier 314, Clorox 391, CSC 482, Emerson 597, HMK 886, Hubbell 908, Koch 1045, Kysor 1054, Lennox 1087, Marley 1145, Maytag 1165, Mueller 1283, Nortek 1350, North American 1351, Parker 1438, Shaklee 1666, Slant/Fin 1695, Stout 1767, Sundstrand 1777, Tennant 1808, Tokheim 1840, Triangle 1858, Venture 1931, Vilter 1938, Vogt 1941, Wagner 1950, Whirlpool 1993, White 1995, Williamson 2004, Wittern 2019

Machinery, special industry, Acme-Cleveland 7, Albany 26, Alco 30, Alliant 39, AMPCO-Pittsburgh 84, Applied 101, AXIA 132, Batson-Cook 177, Cincinnati 369, Cline 390, Cranston 471, Crompton 479, DEC 508, Duriron 568, Farr 632, FMC 704, French 729, Hamischfeger 853, Horix 902, KBA-Motter 1009, Koch 1045, Matthews 1160, McCormick 1171, Monarch 1251, Morgan 1266, Nordson 1347, Old Dominion 1391, Quaker 1537, R & B 1543, Rexham 1576, Universal Cooperatives 1906, Venture 1931, Wallace 1954

Mailing, reproduction, commercial art, photography, and stenographic service, Banta 162, Gerber 772

Management and public relations services, Aeroflex 14, Aerospace 15, APCOA 97, Asea 119, Barton-Malow 175, BDM 184, Bechtel 188, Bernstein 208, CIGNA 366, CIT 371, Commerce 417, Computer 425, Coopers 451, Deloitte 514, Deutsch 525, DynCorp 572, Foote 711, IBM 921, Independent 935, Kaiser 1004, Kearney 1010,

130

giving, they can aid you in shaping an appeal. Business reports often present a company's philosophy and its plans for the future, which in turn may prove helpful when it comes to linking a grant request to a corporation's interests. You should also stay abreast of economic conditions and the local business news. A company that is laying off employees or running a deficit may not be the best one to ask for a donation.

Follow a corporate giver's printed guidelines to the letter—especially in regard to submission deadlines. Find out to whom the request should be addressed, as well as the preferred format. Understanding the corporate hierarchy can be helpful. At some companies, sponsorships and nonmonetary support may be handled by the marketing department, while employee voluntarism may be coordinated in the human resources department. Some companies like to receive a preliminary letter of inquiry; others have application forms, and still others require multiple copies of formal proposals. It is important to find this out in advance.

Presenting Your Ideas to a Corporate Giver

Your proposal should be honest, clear, concise, and appropriate in tone. Draw up a realistic budget and be prepared to divulge your sources of income. Corporate grantmakers emphasize the bottom line, and many will ask for evidence of fiscally responsible, efficient management. Be explicit. State your program and goals, plan of action, timetable, and method of evaluation. Be brief but comprehensive. (See Chapter 10 for more on presenting your ideas to grantmakers.)

The potential benefits of your work to the company should also be spelled out. Consider what a business stands to gain from your program, now or in the future, directly or indirectly. If your program is innovative, tackles an emerging issue, or addresses a need that few other agencies are addressing, emphasize that fact—without undue self-promotion and in as non-controversial a fashion as possible.

Lastly, don't limit yourself to asking only for money. In addition to the "in-kind" support described earlier, look to local businesses as sources for board members and volunteer support. Keep in mind as well that a good relationship with one company may pave the way to good relationships with others.

FIGURE 47. Geographic Index in the *National Directory of Corporate Giving*

WISCONSIN—GEOGRAPHIC INDEX

WEST VIRGINIA
Barboursville
Subsidiaries: Sequa 1660
Beckley
Subsidiaries: Hospital 903
Berkeley Springs
Subsidiaries: U.S. Borax 1872
Bluefield
Plants: Humana 912
Carbon
Plants: Cyprus 488
Charleston
Corporate headquarters: Carbon 306, One 1399
Subsidiaries: AMAX 44, Bell 196, Borden 246, One 1399
Plants: ARCO 105, Union 1882
Foundations: Carbon 306, One 1399
Clarksburg
Subsidiaries: Consolidated 433
Clothier
Plants: Westmoreland 1986
Fairlea
Subsidiaries: UtiliCorp 1923
Grafton
Plants: Georgia-Pacific 771
Hamlin
Plants: Armstrong 114
Harrisville
Plants: Armstrong 114
Huntington
Corporate headquarters: Inco 934
Subsidiaries: Gannett 740, Lee 1080, One 1399
Plants: Betz 214
Corporate giving programs: Inco 934
Institute
Plants: FMC 704
Keyser
Subsidiaries: Westvaco 1987
Lewisburg
Plants: Asea 119, Merck 1199
Martinsburg
Subsidiaries: One 1399
Morgantown
Subsidiaries: One 1399
Plants: EG&G 588, Huntington 915
Moundsville
Plants: Phelps 1464
Neal
Plants: Ashland 120
New Martinsville
Plants: PPG 1501
Oak Hill
Subsidiaries: One 1399
Parkersburg
Plants: Butler 296, Guardian 829
Point Pleasant
Subsidiaries: Multimedia 1284
Princeton
Subsidiaries: One 1399
Ronceverte
Subsidiaries: One 1399
Plants: Humana 912
South Charleston
Subsidiaries: Union 1882
Plants: FMC 704
Summersville
Subsidiaries: One 1399
Weirton
Plants: Illinois 929
Wheeling
Subsidiaries: American Electric 57
Williamstown
Corporate headquarters: Farr 632
Foundations: Farr 632

WISCONSIN
Adams
Subsidiaries: Consolidated 434
Antigo
Plants: Banc One 146
Appleton
Corporate headquarters: Appleton 99, Appleton 100, Riverside 1590
Subsidiaries: Chesapeake 353, PacifiCorp 1429, Reynolds 1579
Plants: Albany 26, Banc One 146, Kimberly-Clark 1034, Piper 1481
Corporate giving programs: Appleton 100
Foundations: Riverside 1590
Ashland
Plants: James 974
Baldwin
Plants: CTS 483, Donaldson 543
Baraboo
Plants: Seneca 1658
Beaver Dam
Plants: Banc One 146
Beloit
Subsidiaries: Harnischfeger 853
Plants: Coltec 412, Ecolab 582, Outboard 1418
Bonduel
Plants: Campbell 301
Brillion
Corporate headquarters: Brillion 263, Endries 600
Foundations: Brillion 263, Endries 600
Brokaw
Plants: Wausau 1971
Brookfield
Corporate headquarters: Harnischfeger 853, North Shore 1353, Northwestern 1365
Subsidiaries: Marshall 1149, Nortek 1350
Plants: Armco 112, Smith 1697
Foundations: Harnischfeger 853, Northwestern 1365
Brown Deer
Subsidiaries: Sunbeam-Oster 1776
Bulter
Subsidiaries: Enerpec 601
Burlington
Subsidiaries: Nestle 1328
Butler
Corporate headquarters: Enerpec 601
Subsidiaries: Enerpec 601
Casper
Plants: Piper 1481
Cecil
Subsidiaries: Rochester 1597
Cedarburg
Subsidiaries: Amcast 46, Emerson 597
Plants: Amcast 46
Clear Lake
Subsidiaries: Union 1882
Clintonville
Corporate headquarters: FWD 737
Subsidiaries: Rochester 1597
Foundations: FWD 737
Coleman
Plants: Chrysler 364
Columbus
Subsidiaries: Mosinee 1274
Cudahy
Corporate headquarters: Ladish 1059
Subsidiaries: Handy 847, Marshall 1149
Foundations: Ladish 1059
Cumberland
Subsidiaries: Firstar 689
Plants: Seneca 1658
Dame
Plants: Menasha 1193
Darlington
Subsidiaries: Barber-Colman 163
De Forest
Subsidiaries: Grace 798
De Pere
Corporate headquarters: U.S. Paper 1873
Foundations: U.S. Paper 1873
Delavan
Subsidiaries: United Dominion 1891, Wicor 1998
Denmark
Subsidiaries: Bemis 203
Eau Claire
Corporate headquarters: National Presto 1311, Northern 1359, Sweet 1784
Subsidiaries: National Presto 1311
Plants: Piper 1481
Corporate giving programs: Northern 1359
Foundations: National Presto 1311, Sweet 1784
Elkhorn
Subsidiaries: Firstar 689
Plants: Banc One 146
Fond du Lac
Corporate headquarters: Castle 322, Giddings 778
Subsidiaries: Brunswick 277
Plants: Banc One 146
Foundations: Castle 322, Giddings 778
Fort Atkinson
Plants: Willis 2005
Glendale
Plants: Briggs 262
Grafton
Plants: Rexnord 1577
Green Bay
Corporate headquarters: Associated 121, Fort Howard 716, Leicht 1084, Prange 1503, Wisconsin 2017
Subsidiaries: Bemis 203, IDS 926, Lipton 1102, Safeguard 1622, Wisconsin 2017
Plants: Banc One 146, FMC 704, GenCorp 754, James 974, Piper 1481, Procter 1518
Foundations: Associated 121, Fort Howard 716, Leicht 1084, Prange 1503, Wisconsin 2017
Green Lake
Plants: Menasha 1193
Hartford
Subsidiaries: Nortek 1350
Plants: Menasha 1193
Horicon
Plants: Deere 509
Jackson
Plants: Seneca 1658
Janesville
Plants: Banc One 146, Seneca 1658, Upjohn 1913
Kenosha
Corporate headquarters: Snap-on 1701
Subsidiaries: Amsted 86, Snap-on 1701
Plants: Chrysler 364, Eaton 579
Corporate giving programs: Snap-on 1701
Kiel
Subsidiaries: Land 1067
Kimberly
Plants: Fuller 733

NATIONAL DIRECTORY OF CORPORATE GIVING 869

Personal Contacts

How important is it to "know someone"? Personal contacts help—if for no other reason than to get information—but their impact varies. Company-sponsored foundations and direct corporate giving programs with separate philanthropy personnel and explicit guidelines or formal procedures are unlikely to require contacts, while companies with informal giving programs and no formal guidelines are likely to be more personal. In particular, this tends to be true of smaller companies.

Grantseekers lacking personal contacts are not necessarily handicapped. Now is the time to build relationships and establish a local presence. Write a letter of introduction to the appropriate contact person at the company you have targeted describing your program and expressing your interest in arranging a meeting. Send along printed literature and articles about your program. Invite corporate decision makers to see your organization in action and/or to attend special events. Ask if you should send a preliminary letter of inquiry or a full proposal; send nothing extraneous. Establishing a rapport with a wary corporate funder can be difficult. Don't allow yourself to be discouraged, and remember: Cultivation requires long-term effort.

When You Get the Grant

If you receive a grant, send a letter of thanks and be sure to submit all required reports according to the agreed-upon timetable. Corporate funders are likely to be insistent on this point and will notice missed deadlines. Keep them informed regardless of the agreement, and suggest ways in which their contribution can be recognized, including printed programs and posters, special receptions or dinners, certificates, plaques, newspaper coverage, and so on. The level of recognition will depend on your resources and the corporate giver's desire for publicity. Given the relatively small size of the average corporate donation, formal recognition will not be required in most cases.

Even if your request is turned down, continue to nurture the relationship. Be sure to thank those in charge for considering your request. It is perfectly acceptable to ask a grantmaker why you weren't funded if they haven't already made it clear. And don't forget to inquire as to whether you can reapply in the next grantmaking cycle.

If at First You Don't Succeed...

Obtaining corporate support requires creativity, ingenuity, and persistence. And though the competition is likely to be stiff in the years ahead, such support is a possibility that the grantseeking nonprofit simply cannot afford to overlook. In the words of James P. Shannon, retired vice president and executive director of the General Mills Foundation:

> Within the past decade corporate support for the nonprofit sector has steadily become more important as government support on the federal, state and local levels has declined. It is reasonable to assume that this trend will continue for the foreseeable future, and that it will pose new challenges to the creative fundraising skills of nonprofit agencies.[2]

---

2. *National Directory of Corporate Giving.* Second edition. New York: The Foundation Center, 1989, pxv.

Chapter 10

Presenting Your
Idea to a Funder

By this point you should have a short list of grantmakers that seem likely to be interested in funding your project on the basis of your subject focus, the geographic area and population groups you serve, and the type and amount of support you require. Now you need to present your idea to those funders and convince them to support it.

While many foundations are quite flexible about the format and timing of grant applications, others have developed specific procedures to facilitate the decision-making process. If this is the case, follow the stated procedures to the letter. You'll want to review the notes you have made about a potential funder during the course of your research and gather together the most recent copy of any annual report, application guidelines, or information brochures issued by that funder. Knowing whom to contact and how to submit your application can be critical in ensuring that your request receives careful consideration.

Timing and Deadlines

Timing is an essential element of the grant-application process. Grant decisions are often tied to board meetings, which can be held as infrequently as once or twice a year. Most foundations need to receive grant applications at least two to three months in advance of board meetings to allow time for review and investigation, and some may require a considerably longer lead time. If the foundation you have targeted has no specified application deadline, try to determine when its board meets and submit your request as far in advance of its next meeting as possible. Then be prepared to wait three to six months for the proposal-review process to run its course.

FIGURE 48.   Getting Ready to Write a Grant Proposal

1. Construct a time line.
2. Commit your grant idea to paper in as succinct a manner as possible.
3. Thoroughly describe your program/organization.
4. Estimate all costs for staff, materials, and equipment.
5. Write job descriptions for all program staff; compile a complete list of board members, volunteers, and/or supporters.
6. Assemble all materials and supporting documents you will need to prepare the proposal.

Remember: A good proposal is based on sound program planning.

Initial Inquiries

Many foundations, both large and small, prefer to have grant applicants send a brief letter of inquiry before, or even in place of, a formal proposal. On rare occasions, grantmakers with staff may offer advice and/or assistance in preparing the final proposal to applicants whose ideas seem particularly relevant to their funding programs. An initial inquiry can also save you and the funder a lot of valuable time if there are specific procedures you must follow in preparing your final proposal, or if the foundation cannot provide funding because of prior commitments or a change in its program focus. Some grantmakers will actually make their funding decisions based solely on a letter of inquiry.

Your letter of inquiry should be brief, no more than two pages, and should describe in clear, concise prose both the purpose of your organization and the parameters of the project for which you are seeking funds. You should be specific about the scope of your project, how it fits into the grantmaker's own program, and the type and amount of support you are seeking. Your opening paragraph should summarize the essential ingredients of your request, including the amount of money and type of support you are seeking. All too often grant applicants bury these important facts in long descriptions of their organization or project. Most grantmakers will also want to see a copy of the IRS letter determining your organization's tax-exempt status. Depending on what you have learned about the funder, offer to send a full proposal for their consideration or ask about the possibility of a meeting with foundation staff or officials to discuss your project.

In these competitive times you need to be somewhat aggressive in your approach to foundations. Give the funder adequate time to respond to your inquiry, but don't be afraid to follow up with a phone call three to four weeks after you've sent your letter to make sure it was received and to ask whether you can supply further information. And remember, there's a fine line between acting in an assertive manner and being perceived as "pushy" by prospective funders. Take care not to cross that line.

The Proposal

The full grant proposal may be your only opportunity to convince a grantmaker that your program is worthy of its support. Depending on what you've uncovered about a funder's application procedures, it will either be your first direct contact with the funder or will follow an initial exchange of letters or conversations with staff and/or trustees. In either case, the proposal should make a clear and concise case for your organization and its programs. Grantmakers receive and review hundreds, sometimes thousands, of proposals every year. They need to be able to identify quickly and efficiently how they can put their money to work to benefit the community or further the causes in which they have an interest.

At this stage your board may feel it's time to turn to outside help, hiring a consultant to develop a proposal. Although bringing in a professional proposal writer can bolster your confidence, it is rarely necessary and may even prove inadvisable, since no one knows your project better than you do. Grantmakers aren't impressed by slick prose and fancy packages. They want the facts, presented clearly and concisely, and they want to get a feeling for the organization and its people.

There are a number of excellent books on the proposal-writing process, and you may find it useful to review several of them before you get started. Some of the better-known works are listed in the bibliography in Appendix A. Many of these titles can be found at a Foundation Center library or Cooperating Collection, as well as in your local public library.

While application criteria and proposal formats vary, most funders expect to see the following components in a grant proposal:

- **A cover letter.** The cover letter, which should be on letterhead and signed by your board chairman, president, or chief executive officer, highlights the features of your proposal most likely to be of interest to the grantmaker. It should point out how you selected the funder and why you believe they will be interested in your proposal, thus establishing a link between the two organizations. It should also include the amount of money and type of support you are seeking.

- **A table of contents.** The table of contents makes it easier for the prospective funder to find specific components of the proposal. While your proposal should be brief (most funders recommend limiting it to ten pages or less), a table of contents helps you organize your presentation and outline the information therein.

- **An executive summary.** The summary briefly describes the problem or need your project hopes to address; your plan of action, including how and where the program will operate, its duration, and how it will be staffed; the budget for the project, including the specific amount requested from the funder and your plans for future funding; and the anticipated results. The summary should be presented as the first section of your proposal and can be as short as one or two paragraphs; it should never be longer than a page.

  Even though the executive summary is the first thing (after the cover letter) in the proposal, it should be the last thing you actually write. By that point you will have thought through and thoroughly documented the need you plan to address, your plan of action, and the projected outcomes of your project, making it easier to pull out the most important facts for the summary.

■ **An introduction to your organization.** Even if your organization is large and relatively well known, you shouldn't assume that the decision makers reading your proposal will be familiar with your programs or accomplishments. In fact, they may not be aware of your existence. Therefore, you need to provide them with enough background information to build confidence in your group and its ability to carry out the program you are proposing.

State the mission of your organization and provide a brief history of your activities, stressing relevant accomplishments and awards as well as your present sources of support. While you should include a list of your board of directors in the appendix to the proposal (see below), you may want to call attention here to well-known individuals on your board or staff who have played a major role in your organization. Remember, your purpose is to convince the prospective funder that you are capable of producing the proposed program results and are deserving of their support.

You can do the groundwork for this section by keeping a "credibility file" that documents your progress and activities. Save letters of encouragement and praise, newspaper articles, and studies that support your work. Soliciting letters of endorsement from individuals and organizations that have benefited from your work is perfectly acceptable, and you may want to include some in the appendix.

Again, keep it short and to the point: The introduction should be no longer than a page.

■ **A statement of need.** State as simply and clearly as possible the problem or need your project will address. Be sure to narrow the problem to limits that are solvable within the scope of your project. A broad picture of the many problems that exist within your community will only detract from your presentation. Once again, there's a fine line between painting a compelling picture of a pressing need and describing a problem that is overwhelming in its size and/or complexity.

Be sure to document your description of the problem with citations from recent studies and current statistics, statements by public officials and/or professionals, and previous studies by other agencies.

Your object is to convince the funder that the problem or need is *real* and that your approach builds upon the lessons others have learned. Show the funder that you have researched the problem carefully and that you have a new or unique contribution to offer toward its resolution. And remember: No matter how well you document a specific need, you are unlikely to convert a funder that has no interest in your specific subject area.

- **Goals and objectives.** Now that you've stated the problem, you need to clarify exactly what it is you hope to accomplish. Goals are abstract and subject to conditions. As such, they are not always entirely attainable. Objectives, on the other hand, are based on realistic expectations and therefore should be more specific. Clearly stated objectives also provide the basis for evaluating your program, so be sure to make them measurable and time limited. The realization of each stated objective will be a step toward achieving your goal. For example, if the problem you've identified is high unemployment among teenagers in your area, your objective might be to provide 100 new jobs for teenagers over the next two years. The goal of the project would be a significant reduction in or even the elimination of teenage unemployment in your community.

  Don't confuse the objective of a program with the means to be used in achieving that end (see Figure 49). You might achieve your objective of providing 100 new jobs for teenagers through a variety of methods, including working with local businesses to create jobs, running a job placement or employment information center, or providing jobs within a program operated by your agency. But your measurable objective remains the same: to provide 100 new jobs for teenagers over the next two years.

- **Implementation methods and schedule.** The methods section of your proposal should describe the plan of action for achieving your goals and objectives, as well as how long it will take. Why have you chosen this particular approach? Who will actually implement the plan? If you're involving staff or volunteers already active in your program or consultants from outside your organization, note their qualifications and include abbreviated versions of their resumes in the appendix to your proposal. If you'll need to hire new staff, include job descriptions and describe your plans for recruitment and training. You should also provide a timetable for the project, making sure to note the projected starting and completion dates for each phase of the program. Be sure to allow ample time for each stage, bearing in mind the possibility of delays while you await funding.

FIGURE 49. Proposal Writer's Flow Chart

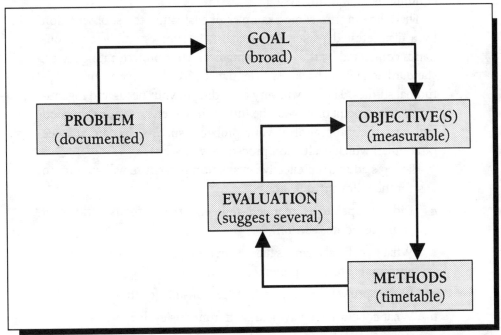

- **Evaluation criteria and procedures.** Evaluation criteria provide a measure for determining how effective your project has been in achieving its stated objectives. If your objectives are specific and measurable, it will be easier to evaluate your success. Although evaluating the outcome and end results of a project is a primary concern, don't overlook the need to evaluate the process or procedures as well. A good evaluation plan will enable you and others to learn from your efforts.

The evaluation component of a proposal often presents a major stumbling block to the inexperienced grantseeker. Try to remember that evaluation is nothing more than an objective means by which both you and the funder determine whether or not you have accomplished what you set out to do. It is an important part of your proposal because, among other things, it demonstrates that you are aware of the responsibility implicit in receiving a grant. It should *not* be an afterthought. It *should* be built into the design of your procedures as a continuous monitoring system.

The following are some examples of evaluation tools: observation by a disinterested person or specialist, interviews and/or questionnaires completed by those benefiting from your project, rating scales, standardized tests, checklists, attendance records, surveys, and longitudinal studies. The list will vary according to your needs and ingenuity. From the point of view of the funder, however, it is your own good faith and their appraisal of your probable success that are at issue rather than which evaluation procedure you select.

Having said this, an effective evaluation procedure will attempt to answer the following questions:

- Did you operate as intended, following the methods outlined in your procedures section?

- What beneficial changes have been brought about that are directly attributable to your project?

- Is your project the only variable responsible for these changes?

- What conclusions may be drawn from this evaluation?

- What future directions may be projected for your field as a result of your accomplishments under this grant?

- **A budget.** Developing a budget requires both candor and common sense. For example, if your proposal involves hiring staff, don't forget that social security payments, worker's compensation, and benefits have to be included. Try to anticipate your expenses in advance. It's unrealistic to expect additional funding at a later date to cover needs overlooked in your initial request.

Remember, too, that foundation and corporate donors are experienced in evaluating costs. Don't pad your budget, but don't underestimate the amount you need, either. If other funders will be contributing to your program, be sure to say so. The fact that others have confidence in your organization is a plus. If you expect to receive "in-kind" donations of equipment, office space, or volunteer time, be sure to mention these as well.

When seeking funds for a specific project, be sure to supply both the budget for your project and, in the appendix, the overall operating budget of your organization. Typically, the budget for a nonprofit organization includes two sections: personnel and nonpersonnel costs (see Figure 50). When in doubt, seek professional assistance from an accountant or someone with financial expertise.

■ **Future funding plans.** Most funders will want to know how you plan to support your project after their grant money has run out. Even with requests for one-time support (e.g., the purchase of equipment), you should describe how you'll handle related expenditures such as ongoing maintenance. Vague references to alternative funding sources are not enough. Foundations want *specifics*. Do you expect the program to become self-supporting through client fees or sales of products or services? Do you plan to solicit support from the public or other grantmakers? Is there a local institution or government agency that will support your program once it has demonstrated its value? Show the funder that you have thought through the question of future funding and outline specific alternatives.

■ **Appendix.** The appendix should include all appropriate supporting documents for your request, including a copy of your agency's tax-exempt determination letter from the IRS, a list of your board of directors, your current operating budget and an audited financial statement, a list of recent and current funding sources (both cash and in-kind), resumes of key staff members and consultants, and letters of endorsement and relevant news clippings. Remember, appendixes may not be read that carefully by grant decision makers. If something is essential, include it in the body of the text.

FIGURE 50.　Sample Budget Format for a Nonprofit Organization's Grant Project

Personnel:
    Salaries (may be prorated)
    Benefits
    Consulting fees   Subtotal:_____

Nonpersonnnel:
    Rent
    Utilities
    Equipment (lease or purchase)
    Supplies
    Travel and meetings
    Publicity
    Insurance
    Postage
    Printing
    Other   Subtotal:_____

                                    Total: _____

Writing Style and Format

Make your proposal as readable as possible by using active language and by being specific about what it is you hope to accomplish. Keep your proposal succinct and to the point. Use the group approach to generate ideas, but let one writer draft the proposal. Writing by committee doesn't work when you need a concise and well-organized final product (see Figure 51).

Ask colleagues who have been successful in securing foundation grants to review the proposal. You may also want to have someone unfamiliar with your project read the proposal to be sure it is clear and avoids specialized jargon.

Prior to submission, review the application procedures issued by the grantmaker. Have you fulfilled their requirements and addressed their concerns? Do your proposal and cover letter establish the connections between your project and their interests? Grantseekers often ask whether they should tailor proposals to individual funders. Unfortunately, the answer to this question is "yes and no." While it is generally not a

FIGURE 51.   Stylistic Hints for Proposal Writers

1. Use the active rather than the passive voice.

2. Avoid jargon; use acronyms only when absolutely necessary.

3. Stick to simple declarative sentences.

4. Keep your paragraphs short; employ headings and subheadings.

5. Address yourself to a human being: Picture the grant decision maker across the desk from you as you write. Always address your cover letter to an individual. Never begin with "Dear Sir" or "To Whom It May Concern."

6. Write with the needs of the people you hope to help in mind, making sure to demonstrate how your program will be of benefit to them.

7. Unless you have evidence to the contrary, assume that the reader is unfamiliar with your organization.

8. Do not resort to emotional appeals; base your arguments on documented facts.

good idea to develop a proposal or make major adjustments in your operations to conform to the interests of a particular funding source, you should let your proposal reflect any connections that exist between you and the grantmaker you have targeted. Establishing links is what fundraising is all about.

What Happens Next?

Submitting your proposal is nowhere near the end of your involvement in the grantmaking process. A few weeks after you have submitted your proposal, follow up with a phone call to make sure your materials were received. If they seem open to the idea, you may want to arrange a meeting with foundation representatives to discuss your program or project.

Grant review procedures vary widely, and the decision-making process can take anywhere from a few weeks to six months. During the review process, the funder may ask for additional information either directly from you or from outside consultants or professional references. This is a difficult time for the grantseeker. You need to be patient but persistent. Some foundations outline their review procedures in annual reports or application guidelines. If you are unclear about the process or timetable, don't hesitate to ask.

REJECTION IS NOT THE END

Most grantmakers receive many more worthwhile proposals than they can possibly fund in a given year. In an annual report several years back, the M. J. Murdock Charitable Trust described the situation as follows:

> It is seldom that the Trust is faced with having to decline a poor proposal. Rather, it is a matter of having to decide among a great many worthy proposals. A denial, therefore, is hardly ever a rejection on the merits of a proposal, but it is simply the result of a highly competitive system and the limitation of financial resources.

Just because a grantmaker is unable to fund a particular proposal does not mean the door is closed forever. If you are unsure why your proposal was rejected, ask. Did the funder need additional information? Would they be interested in considering the proposal at a future date? Could they suggest other sources of support you should pursue? Such follow-up discussions can be particularly helpful if the grantmaker has demonstrated a commitment to funding in your geographic area or subject field.

Rejection, too, is not necessarily the end of the process. Now might be the time to begin cultivation of a prospective funder. Put them on your mailing list so that they can become further acquainted with your organization. Remember, there's always next year.

WHEN YOU GET THE GRANT

Congratulations! You have received formal notification of your grant award and are ready to implement your program. Before you begin to hire staff or purchase supplies, take a few moments to acknowledge the funder's support with a letter of thanks. You also need to find out if the funder has specific forms, procedures, and deadlines for reporting the progress of your project. Clarifying your responsibilities as a grantee at the outset, particularly with respect to financial reporting, will prevent misunderstandings and more serious problems later. So be sure you understand all the strings attached to your grant before you start to spend the money.

Some grantmakers request, and most appreciate, acknowledgment of their support in press releases, publications, and other products resulting from or concerning grant-related activities. A few of the larger, staffed foundations offer assistance to grantees in developing press releases and other publicity materials. Again, if you are unsure about the grantmaker's expectations, don't hesitate to ask.

Keep detailed records of all grant-related activities, including contacts with and payments from the funder. Prepare a schedule of deadlines for reports and follow-up phone calls. Communicate with funders selectively. Don't inundate them with mail or invitations, but don't forget to keep them "in the loop" regarding important events or developments relating to your project. This is the beginning of what you hope will be a long and fruitful relationship. Treat it with the care and attention it deserves.

For further recommendations on this subject see *The Foundation Center's Guide to Proposal Writing*. The authors of the guide take you step by step through the proposal-writing process, illustrating their advice with excerpts from actual proposals and offering helpful hints from grantmakers interviewed in the preparation of the guide. A number of other proposal-writing books are listed in Appendix A.

Appendix A

Additional Readings

The Foundation Center's New York library has one of the most comprehensive collections of materials on philanthropy, fundraising, and nonprofit management in the country. In preparing this reading list, we did not attempt to include the thousands of titles published in the aforementioned subject areas and available in our libraries, but instead concentrated on the most frequently used or recently published materials that shed light on some of the topics covered by this guide. We provide basic bibliographic citations and, in some cases, a brief abstract as a further indication of the contents and coverage of the work in question. The inclusion or omission of a particular title does not imply an endorsement or lack thereof by the Foundation Center.

The list of additional readings is arranged in the following categories:

- Company foundations and corporate giving
- Laws regulating foundations and nonprofits
- Proposal development
- Fundraising—General

- Fundraising—Specialized guides
- Periodicals on philanthropy, foundations, and fundraising

Copies of most of the titles listed here may be found in the Foundation Center's New York and Washington, D.C., libraries; many will also be found in the Atlanta, Cleveland, and San Francisco libraries, and on a more selective basis in the various libraries in the Cooperating Collections network. Anyone may examine and use the publications in our libraries free of charge.

By its very nature a printed bibliography of this sort becomes obsolete almost as soon as it is issued. The reader is advised always to check for a more recently published or revised edition, especially in the case of funding directories or materials relating to tax laws. In general, we have not included books published prior to 1989. Exceptions are made for "classics" and for those works, especially in the area of proposal development, that have stood the test of time. For a comprehensive listing and detailed abstracts of books and articles on these and related subjects, please refer to *The Literature of the Nonprofit Sector: A Bibliography with Abstracts* and its annual supplements.

Corporate Foundations and Corporate Giving

Bergin, Ron. *Sponsorship and the Arts: A Practical Guide to Corporate Sponsorship of the Performing and Visual Arts*. Evanston, IL: Entertainment Resource Group, 1990.
  Examines the general principles of corporate sponsorship: contemporary applications, proposal considerations, and legal issues; provides several case studies and examples.

Berriault, Julie, ed. *Corporate Five Hundred: Directory of Corporate Philanthropy*. 11th edition. San Francisco: Public Management Institute, 1992.
  Reports on nearly 590 companies active in U.S. philanthropy.

Close, Arthur C., Gregory L. Bologna, and Curtis W. McCormick, eds. *National Directory of Corporate Public Affairs*. 11th edition. Washington, D.C.: Columbia Books, 1990.
  Provides profiles of 1,600 companies identified as having public affairs programs and lists approximately 12,000 corporate officers engaged in the informational, political, and philanthropic aspects of public affairs.

Corporate Giving Directory. 14th edition. Rockville, MD: The Taft Group, 1992.
Contains profiles of more than 600 corporate giving programs making
contributions of at least $250,000 annually.

Corporate Foundation Profiles. 8th edition. New York: The Foundation Center, 1994.
Provides detailed profiles of more than 220 of the largest corporate foundations in the United States and brief descriptive profiles of some 1,000
smaller corporate foundations.

Directory of Japanese Giving. Seattle, WA: Corporate Philanthropy Report, 1991.
Profiles Japanese corporations and their philanthropic activities in the U.S.
and Japan.

Hicks, S. David. *Corporate Giving Yellow Pages*. Rockville, MD: The Taft Group, 1993.
Alphabetically arranged corporate entries include both direct corporate
giving programs and corporate foundations.

Jankowski, Katherine E., ed. *Directory of International Corporate Giving in America*.
4th edition. Rockville, MD: The Taft Group, 1993.
Provides information on more than 350 foreign-owned U.S. companies that
support U.S. nonprofits.

Japanese Corporate Connection: A Guide for Fundraisers. Seattle, WA: Corporate
Philanthropy Report, 1991.
Presents a five-step process derived from interviews with U.S. nonprofits
that have built long-term relationships with overseas Japanese funders.

Klepper, Anne. *Corporate Contributions*. 26th edition. Research Report, no. 1014.
New York: The Conference Board, 1992.
This survey of major U.S. corporations provides a detailed overview, com-
plete with charts and tables on their 1991 contribution practices.

National Directory of Corporate Giving. 3rd edition. New York: The Foundation
Center, 1993.
A directory of more than 2,300 corporations that make contributions to
nonprofit organizations through corporate foundations or direct-giving
programs.

Rolen, Dawn A. *Matching Gift Details: The Guidebook to Corporate Matching Gift Programs*. Washington, D.C.: Council for Advancement and Support of Education, 1993.
Lists corporations that match employee gifts to educational institutions.

Laws Regulating Foundations and Nonprofits

Bromberger, Allen, R., ed. *Getting Organized*. Mt. Kisco, NY: Moyer Bell, 1989.
Introductory manual for organizations that wish to incorporate and secure recognition of federal and state tax-exempt status.

Drucker, Peter F. *Managing the Nonprofit Organization: Principles and Practices*. New York: HarperCollins Publishers, 1990.

Freeman, David. *The Handbook on Private Foundations*. Revised edition. The Foundation Center, 1991.
Offers advice on establishing, staffing, and governing foundations, with insights into tax and legal issues.

Hopkins, Bruce R. *Starting and Managing a Nonprofit Organization: A Legal Guide*. New York: John Wiley, 1989.
A readable exploration of the fundamental laws affecting the operation of nonprofit organizations.

Kirschten, Barbara, L. *Nonprofit Corporation Forms Handbook*. 3rd edition. New York: Clark Boardman, 1992.
Provides model corporate documents to facilitate the incorporation of nonprofit organizations in various jurisdictions, as well as guidance in applying to the IRS for recognition of exemption from federal income tax.

Oleck, Howard. *Nonprofit Corporations, Organizations, and Associations*. 5th edition. Englewood Cliffs, NJ: Prentice-Hall, 1988. Supplement, 1990.
Widely regarded as the definitive authority on the law and operation of nonprofit enterprises of all kinds, this book offers practical information concerning every aspect of nonprofit organization, administration, regulation, and taxation.

Olenick, Arnold J., and Philip R. Olenick. *A Nonprofit Organization Operating Manual: Planning for Survival and Growth*. New York: The Foundation Center, 1991.
Leads nonprofits through the maze of tax and legal codes and offers advice on accounting procedures.

United States Department of the Treasury. Internal Revenue Service. *Tax-Exempt Status for Your Organization*. Washington, D.C.: Government Printing Office, 1989.
Discusses the rules and procedures for organizations seeking exemption from federal income tax under Section 501(a) of the Internal Revenue Code.

Proposal Development

The following titles are intended for the novice grantseeker:

Brooklyn In Touch Information Center. *Fundraising with Proposals*. Brooklyn, NY: Brooklyn In Touch Information Center, 1988.
A basic guide for the novice fundraiser. Includes a sample proposal letter and outline.

Burns, Michael E. *Proposal Writer's Guide*. Revised edition. Hartford, CT: D.A.T.A., 1993.
A step-by-step approach to preparing written fund requests. Includes two sample proposals.

Coggins, Christiana. *A User's Guide to Proposal Writing: Or How to Get Your Project Funded*. New York: International Planned Parenthood Federation/Western Hemisphere Region, Inc., 1990.
Intended primarily for use in submitting a proposal to the Planned Parenthood Federation, this brief how-to guide is organized according to the eight components of a proposal. Concludes with a useful sample proposal. Also available in Spanish.

Conrad, Daniel Lynn. *The Quick Proposal Workbook*. San Francisco: Public Management Institute, 1980.

A workbook on project planning, proposal writing, and evaluation techniques.

Kiritz, Norton J. *Program Planning and Proposal Writing: Expanded Version.* Grantsmanship Center Reprint Series on Program Planning & Proposal Writing. Los Angeles: The Grantsmanship Center, 1980.

A step-by-step guide to a widely used format written in clear, concise language.

For more advanced readers:

Belcher, Jane C., and Julia M. Jacobsen. *From Idea to Funded Project: Grant Proposals That Work*. 4th edition, revised. Phoenix, AZ: Oryx Press, 1992.

Presents a method for nurturing an idea from inception through the development of a proposal; finding sources of support; administering grants; and evaluating your program. The second part provides information on basic resources and includes several forms and regulations for government funding sources.

Bowman, Joel P., and Bernardine P. Branchaw. *How to Write Proposals That Produce*. Phoenix, AZ: Oryx Press, 1992.

A detailed and technical treatment of the process of writing proposals. Directed toward readers from both the corporate and nonprofit sectors.

Browning, Beverly A. *Successful Grant Writing Tips: The Manual*. Burton, MI: Grantsline Inc., 1991.

Covers each element of a proposal; includes examples, tables, and helpful graphics.

Knight, Lucy. "Write on the Money: The Basics of Effective Proposal Writing, from Content to Structure to Length." *Currents* (October 1988): 10-12, 14-17.

Working from the premise that the objective of a proposal is to persuade, this article provides advice on the basics of effective proposal writing.

Coley, Soraya M., and Cynthia A. Scheinberg. *Proposal Writing*. Sage Human Services Guides, no. 63. Beverly Hills, CA: Sage Publications, 1990.
    Intended primarily for the moderately experienced grantseeker, this guide provides step-by-step advice on how to develop proposals. Examples and worksheets throughout.

Geever, Jane C., and Patricia McNeill. *The Foundation Center's Guide to Proposal Writing*. New York: The Foundation Center, 1993.
    This in-depth manual guides the grantseeker from pre-proposal planning to post-grant follow-up. Incorporates excerpts from actual grant proposals and interviews with foundation and corporate grantmakers revealing what they look for in a proposal.

Gooch, Judith Mirick. *Writing Winning Proposals*. Washington, D.C.: Council for the Advancement and Support of Education, 1987.
    While it focuses primarily on college and university proposal writing, Mirick's book provides general information useful to all grantseekers. Includes a case study, samples, and a bibliography.

Hall, Mary S. *Getting Started: A Complete Guide to Proposal Writing*. 3rd edition. Portland, OR: Continuing Education Press, 1988.
    This soup-to-nuts guidebook offers a logical plan for writing a proposal. Each chapter of the actual proposal-writing section focuses on a specific component of the process. Includes resource lists, case studies, checklists, and sample formats.

Kalish, Susan Ezell, ed. *The Proposal Writer's Swipe File: 15 Winning Fund-raising Proposals...Prototypes of Approaches, Styles, and Structures*. 3rd edition. Rockville, MD: The Taft Group, 1984.
    As the title indicates: 15 complete sample proposals submitted by education, science, and arts and humanities organizations to foundations and corporate giving programs.

Meador, Roy. *Guidelines for Preparing Proposals*. 2nd edition. Chelsea, MI: Lewis Publishers, 1991.

> An advanced manual covering proposals for business, government, and foundations. Contains the usual proposal-writing guidelines and added pointers for highly technical or scientific projects.

Fundraising—General

Adams-Chu, Lynda Lee. *The Professionals' Guide to Fund-Raising, Corporate Giving, and Philanthropy: People Give to People*. Westport, CT: Greenwood Press, 1988.

> An introduction to philanthropic activities in the U.S., with an emphasis on understanding the fundraising process in relation to nonprofit organizations.

American Association of Fund-Raising Counsel Trust for Philanthropy. *Giving USA*. New York: AAFRC Trust for Philanthropy, 1993.

> The annual yearbook of statistics on private philanthropy.

Bayley, Ted D. *The Fund Raiser's Guide to Successful Campaigns*. New York: McGraw-Hill, 1988.

> A general guide for the novice fundraiser, including how to organize and motivate volunteers.

Bergan, Helen. *Where the Money Is: A Fund Raiser's Guide to the Rich*. 2nd edition. Alexandria, VA: BioGuide Press, 1992.

> Provides a complete course in prospect and donor research.

Bobo, Kim, Jackie Kendall, and Steve Max. *Organizing for Social Change: A Manual for Activists in the 1990s*. Bethesda, MD: Seven Locks Press, 1991.

> Covers the techniques involved in raising support for groups dedicated to social change.

Collins, Sarah, and Charlotte Dion, eds. *The Foundation Center's User-Friendly Guide: A Grantseeker's Guide to Resources*. Revised edition. New York: The Foundation Center, 1994.
    A primer for novice grantseekers, introducing them to available resources and the fundamentals of identifying potential funders.

Dove, Kent E. *Conducting a Successful Capital Campaign: A Comprehensive Fundraising Guide for Nonprofit Organizations*. San Francisco: Jossey-Bass Publishers, 1988.
    Written for executives and staff of a wide range of nonprofit organizations, this book covers the fundamental issues and challenges of capital campaigns.

Flanagan, Joan. *The Grass Roots Fundraising Book: How to Raise Money in Your Community*. 3rd edition. Chicago: Contemporary Books, 1992.
    A basic guide on how to set up a fundraising program, choose the right strategy for your group, and raise money through a variety of approaches.

Hauman, David J. *The Capital Campaign Handbook: How to Maximize Your Fund Raising Campaign*. Rockville, MD: The Taft Group, 1988.
    Integrates the theory and practice of managing a capital campaign, explaining not only what should happen, but why what happens is necessary to the success of the campaign.

Mellon Bank Corporation. *Discover Total Resources: A Guide for Nonprofits*. Pittsburgh, PA: Mellon Bank, 1985.
    A guide written to help board members, staff, and volunteers evaluate their use of community resources: money, people, goods, and services.

New, Anne L. *Raise More Money for Your Nonprofit Organization: A Guide to Evaluating and Improving Your Fundraising*. New York: The Foundation Center, 1991.
    A workbook of questionnaires designed to help nonprofits evaluate and improve their fundraising.

Nichols, Judith E. *Changing Demographics: Fund Raising in the 1990s: Using Demographics and Psychographics to Improve Your Fund Raising Efforts*. Chicago: Bonus Books, 1990.
 This how-to book provides background information and practical advice about the use of demographic and psychographic tools to target significant segments of the population.

Panas, Jerold. *Official Fundraising Almanac: Facts, Figures, and Anecdotes from and for Fundraisers*. Chicago: Pluribus Press, 1989.
 This fundraising resource and reference book provides wide-ranging information to help fundraisers become more effective and productive.

Raybin, Arthur D. *How to Hire the Right Fund Raising Consultant*. Rockville, MD: The Taft Group, 1985.
 Selecting and working with a fundraising firm or an independent consultant.

Seltzer, Michael. *Securing Your Organization's Future: A Complete Guide to Fundraising Strategies*. New York: The Foundation Center, 1987.
 A step-by-step approach to creating and sustaining a network of funding sources.

Seymour, Harold James. *Designs for Fund-Raising*. 2nd edition. Ambler, PA: Fund-Raising Institute, 1988.
 A highly readable classic on general fundraising principles, patterns, and techniques, updated to reflect the changes in statistics since it was first published in 1966.

Strand, Bobbie J., and Susan Hunt, eds. *Prospect Research: A How-to Guide*. Washington, D.C.: Council for the Advancement and Support of Education, 1986.
 Presents a step-by-step method for locating and uncovering information on prospective donors (foundation, corporate, and individual).

Fundraising—Specialized Guides

AIDS Funding. 3rd edition. New York: The Foundation Center, 1993.

Allen, Anne, ed. *Search for Security: the Access Guide to Foundations in Peace, Security, and International Relations.* Washington, D.C.: Access, 1989.

Corry, Emmet, O.S.F. *Grants for Libraries: A Guide to Public and Private Funding Programs and Proposal Writing.* 2nd edition. Littleton, CO: Libraries Unlimited, 1986.

Compendium: U.S. Nonprofit Assistance to Central and Eastern Europe and the Commonwealth of Independent States. Washington, D.C.: Citizens Democracy Corps, 1992.

Computer Resource Guide: Computer Grants Directory. 4th edition. San Francisco: Public Management Institute, 1991.

Eckstein, Richard M., ed. *Directory of Grants for Organizations Serving People with Disabilities.* 8th edition. Margate, FL: Research Grant Guides, 1993.

The Environmental Grantmakers Association Directory. 4th edition. New York: Environmental Grantmakers Association, 1992.

Environmental Grantmaking Foundations. Rochester, NY: Environmental Data Research Institute, 1992.

Ferguson, Jacqueline. *Grants for Schools: How to Find and Win Funds for K-Twelve Programs.* 2nd edition. Alexandria, VA: Capitol Publications, 1993.

Foundation Grants to Individuals. 8th edition: New York: The Foundation Center, 1993.

Guide to Funding for International and Foreign Programs. 2nd edition. New York: The Foundation Center, 1994.

Hartman, Hedy A. *Fund Raising for Museums: The Essential Book for Staff and Trustees.* 2nd edition. Bellevue, WA: Hartman Planning and Development Group, 1987.

Hicks, S. David, ed. *Fund Raiser's Guide to Human Services Funding*. Rockville, MD: The Taft Group, 1993.

Klein, Kim. *Fundraising for Social Change*. 2nd edition. Inverness, CA: Chardon Press, 1988.
   This primer explains community-based fundraising techniques for small nonprofit groups with budgets under $500,000.

Marshall, Marylyn J., and Robert K. Jenkins, eds. *The Health Funds Grant Resources Yearbook*. 5th edition. Wall Township, NJ: Health Resources Publishing, 1990.
   Contains articles that describe and analyze trends and statistics in federal, corporate, and foundation health-grants programs.

Meiners, Phyllis A., ed. *National Directory of Philanthropy for Native Americans*. Kansas City: Corporate Resource Consultants, 1992.

National Guide to Funding in Aging. 3rd edition. New York: The Foundation Center, 1992.

National Guide to Funding in Arts and Culture. 3rd edition. New York: The Foundation Center, 1994.

National Guide to Funding in Health. 3rd edition. New York: The Foundation Center, 1993.

National Guide to Funding in Higher Education. 3rd edition. New York: The Foundation Center, 1994.

National Guide to Funding in Religion. 3rd edition. New York: The Foundation Center, 1993.

National Guide to Funding for Children, Youth and Families. 2nd edition. New York: The Foundation Center, 1993.

National Guide to Funding for the Economically Disadvantaged. New York: The Foundation Center, 1993.

National Guide to Funding for Elementary and Secondary Education. 2nd edition. New York: The Foundation Center, 1993.

National Guide to Funding for the Environment and Animal Welfare. 2nd edition. New York: The Foundation Center, 1994.

National Guide to Funding for Women and Girls. 2nd edition. New York: The Foundation Center, 1993.

Paul, Mary Eileen, and Linda Clements, ed. *Church Funding Resource Guide*. 10th edition. Washington, D.C.: ResourceWomen, 1993.

Reyes, Rosana, ed. *Activist's Guide to Religious Funders*. 3rd edition. Oakland, CA: Center for Third World Organizing, 1993.

Robinson, Kerry, ed. *Foundation Guide for Religious Grant Seekers*. 4th edition. Decatur, GA: Scholars Press, 1992.
   Provides introductory essays for the religious grantseeker as well as infor-
   mation on foundations with a history of religious grantmaking.

Shellow, Jill R., and Nancy C. Stella, eds. *Grant Seekers Guide*. 3rd edition. Mt. Kisco, NY: Moyer Bell, 1989.
   Lists more than 230 grantmakers that award grants to nonprofit organiza-
   tions advocating social and economic justice.

Siemon, Dorothy. *Creative Sources of Funding for Programs for Homeless Families*. Washington, D.C.: Georgetown University Child Development Center, 1990.

Stolper, Carolyn L., and Karen Brooks Hopkins. *Successful Fundraising for Arts and Cultural Organizations*. Phoenix, AZ: Oryx Press, 1989.

Women and Foundations/Corporate Philanthropy, comp. *Directory of Women's Funds*. Revised edition. New York: Women and Foundations/Corporate Philanthropy, 1988.

Periodicals on Foundations and Fundraising

The Chronicle of Philanthropy. 1255 23rd Street NW, Washington, D.C. 20037. Biweekly.
> Reports on issues and trends in the nonprofit sector, covering corporate and individual giving, foundation profiles, updates on fundraising campaigns, taxation, regulation, and management.

Corporate Giving Watch. The Taft Group, 12300 Twinbrook Parkway, Rockville, MD 20852-1607. Monthly.
> Articles analyzing corporate philanthropy, corporate sources of support, and fundraising ideas.

Corporate Philanthropy Report. Capitol Publications, 1101 King Street, Suite 444, Alexandria, VA 22314. Monthly.
> Articles on issues and trends, reviews of current giving by companies and industry, and news items.

Currents. Council for the Advancement and Support of Education, 11 Dupont Circle, Suite 400, Washington, D.C. 20036-1262. 10/yr.
> Articles on management, fundraising, and development for educational institutions. Book reviews and conference listings included.

Foundation Giving Watch. The Taft Group, 12300 Twinbrook Parkway, Rockville, MD 20852-1607. Monthly.
> Brief reports on new foundation programs, giving trends, and recent grants. Updates the annual *Foundation Reporter*.

Foundation News. Council on Foundations, 1828 L Street NW, Washington, D.C. 20077-6013. Bimonthly.
> Articles on grantmaking activities, book reviews, and people in the news.

FRI Monthly Portfolio. Fund Raising Institute, The Taft Group, 12300 Twinbrook Parkway, Rockville, MD 20852-1607. Bimonthly.
> Provides practical advice to fundraisers, with a focus on direct mail and capital campaigns.

Fund Raising Management. Hoke Communications, 224 Seventh Street, Garden City, NY 11530-5771. Monthly.
   Articles on all aspects of fundraising, book reviews, and a calendar of events.

Grassroots Fundraising Journal. P.O. Box 11607, Berkeley, CA 94701. Bimonthly.
   Articles on alternative sources of funding, book reviews, and bibliographies.

The NonProfit Times. Davis Information Group, 190 Tamarack Circle, Skillman, NJ 08558. Monthly.
   News articles focusing on trends, legislation, fundraising, and management of nonprofits.

The Philanthropy Monthly. P.O. Box 989, New Milford, CT 06776. 10/yr.
   Articles concentrating on general issues in philanthropy and tax and legal aspects of fundraising.

Washington International Arts Letter. Allied Business Consultants, Inc., P.O. Box 12010, Des Moines, IA 50312. 6/yr.
   Information on festivals, workshops, publications, and grants and awards for the arts and humanities.

Whole Nonprofit Catalog. The Grantsmanship Center, 650 South Spring Street, Suite 507, P.O. Box 6210, Los Angeles, CA 90014. Quarterly.
   Articles, summaries of publications, and listings for Grantsmanship Center training programs and seminars.

Appendix B

State Charities Registration Officers

ALABAMA

Rhonda Barber
Consumer Specialist
Consumer Affairs
Office of the Attorney General
11 South Union Street
Montgomery, AL 36130
Tel: (205) 242-7334
Fax: (205) 242-7458

ALASKA

Gary Amendola, Esq.
Assistant Attorney General
Department of Law
P. O. Box 110300
Juneau, AK 99811
Tel: (907) 465-2398
Fax: (907) 465-2417

Reproduced with permission of *The Philanthropy Monthly*, Box 989, New Milford, CT 06776, Tel: (203) 354-7132, publishers of the SURVEY OF STATE LAWS REGULATING CHARITABLE SOLICITATION, a loose-leaf reporting service since 1977 providing current digests of statutes and information on changes in enforcement personnel.

James Forbes, Esq.
Assistant Attorney General
Department of Law
1031 West 4th Avenue
Anchorage, AK 99501-1999
Tel: (970) 269-5100

ARIZONA

Gale Arriotte, Esq.
Chief Counsel
Office of the Attorney General
1275 West Washington Avenue
Phoenix, AZ 85007
Tel: (602) 542-1719
Fax: (602) 542-1726

ARKANSAS

Wendy Michaelis, Esq.
Deputy Attorney General
Consumer Affairs Division
200 Tower Building
323 Center Street
Little Rock, AR 72201-2610
Tel: (501) 682-2007
Fax: (501) 682-8084

CALIFORNIA

Carole Ritts Kornblum, Esq.
Assistant Attorney General

455 Golden Gate Avenue
Room 7244A
San Francisco, CA 94102
Tel: (415) 703-2019

Larry W. Campbell
Registrar of Charitable Trusts
Office of the Attorney General
P.O. Box 903447
Sacramento, CA 94203-4470
Tel: (916) 445-2021
Fax: (916) 444-3651

COLORADO

Timothy Tymkovitch, Esq.
Solicitor General
Department of Law
110 16th Street
Suite 1000
Denver, CO 80202
Tel: (303) 620-4510
Fax: (303) 620-4130

Neal Richardson, Esq.
Deputy District Attorney
Office of the District Attorney
303 West Colfax Avenue
Suite 1300
Denver, CO 80204
Tel: (303) 575-3555
Fax: (303) 640-3180

CONNECTICUT

David E. Ormstedt, Esq.
Assistant Attorney General
Office of the Attorney General
Public Charities Division
55 Elm Street
Hartford, CT 06106
Tel: (203) 566-5836
Fax: (203) 566-7722

DELAWARE

Steven Blackamore, Esq.
Deputy Attorney General
Department of Justice
State Office Building
820 N. French Street, 8th Floor
Wilmington, DE 19801
Tel: (302) 577-2500
Fax: (302) 577-6630 or 655-0576

DISTRICT OF COLUMBIA

Hampton Cross
Acting Director
Consumer and Regulatory Affairs
614 H Street
Room 1120
Washington, DC 20001
Tel: (202) 727-7170
Fax: (202) 727-8073

person to contact for forms:
Ruby Coston-White
(202) 727-7090

FLORIDA

Mary Helen Shelton
Department of Agriculture
Division of Consumer Affairs
The Mayo Building
Tallahassee, FL 32399-0810
Tel: (904) 488-2221

toll-free Florida only:
(800) 435-7352

Jody Collins, Esq.
Assistant Attorney General
Department of Legal Affairs
400 Hollywood Blvd.
Suite 505 South
Hollywood, FL 33021
Tel: (305) 985-4780

Barbara Edwards, Esq.
Assistant Attorney General
Department of Legal Affairs
The Capitol
Tallahassee, FL 32399-1050
Tel: (904) 488-6851
Fax: (904) 488-2221

GEORGIA

Robert K. Hooks
Director of Business Regulation
Office of the Secretary of State
2 Martin Luther King, Jr., Dr. SE
802 West Tower
Atlanta, GA 30334
Tel: (404) 657-8410
Fax: (404) 651-9530

person to contact for forms:
Debra Ferguson
Tel: (404) 656-4910

HAWAII

John Anderson, Esq.
Deputy Attorney General
Office of the Attorney General
425 Queen Street, 3rd Floor
Honolulu, HI 96813
Tel: (808) 586-1500
Fax: (808) 586-1205

Lorrin K. Kau
Office of Consumer Protection
Dept. of Comm. & Consumer Affairs
828 Forts Street Mall
Suite 600B
Honolulu, HI 96813
Tel: (808) 586-2636
Fax: (808) 586-2640

IDAHO

Terry Anderson, Esq.
Deputy Attorney General
Chief, Business Regulation Division
State House
Boise, ID 83720
Tel: (208) 334-2400
Fax: (208) 334-2530

Brett Delang, Esq.
Deputy Attorney General
Consumer Protection Unit
Business Regulation Division
State House
Boise, ID 83720
Tel: (208) 334-2424
Fax: (208) 334-2830

ILLINOIS

Floyd Perkins, Esq.
Assistant Attorney General
Chief, Charitable Trusts and
    Solicitations Division
100 West Randolph Street
Chicago, IL 60601
Tel: (312) 814-2595
Fax: (312) 814-2549

INDIANA

Lisa Hayes, Esq.
Office of the Attorney General
Consumer Protection Division
219 State House
Indianapolis, IN 46204
Tel: (317) 232-6331

IOWA

Norman Norland
Investigator
Consumer Protection Division
1300 East Walnut
Hoover Building, 2nd Floor
Des Moines, IA 50319
Tel: (515) 281-5926
Fax: (515) 281-6771

KANSAS

Kathy Greenlee, Esq.
Assistant Attorney General
Office of the Attorney General
Kansas Judicial Center
Lower Level
Topeka, KS 66612
Tel: (913) 296-3751
Fax: (913) 296-6296

KENTUCKY

Jean Hanks
Program Coordinator
Consumer Protection Division
Office of the Attorney General
209 St. Clair Street
Frankfort, KY 40601
Tel: (502) 564-2200
Fax: (502) 564-8317

LOUISIANA

Jennifer Johnson
Acting Chief, Consumer Protection
    Division
Department of Justice
P.O. Box 94095
Natural Resources & Lands Building
Baton Rouge, LA 70802
Tel: (504) 342-7013 or 9638
Fax: (504) 342-9637

MAINE

Marlene McFadden
Registrar
Division of Licensing & Enforcement
Department of Prof. & Financial
    Regulation
State House Station #35
Augusta, ME 04333
Tel: (207) 582-8723
Fax: (207) 582-5415

MARYLAND

Susan Elson, Esq.
Legal Officer, Charitable Division
Secretary of State's Office
State House
Annapolis, MD 21401
Tel: (410) 974-5534
Fax: (410) 974-5190

Lois Hug
Director, Charitable Division
Secretary of State's Office
State House
Annapolis, MD 21401
Tel: (410) 974-5534

MASSACHUSETTS

Richard C. Allen, Esq.
Director, Division of Public Charities
Department of the Attorney General
One Ashburton Place, 14th Floor
Boston, MA 02108
Tel: (617) 727-2200, ext. 2101
Fax: (617) 727-2920

MICHIGAN

David W. Silver, Esq.
Assistant Attorney General
Consumer Protection & Charitable
   Trusts Section
Office of the Attorney General

P.O. Box 30214
Lansing, MI 48909
Tel: (517) 373-1152
Fax: (517) 335-1935

for forms:
Charitable Trusts Section
Office of the Attorney General
P.O. Box 30214
Lansing, MI 48909
Tel: (517) 373-1152
Fax: (517) 335-1935

MINNESOTA

Sheila Fishman, Esq.
Assistant Attorney General
Office of the Attorney General
North Central Life Tower
Suite 1200
445 Minnesota Street
St. Paul, MN 55101-2130
Tel: (612) 297-4613
Fax: (612) 296-7438

Jody Wahl
Investigator
Office of the Attorney General
North Central Life Tower
Suite 1200
445 Minnesota Street
St. Paul. MN 55101
Tel: (612) 297-4613
Fax: (612) 296-7438

person to contact for forms:
Cyndie Hagemeister
Tel: (612) 297-4613

215 North Sanders
Helena, MT 59620-1401
Tel: (406) 444-2026

MISSISSIPPI

Leslie A. Staehle, Esq.
Special Assistant to the Attorney
    General
Office of Consumer Protection
P.O. Box 22947
Jackson, MS 39225-2947
Tel: (601) 354-6018
Fax: (601) 354-6295

MISSOURI

Cathy Westergaard
Investigator
Office of the Attorney General
Consumer Protection Division
P.O. Box 899
Jefferson City, MO 65102
Tel: (314) 751-3321
Fax: (314) 751-7948

MONTANA

Honorable Joseph P. Mazurek
Attorney General of Montana
Office of the Attorney General
Justice Building

NEBRASKA

L. Steven Grasz, Esq.
Deputy Attorney General
Attorney General's Office
2115 State Capitol
Lincoln, NE 68509
Tel: (402) 471-2682
Fax: (402) 471-3297

Cynthia A. Keenportz
Administrative Secretary
Secretary of State's Office
P.O. Box 94608
State Capitol
Lincoln, NE 68509
Tel: (402) 471-2554
Fax: (402) 471-3666

NEVADA

Melanie Meehan-Crossley, Esq.
Deputy Attorney General
Office of the Attorney General
Heroes' Memorial Building
198 South Carson Street
Carson City, NV 89710
Tel: (702) 687-3514
Fax: (702) 687-5798

NEW HAMPSHIRE

William Cullimore, Esq.
Director, Division of Charitable Trusts
Office of the Attorney General
State House Annex
25 Capitol Street
Concord, NH 03301-6397
Tel: (603) 271-3591
Fax: (603) 271-2110

Terry M. Knowles
Registrar
Register of Charitable Trusts
State House Annex
25 Capitol Street
Concord, NH 03301-6397
Tel: (603) 271-3591
Fax: (603 271-2110

NEW JERSEY

John J. Chernowski, Esq.
Deputy Attorney General
Division of Law
R. J. Hughes Justice Complex CN112
Market Street
Trenton, NJ 08625
Tel: (609) 292-8564
Fax: (609) 777-3112

Charles Tatum
Charitable Registrations &
   Investigations
P.O. Box 45021

Division of Consumer Affairs
124 Halsey Street, 7th Floor
Newark, NJ 07101
Tel: (201) 648-2807
Fax: (201) 648-2807

NEW MEXICO

John B. Hiatt, Esq.
Assistant Attorney General
Office of the Attorney General
P.O. Drawer 1508
Santa Fe, NM 87504-1508
Tel: (505) 827-6060
Fax: (505) 827-6685

Terri Rodriquez
Registry of Charitable Organizations
Office of the Attorney General
P.O. Drawer 1508
Santa Fe, NM 87504-1508
Tel: (505) 827-6060
Fax: (505) 827-6685

NEW YORK

Pamela Mann, Esq.
Assistant Attorney General
Chief, Charitable Trusts and Estates
   Bureau
Department of Law
120 Broadway
New York, NY 10271
Tel: (212) 416-8400

Douglas M. Williams
Director, Office of Charities
   Registration
Department of State
162 Washington Avenue
Albany, NY 12231
Tel: (518) 474-3820

NORTH CAROLINA

George Boylan, Esq.
Special Deputy Attorney General
Department of Justice
Suite 606, Revenue Building
P.O. Box 629
Raleigh, NC 27602
Tel: (919) 733-3252
Fax: (919) 715-3550

Lionel Randolph
Branch Head, Sol. Licensing Branch
Division of Fac. Service
Department of Human Resources
701 Barbour Drive
Dorothea Dix Hospital Campus
Raleigh, NC 27603
Tel: (919) 733-4512

Sherri Dorsett, Esq.
Special Deputy Attorney General
Department of Justice
701 Barbour Drive
Dorothea Dix Hospital Campus
Raleigh, NC 27603
Tel: (919) 733-4512

NORTH DAKOTA

David W. Huey, Esq.
Assistant Attorney General
Consumer Protection and Antitrust
   Division
600 East Boulevard
Bismarck, ND 58505
Tel: (701) 224-3404
Fax: (701) 224-3535

OHIO

Donna Rogers, Esq.
Acting Section Chief
Charitable Foundations Section
Attorney General's Office
101 East Town Street
Columbus, OH 43266-0900
Tel: (614) 466-3180
Fax: (614) 644-9973

OKLAHOMA

Aaron Craig
Administrator
Oklahoma Tax Commission
Income Tax
2501 Lincoln Boulevard
Oklahoma City, OK 73194-0009
Tel: (405) 521-3150
Fax: (405) 521-3826

OREGON

Ross Laybourn, Esq.
Administrator of Charitable Trusts
Department of Justice
1515 S.W. 5th Avenue
Suite 410
Portland, OR 97201
Tel: (503) 229-5725
Fax: (503) 229-5120

PENNSYLVANIA

Janice L. Anderson, Esq.
Chief Deputy Attorney General
Charitable Organizations Section
Office of the Attorney General
Strawberry Square, 14th Floor
Harrisburg, PA 17120
Tel: (717) 783-2853
Fax: (717) 787-1190

Richard H. Utley
Director, Bureau of Charitable
   Organizations
Department of State
North Office Building
Room 308
Harrisburg, PA 17120
Tel: (717) 783-3077 or 1720
Fax: (717) 787-1734

RHODE ISLAND

David J. Flanagan, Esq.
Special Assistant Attorney General
Administrator of Charitable Trusts
Office of the Attorney General
72 Pine Street
Providence, RI 02903
Tel: (401) 274-2294
Fax: (401) 277-1331

SOUTH CAROLINA

C. Havird Jones, Esq.
Assistant Attorney General
Office of the Attorney General
P.O. Box 11549
Columbia, SC 29211
Tel: (803) 734-3651
Fax: (803) 253 6283

Charles E. Brown
Director, Division of Public Charities
Secretary of State
P.O. Box 11350
Columbia, SC 29211
Tel: (803) 734-2169
Fax: (803) 734-2164

SOUTH DAKOTA

Ann Meyer, Esq.
Assistant Attorney General
Office of the Attorney General
State Capitol Building
500 East Capitol
Pierre, SD 57501-5070
Tel: (605) 773-3215
Fax: (605) 773-4106

TENNESSEE

Elizabeth McCarter, Esq.
Assistant Attorney General
Office of the Attorney General
450 James Robertson Parkway
Nashville, TN 37243-0485
Tel: (615) 741-3549
Fax: (615) 532-2910

Judy Bond-McKissack
Director, Division of Charitable
   Solicitations
Office of the Secretary of State
James K. Polk Building
Suite 500
Nashville, TN 37243-0308
Tel: (615) 741-2555
Fax: (615) 741-1278

for forms call:
(615) 741-2555

TEXAS

Rose Ann Reeser, Esq.
Assistant Attorney General
Chief, Charitable Trusts Section
P.O. Box 12548
Austin, TX 78711
Tel: (512) 475-4181
Fax: (512) 322-0578

UTAH

Francine A. Giani
Director, Division of Consumer
   Protection
Department of Commerce
P.O. Box 45804
Salt Lake City, UT 84145
Tel: (801) 530-6601
Fax: (801) 530-6001

VERMONT

Debra Leahy, Esq.
Assistant Attorney General
Office of the Attorney General
109 State Street
Montpelier, VT 05609-1001
Tel: (802) 828-3171
Fax: (802) 828-2154

VIRGINIA

Edward P. Nolde, Esq.
Assistant Attorney General
Office of the Attorney General
101 North 8th Street, 5th Floor
Richmond, VA 23219
Tel: (804) 786-2115
Fax: (804) 371-2087

J. Michael Wright, Esq.
Manager of Registration
Department of Agriculture and
    Consumer Services
P.O. Box 1163
Richmond, VA 23209
Tel: (804) 786-1343
Fax: (804) 371-7479

WASHINGTON

Stacia Hollar, Esq.
Assistant Attorney General
Office of the Attorney General
Highways Licenses Building
1125 Washington
P.O. Box 40100
Olympia, WA 98504-0100
Tel: (206) 586-0812
Fax: (206) 586-8474

Michelle Burkheimer
Special Assistant to the Secretary of
    State
Office of the Secretary of State

P.O. Box 40220
Olympia, WA 98504-0220
Tel: (206) 753-7121
Fax: (206) 586-5629

David Horner, Esq.
Consumer Resource Center
Office of the Attorney General
900 4th Avenue
Suite 2000
Seattle WA 98164
Tel: 9206) 464-7030
Fax: (206) 464-6451

WEST VIRGINIA

James P. Carbone, Esq.
Assistant Attorney General
Division of Consumer Protection
Office of the Attorney General
812 Quarrier Street, 6th Floor
Charleston, WV 25301-2617
Tel: (304) 558-8986
Fax: (304) 558-0184

Cathy Frerotte
Administrative Assistant, Charitable
    Organizations
Office of the Secretary of State
Building 1, Suite 157K
1900 Kanawha Boulevard East
Charleston, WV 25305-0770
Tel: (304) 558-6000
Fax: (304) 558-0900

WISCONSIN

Robert W. Larson, Esq.
Assistant Attorney General
Department of Justice
123 West Washington Avenue
Madison, WI 53707
Tel: (608) 266-3076

Mark E. Smith, Esq.
Assistant Attorney General
Department of Justice
123 West Washington Avenue
Madison, WI 53702
Tel: (608) 266-3968

Marlene Maly
Registrar for Fund Raisers
Dept. of Regulation and Licensing
1400 East Washington Avenue
P.O. Box 8935
Madison, WI 53708-8935
Tel: (608) 266-0648
Fax: (608) 267-0644

Michelle Krisher
Registrar for Charitable
    Organizations, M-Z
Dept. of Regulation and Licensing
1400 East Washington Avenue
P.O. Box 8935
Madison, WI 53708
Tel: (608) 266-0829
Fax: (608) 267-0644

Donna Williams
Registrar for Charitable
    Organizations, A-L
Dept. of Regulation and Licensing
1400 East Washington Avenue
P.O. Box 8935
Madison, WI 53708
Tel: (608) 266-0829
Fax: (608) 267-0644

WYOMING

Honorable Joseph B. Meyer
Attorney General of Wyoming
Office of the Attorney General
State Capitol Building
Cheyenne, WY 82002
Tel: (307) 777-7841

Appendix C

Publications and Services of the Foundation Center

The Foundation Center is a national service organization funded and supported by foundations to provide a single authoritative source of information on foundation and corporate giving. The Center's programs are designed to help grantseekers as they begin to select those funders who may be interested in their projects from the more than 35,000 active U.S. foundations. Among its primary activities toward this end are publishing reference books on foundation and corporate philanthropy and disseminating information on grantmaking through a nationwide program of public services.

Publications of the Foundation Center are the primary working tool of every serious grantseeker. They are also used by grantmakers, scholars, journalists, and legislators—in short, by anyone seeking factual information on philanthropy. All private foundations and a significant number of corporations actively engaged in grantmaking, regardless of size or geographic location, are included in one or more of the Center's publications. The publications are of three kinds: general reference directories that describe specific funders, characterizing their program interests and providing fiscal and personnel data; grants indexes that list and classify by subject recent foundation and corporate awards; and guides, monographs, and bibliographies that introduce the reader to funding research, elements of proposal writing, and nonprofit management issues. The majority of the reference titles are updated annually. The information that follows describes the most current available editions of these publications.

Foundation Center publications may be ordered from the Foundation Center, 79 Fifth Avenue, New York, NY 10003-3076. For information about any aspect of the Center's program or for the name of the Center's library or Cooperating Collection nearest you, call (212) 620-4230.

General Reference Directories

THE FOUNDATION DIRECTORY, 1994 edition

The Foundation Directory has been widely known and respected in the field for more than 30 years. It includes the latest information on all foundations whose assets exceed $2 million or whose annual grants total $200,000 or more. The 1994 edition includes more than 6,700 foundations, 800 of which are new to this edition. *Directory* foundations hold more than $160 billion in assets and award over $9 billion in grants annually, accounting for 90 percent of all U.S. foundation dollars awarded in 1991.

Each *Directory* entry lists the grantmaker's address, telephone number, officers and directors, and financial data, in addtion to information on its application procedures, fields of interest, giving limitations, and types of support awarded. Almost half the entries also include descriptions of recently awarded grants—often the best indication of a grantmaker's giving interests. The Foundation Center works closely with foundations to ensure the accuracy and timeliness of the information provided.

The *Directory* includes indexes by foundation name; subject areas of interest; names of donors, trustees, and officers; geographic location; and the types of support awarded. Also included are analyses of the foundation community by geography, asset and grant size, and the different foundation types.

March 1994
Softbound: ISBN 0-87954-545-3/$170
Hardbound: ISBN 0-87954-544-5/$195
Published annually

THE FOUNDATION DIRECTORY PART 2: A Guide to Grant Programs $50,000–$200,000, 1994 (3rd) edition

The Foundation Directory Part 2 covers the next largest set of foundations, those with grant programs between $50,000 and $200,000. It includes information on some 4,000 mid-sized foundations and more than 30,000 recently awarded grants. Access to foundation entries is facilitated by five indexes organized by city and state; donors, officers, and trustees; types of support; foundation names; and more than 200 specific subject areas.

March 1994/ISBN 0-87954-547-X/$170
Published annually

THE FOUNDATION DIRECTORY SUPPLEMENT

The Foundation Directory Supplement provides the latest information on *Foundation Directory* and *Foundation Directory Part 2* grantmakers six months after those books are published.

September 1994/ISBN 0-87954-555-0/$110

GUIDE TO U.S. FOUNDATIONS, THEIR TRUSTEES, OFFICERS, AND DONORS

The *Guide to U.S. Foundations* provides fundraisers with current, accurate information on all 35,000 + active grantmaking foundations in the United States, including more than 20,000 grantmakers not covered in other Foundation Center publications. The two-volume set also includes a master list of the names of the people who establish, oversee, and manage those institutions. Each entry includes asset and giving amounts as well as geographic limitations, and tells you whether you can find more extensive information on a grantmaker in another Foundation Center reference work.

April 1994/ISBN 0-87954-549-6/$195

THE FOUNDATION 1000

The Foundation 1000 provides access to extensive and accurate information on the largest U.S. grantmakers, which together distribute more than 60 percent of all foundation grant dollars. *Foundation 1000* grantmakers hold more than $100 billion in assets and each year award some 190,000 grants worth $6 billion to nonprofit organizations nationwide.

The Foundation 1000 provides thorough analyses of the 1,000 largest foundations and their grant programs. Each profile in the volume features a complete foundation description, a detailed breakdown of its grant program, and examples of its recently awarded grants.

There are, in addition, indexes by subject field, type of support, and geographic location. A special new index locates grantmakers by the names of their officers, donors, and trustees.

October 1993/ISBN 0-87954-503-8/$225
Published annually

NATIONAL DIRECTORY OF CORPORATE GIVING, 3rd edition

The 3rd edition of the *National Directory of Corporate Giving* offers authoritative information on approximately 2,300 corporate foundations and direct-giving programs.

The *Directory of Corporate Giving* features detailed portraits of 1,700 corporate foundations plus an additional 600 direct-giving programs, and includes application information, key personnel, types of support generally awarded, giving limitations, financial data, and purpose and activities statements. More than 1,100 entries in the 3rd edition also include sample grants. The volume also provides data on corporations that sponsor foundations and those that have direct-giving programs. Each entry gives the company's name and address, a review of its types of business, its financial data (complete with *Forbes* and *Fortune* ratings), all plant and subsidiary locations, and a charitable-giving statement.

The *National Directory of Corporate Giving* features an extensive bibliography of additional reference works on corporate funding. The six indexes help you target funding prospects by geographic region; types of support funded; subject area; officers, donors, and trustees; types of business; and the names of corporations and their foundations or direct-giving programs.

October 1993/ISBN 0-87954-485-6/$195

CORPORATE FOUNDATION PROFILES, 8th edition

This volume includes comprehensive information on 228 of the largest corporate foundations in the United States, grantmakers that each give at least $1.25 million annually. Each profile includes foundation giving interests, application guidelines, recently awarded grants, information on the sponsoring company, and many other essential fundraising facts. Three indexes help grantseekers search for prospective funders by subject area, geographic region, and types of support.

February 1994/ISBN 0-87954-505-4/$145
Published biennially

NEW YORK STATE FOUNDATIONS: A Comprehensive Directory, 3rd edition

This volume helps fundraisers identify the giving interests and funding policies of some 5,200 foundations in New York State. Entries have been drawn from the most current sources of information available, including IRS 990-PF returns and, in many cases, the foundations themselves. Many include descriptions of recently awarded grants. A separate section covers several out-of-state grantmakers that fund nonprofits in New York State. Five indexes offer quick access to foundations according to their fields of interest; types of support awarded; city and county location; names of donors, officers, and trustees; and foundation names.

July 1993/ISBN 0-87954-501-1/$165
Published biennially

FOUNDATION GRANTS TO INDIVIDUALS, 8th edition

The 8th edition of this volume provides full descriptions of the programs of more than 2,250 foundations, all of which award grants to individuals. Entries include foundation addresses and telephone numbers, financial data, giving limitations, and application guidelines.

April 1993/ISBN 0-87954-493-7/$55

Subject Directories

AIDS FUNDING: A Guide to Giving by Foundations and Charitable Organizations, 3rd edition

The more than 500 foundations, direct corporate giving programs, and public charities covered by this volume have, together, awarded some $97 million to AIDS- and HIV-related nonprofit organizations involved in direct relief, medical research, legal aid, preventative education, and other programs aimed at helping people with AIDS and AIDS-related diseases. Grants lists accompany more than half the entries.

November 1993/ISBN 0-87954-507-0/$75

GUIDE TO FUNDING FOR INTERNATIONAL AND FOREIGN PROGRAMS, 2nd edition

The 2nd edition of the *Guide to Funding for International and Foreign Programs* includes lists of grants recently awarded by grantmakers to projects with an international focus, both within the United States and abroad. The foundations featured have supported projects concerned with international relief, disaster assistance, human rights, civil liberties, community development, and education. The guide provides the facts fundraisers need, including foundation addresses, financial data, giving priorities, application procedures, contact names, and key officials; sample grants; and a range of indexes that help fundraisers target funders by specific program areas and geographic preferences.

April 1994/ISBN 0-87954-546-1/$85

NATIONAL GUIDE TO FUNDING IN AGING, 3rd edition

The *National Guide to Funding in Aging* covers the many public and private sources of funding support and technical assistance for programs for the aging. The 3rd edition of this volume provides essential facts on more than 1,000 grantmakers, including federal funding programs; state government funding programs (with listings for all 50 states and U.S. territories); foundations that have demonstrated or expressed an interest in the field (many entries include lists of sample grants); and other academic, religious, and service agencies that provide funding and technical aid to aging-related nonprofits.

December 1992/ISBN 0-87954-444-9/$80

NATIONAL GUIDE TO FUNDING IN ARTS AND CULTURE, 3rd edition

The 3rd edition of this subject guide covers those foundations and corporate giving programs that have demonstrated a commitment to funding art colonies, dance companies, museums, theaters, and many other types of arts and culture projects and institutions. With more than 4,000 grantmakers listed, six indexes, and a special bibliography, the volume facilitates rapid and accurate research. To illustrate the kinds of projects currently receiving support from grantmakers, the 3rd edition also lists thousands of actual grants recently awarded by foundations in the field.

April 1994/ISBN 0-87954-548-8/$135

NATIONAL GUIDE TO FUNDING FOR CHILDREN, YOUTH AND FAMILIES, 2nd edition

The 2nd edition of this guide covers some 3,600 foundations and corporate giving programs that, together, award millions of dollars each year to organizations committed to causes involving children, youth, and families. Each entry includes the grantmaker's address and a contact name, a statement of purpose, and application guidelines. There are, in addition, descriptions of more than 9,300 sample grants recently awarded by many of these foundations. Six indexes help grantseekers target appropriate sources of funding, and a bibliography facilitates further research in the field.

April 1993/ISBN 0-87954-491-0/$135

NATIONAL GUIDE TO FUNDING FOR THE ECONOMICALLY DISADVANTAGED

This volume covers more than 1,400 foundations and direct corporate giving programs, each with a history of awarding grant dollars to projects and institutions that aid the economically disadvantaged in the areas of employment programs, homeless shelters, hunger relief, welfare initiatives, and hundreds of other subject categories.

The guide features portraits that include the grantmaker's address, financial data, giving priorities statement, application procedures, contact names, and key officials. It also includes descriptions of some 2,000 actual grants recently awarded by foundations or corporate givers.

May 1993/ISBN 0-87954-494-5/$85

NATIONAL GUIDE TO FUNDING FOR ELEMENTARY AND SECONDARY EDUCATION, 2nd edition

This guide covers more than 2,000 foundations and corporate giving programs that fund nursery schools, bilingual education initiatives, programs for gifted children, remedial reading/math programs, drop-out prevention services, educational testing programs, and a variety of nonprofit organizations and activities. The volume also includes more than 4,700 descriptions of recently awarded grants.

June 1993/ISBN 0-87954-495-3/$135

NATIONAL GUIDE TO FUNDING FOR THE ENVIRONMENT AND ANIMAL WELFARE, 2nd edition

This volume features some 1,300 foundations and corporate giving programs and includes lists of environmental grants recently awarded to projects and organizations involved in international conservation, ecological research, litigation and advocacy, waste reduction, animal welfare, and much more. The *National Guide to Funding for the Environment and Animal Welfare* provides foundation addresses, financial data, giving priorities, application procedures, contact names, and key officials; sample grants; and a range of indexes that help fundraisers target funders by specific program areas and geographic preferences.

May 1994/ISBN 0-87954-551-8/$85

NATIONAL GUIDE TO FUNDING IN HEALTH, 3rd edition

The 3rd edition of this volume covers some 3,300 foundations and corporate giving programs, all of which have a documented or stated interest in funding hospitals, universities, research institutes, community-based agencies, national health associations, and a broad range of other health-related programs and services. It includes facts on grantmakers' program interests, contact persons, and application guidelines. Many entries also include descriptions of recently awarded grants—the volume features more than 9,000 sample grants in all. Six indexes help fundraisers target prospective funding sources. A bibliography of publications on health issues and philanthropic initiatives in the field is included as a guide to further study.

April 1993/ISBN 0-87954-490-2/$135

NATIONAL GUIDE TO FUNDING IN HIGHER EDUCATION, 3rd edition

The 3rd edition of this guide covers more than 3,600 foundations and corporate giving programs, all with a demonstrated history of awarding grants to colleges, universities, graduate programs, and research institutes. Each entry gives a thorough portrait of the grantmaker, including its address, contact person, financial data, statement of purpose, preferred types of support, and geographic limitations. The 3rd edition also includes more than 10,000 descriptions of recently awarded grants as well as a selective bibliography to direct you to additional reference works on higher education and philanthropy.

May 1994/ISBN 0-87954-550-X/$135

NATIONAL GUIDE TO FUNDING FOR LIBRARIES AND INFORMATION SERVICES, 2nd edition

The 2nd edition of this volume covers some 600 foundations and corporate giving programs. Each entry includes the grantmaker's address, contact person, financial data, statement of purpose, preferred types of support, and geographic limitations. The guide also features more than 800 descriptions of recently awarded grants. The *National Guide to Funding for Libraries and Information Services* offers data on funders of a wide range of organizations and projects, from the smallest pubic libraries to major research institutions; art, law, and medical libraries; and other specialized information centers.

May 1993/ISBN 0-87954-497-X/$85

NATIONAL GUIDE TO FUNDING IN RELIGION, 2nd edition

The 2nd edition of this guide covers more than 4,200 foundations and corporate giving programs, all of which have demonstrated or stated an interest in funding churches, missionary societies, and/or religious welfare and education programs. Entries include the grantmaker's address, financial data, giving priorities, application procedures, contact names, and key officials. Many entries also include descriptions of grants recently awarded by the foundation or corporate giver.

June 1993/ISBN 0-87954-496-1/$135

NATIONAL GUIDE TO FUNDING FOR WOMEN AND GIRLS, 2nd edition

The 2nd edition of this guide covers some 1,000 foundations and corporate giving programs, all of which have demonstrated or stated an interest in funding scholarships, shelters for abused women, girls' clubs, health clinics, employment centers, and a variety of other programs. Entries include the grantmaker's address, financial data, giving priorities, application procedures, contact names, and key officials. The *National*

Guide to Funding for Women and Girls also lists more than 3,000 grants recently awarded by foundations or corporate givers.

May 1993/ISBN 0-87954-498-8/$95

Grant Directories

GRANT GUIDES

The *Grant Guides* series lists actual foundation grants in 30 key areas of grantmaking. These research tools bring together thousands of grants of $10,000 or more, all of them recently awarded by many of the top funders in each field. Each volume includes the names, addresses, and giving limitations of the foundations listed. The grant descriptions provide the grant recipient's name and location, the amount of the grant, the date the grant was authorized, and a description of the grant's intended use.

Each *Grant Guide* includes three indexes organized as follows: by recipient type; by the subject focus of the foundation's grants; and by the geographic area in which the foundation has already funded projects. In addition, each volume uses a series of statistical tables to document the 25 top funders in that particular area of interest; the 15 largest grants reported; the total dollar amount and number of grants awarded for specific types of support, recipient organization type, and population group; and the total grant dollars received in each U.S. state and many foreign countries.

Series published annually in October/1993/1994
Editions/$65 each

THE FOUNDATION GRANTS INDEX, 1994 edition

The 1994 (22nd) edition of *The Foundation Grants Index* covers the grantmaking programs of more than 950 of the largest independent, corporate, and community foundations in the U.S., and includes more than 60,000 grant descriptions in all. Grant descriptions are divided into 28 broad subject areas (e.g., health, higher education, and arts and culture). Within each of these broad fields the grant descriptions are listed geographically by state and alphabetically by the name of the foundation. The grant descriptions provide fundraisers with the grant recipient's name and location, the grant amount, the date the grant was authorized, and a description of the grant's intended use.

December 1993/ISBN 0-87954-508-9/$135

THE FOUNDATION GRANTS INDEX QUARTERLY

This subscription service provides new information on foundation funding every three months. Each issue of the *Quarterly* offers descriptions of more than 5,000 recently awarded foundation grants arranged by state and indexed by subjects and recipients. The *Quarterly* also notes changes in foundation addresses, personnel, program interests, and application procedures. Included is a list of grantmakers' recent publications, from annual reports and information brochures to grants lists and newsletters.

Annual subscription $85/4 issues/ISBN 0735-2522

WHO GETS GRANTS/WHO GIVES GRANTS: Nonprofit Organizations and the Foundation Grants They Received, 2nd edition

With more than 18,000 nonprofit organizations and 54,000 grants listed, the second edition of *Who Gets Grants* provides direct access to a wealth of grant recipient information. The book is divided into 19 different subject areas; within each subject area the grant recipients are listed by geographic area. The grant recipient entries include the amount of the grant, its duration and use, and the name of the grantmaker. The index provides a list of all the grants made by each foundation covered, giving grantseekers a sense of a grantmaker's larger funding priorities. An appendix lists foundation addresses and funding limitations.

April 1994/ISBN 0-87954-542-9/$95

Guidebooks

THE FOUNDATION CENTER'S USER-FRIENDLY GUIDE: A Grantseeker's Guide to Resources, Revised edition
Edited by Sarah Collins and Charlotte Dion

This book answers the most commonly asked questions about grantseeking in an up-beat, easy-to-read style. Specifically designed for novice grantseekers, the *User-Friendly*

Guide leads the reader through the wide range of research directories and resources used successfully by professional fundraisers.

March 1994/ISBN 0-87954-541-0/$14.95

FOUNDATION GIVING: Yearbook of Facts and Figures on Private, Corporate and Community Foundations, 1994 edition

Foundation Giving includes data on more than 35,000 grantmaking foundations in the U.S. Using a range of statistical tables to chart foundation giving by subject area and type of support, to categorize foundations by asset and giving amount, and to document other noteworthy data such as the breakdown of grants awarded by the largest foundations, the study offers a comprehensive review of foundation activity over the past year.

June 1994/ISBN 0-87954-554-2/$19.95

THE FOUNDATION CENTER'S GUIDE TO PROPOSAL WRITING

The *Guide to Proposal Writing* takes fundraisers through each step of the process, from pre-proposal planning to the writing itself to the essential post-grant follow-up. Written by Jane Geever and Patricia McNeill, professional fundraisers who have themselves been creating successful proposals for more than 25 years, the book offers invaluable tips, candid advice, and in-depth practical instruction in addition to excerpts from actual grant proposals.

August 1993/ISBN 0-87954-492-9/$29.95

Benchmark Studies

AGING: The Burden Study on Foundation Grantmaking Trends

This in-depth analysis of foundation funding for programs that benefit the elderly covers private, corporate, and community grantmakers while considering such pertinent topics as the availability of support for caregivers, the frail elderly, and Alzheimer's patients; a renewed interest in support services and institutional long-term care; and inter-generational programs.

September 1991/ISBN 0-87954-389-2/$40

ALCOHOL AND DRUG ABUSE FUNDING: An Analysis of Foundation Grants, 1983–1987

This report provides an authoritative study of independent, corporate, and community foundation grants awarded between 1983 and 1987 for drug and alcohol abuse programs. The study examines the historical background, present status, and future directions of grantmaking in this critical field, and is designed for foundation policymakers, grantseekers, and researchers in the fields of health care and prevention, education, and social service.

August 1989/ISBN 0-87594-286-1/$45

ARTS FUNDING: A Report on Foundation and Corporate Grantmaking Trends

Commissioned by Grantmakers in the Arts, *Arts Funding* documents notable shifts in arts and culture funding patterns through the 1980s. The study covers funding for the performing and visual arts, museums, ethnic arts, media, journalism, historic preservation, and arts-related humanities, and includes profiles of more than 60 top foundation and corporate grantmakers in the field.

April 1993/ISBN 0-87954-448-1/$40

CRIME AND JUSTICE: The Burden Study on Foundation Grantmaking Trends

This comprehensive work examines foundation funding for programs involved with crime prevention, juvenile justice, law enforcement, correction facilities, rehabilitation, and victim assistance. It also looks at significant developments in the criminal justice field, changing public perceptions of crime, and the growth of funding for programs combating spouse and child abuse.

April 1991/ISBN 0-87954-381-7/$35

Bibliographies

THE LITERATURE OF THE NONPROFIT SECTOR: A Bibliography with Abstracts, Volumes I–V

This bibliographical series covers references on fundraising, foundations, corporate giving, nonprofit management, and more. The entries are divided into 12 broad subject fields, and each volume includes subject, title, and author indexes. Many entries are abstracted to give readers a clear idea of the material covered in each work. Volume V expands the coverage to more than 10,700 titles.

Volume V, December 1993/ISBN 0-87954-509-7/$45
Volume IV, September 1992/ISBN 0-87954-447-3/$45
Volume III, September 1991/ISBN 0-87954-386-8/$45
Volume II, July 1990/ISBN 0-87954-343-4/$45
Volume I, August 1989/ISBN 0-87954-287-X/$55
Volumes I–V Set/$180

Other Publications

AMERICA'S NONPROFIT SECTOR: A Primer
by Lester M. Salamon

In this informative book, Lester M. Salamon provides a basic, easy-to-understand handbook for government officials, journalists, and students—in short, for anyone who wants to understand the makeup of America's nonprofit sector. Generously illustrated with charts and tables.

August 1992/ISBN 0-87954-451-1/$14.95

AMERICA'S VOLUNTARY SPIRIT: A Book of Readings
edited by Brian O'Connell

Editor Brian O'Connell brings together 45 selections that celebrate the richness and variety of America's unique voluntary sector. O'Connell researched nearly 1,000 selections spanning 300 years to identify those speeches, articles, and papers that best define and characterize the roles philanthropy and voluntary action play in our society. Contributors as diverse as de Tocqueville and John D. Rockefeller, Thoreau and Max Lerner, Erma Bombeck and Vernon Jordan provide a common examination of this important dimension of American life. The anthology includes a bibliography of some 500 important writings and a detailed subject index.

October 1983/ISBN 0-87954-079-6/$19.95

THE BOARD MEMBER'S BOOK, 2nd edition
by Brian O'Connell, President, INDEPENDENT SECTOR

Based on his extensive experience working with and on the boards of voluntary organizations, Brian O'Connell has developed this guide to the essential functions of voluntary boards. O'Connell offers practical advice on how to be a more effective board member as well as on how board members can help their organizations make a difference.

October 1993/ISBN 0-87954-502-X/$24.95

CAREERS FOR DREAMERS AND DOERS: A Guide to Management Careers in the Nonprofit Sector
by Lilly Cohen and Dennis Young

Co-authors Lilly Cohen and Dennis Young explain how to build a professional career on a foundation of idealism, offering practical advice for starting a job search as well as strategies tested by successful nonprofit managers. *Careers for Dreamers and Doers* draws on the experience of 27 established professionals, offering profiles of nonprofit CEOs, development officers, and consultants in the "third sector."

November 1989/ISBN 0-87954-294-2/$24.95

THE CHARITABLE IMPULSE: Wealth and Social Conscience in Communities and Cultures Outside the United States
by James A. Joseph

The Charitable Impulse is the product of author James Joseph's life-long interest in how compassionate values are developed, nurtured, and activated. In his quest to identify the motives and personal attributes that lead to a caring society, he has traveled from South America to South Africa, from England to the Middle East, interviewing men and women who contribute to the public good. *The Charitable Impulse* adds a much-needed international dimension to the growing body of literature on philanthropy and voluntarism.

September 1989
Softbound: ISBN 0-87954-301-9/$19.95
Hardbound: ISBN 0-87954-300-0/$24.95

HISPANICS AND THE NONPROFIT SECTOR
by Herman E. Gallegos and Michael O'Neill

Co-authors Herman Gallegos and Michael O'Neill look at economic development groups, legal rights and advocacy organizations, unions, cultural and educational programs, and other types of nonprofits that address the needs of the increasingly large and diverse group of Spanish-speaking citizens and immigrants to the U.S. Their book traces the roots of Hispanic nonprofit organizations to the *mutualistas* of the 19th century and considers such modern responses as the National Council of La Raza and the Mexican American Legal Defense and Educational Fund.

April 1991/ISBN 0-87954-398-1/$24.95

MANAGING FOR PROFIT IN THE NONPROFIT WORLD
by Paul Firstenberg

Drawing upon his extensive for-profit experience as well as his 14 years of experience as a nonprofit professional at the Children's Television Workshop, the Ford Foundation, Princeton, Tulane, and Yale, author Paul Firstenberg outlines innovative ways in which nonprofit managers can utilize the same state-of-the-art management techniques developed by the most successful for-profit enterprises.

September 1986/ISBN·0-87954-159-8/$19.95

THE NONPROFIT ENTREPRENEUR: Creating Ventures to Earn Income
by Edward Skloot

In this well-organized, topic-by-topic analytical approach to nonprofit venturing, Edward Skloot demonstrates how nonprofits can launch successful earned income enterprises without compromising their missions. Topics in this collection include legal issues, marketing techniques, business planning, the pitfalls of venturing for smaller nonprofits, and a special section on museums and their retail operations.

September 1988/ISBN 0-87594-239-X/$19.95

A NONPROFIT ORGANIZATION OPERATING MANUAL: Planning for Survival and Growth
by Arnold J. Olenick and Philip R. Olenick

This desk manual for nonprofit executives covers all aspects of starting and managing a nonprofit. The authors discuss legal problems, tax exemption, organizational planning and development; board relations; operational, proposal, cash, and capital budgeting; marketing; grant proposals, fundraising, and for-profit ventures; accounting; computerization; and tax planning and compliance.

July 1991/ISBN 0-87954-293-4/$29.95

PROMOTING ISSUES AND IDEAS: A Guide to Public Relations for Nonprofit Organizations
by Public Interest Public Relations

In this manual, PIPR, specialists in promoting the issues and ideas of nonprofit groups, presents proven strategies, including the "nuts-and-bolts" of advertising, publicity, speechmaking, lobbying, and special events; how to write and produce informational literature that leaps off the page; public relations on a shoestring budget; how to plan and evaluate public relations efforts; and the use of new communications technologies.

March 1987/ISBN 0-87954-192-X/$24.95

RAISE MORE MONEY FOR YOUR NONPROFIT ORGANIZATION: A Guide to Evaluating and Improving Your Fundraising
by Anne L. New

Author Anne New lays out guidelines for a fundraising program that will benefit the incipient as well as the established nonprofit organization. Her book is divided into three sections: "The Basics" delineates the steps a nonprofit must take before launching a development campaign; "Fundraising Methods" encourages organizational self-analysis and points the way to an effective program involving many sources of funding; and "Fundraising Resources" highlights the most useful research and funding directories.

January 1991/ISBN 0-87954-388-4/$14.95

SECURING YOUR ORGANIZATION'S FUTURE: A Complete Guide to Fundraising Strategies
by Michael Seltzer

Michael Seltzer, a pioneer in the field of nonprofit management and fundraising, provides bottom-line facts and easy-to-follow worksheets for beginners, along with a complete review of the basics and new money-making ideas for veteran fundraisers.

Seltzer's work is supplemented with an extensive bibliography of selected readings and resource organizations.

March 1987/ISBN 0-87954-190-3-/$24.95

SUCCEEDING WITH CONSULTANTS: Self-Assessment for the Changing Nonprofit
by Barbara Kibbe and Fred Setterberg

Succeeding with Consultants provides practical advice for nonprofit executives eager to improve their organization's performance. Written by Barbara Kibbe and Fred Setterberg, and supported by the David and Lucile Packard Foundation, it guides nonprofits through the process of selecting and utilizing consultants to strengthen their organization's operations. In the process the authors emphasize self-assessment tools and look at six areas in which a nonprofit organization might benefit from a consultant's advice: governance, planning, fund development, financial management, public relations and marketing, and quality assurance.

April 1992/ISBN 0-87954-450-3/$19.95

VOLUNTEERS IN ACTION
by Brian O'Connell and Ann Brown O'Connell

Authors Brian O'Connell and Ann Brown O'Connell illustrate the impact of ordinary citizens and how their dedication to voluntary action enriches their lives and changes their communities, the country, and the world. Using interviews and anecdotes, the authors provide insights into the true nature of the voluntary sector. The book also serves as a call to action, encouraging citizens to involve themselves in this rewarding form of participatory democracy.

September 1989
Softbound: ISBN ISBN 0-87954-292-6/$19.95
Hardbound: ISBN 0-87954-291-8/$24.95

Membership Program

ASSOCIATES PROGRAM

- Annual membership in the Associates Program delivers important information from:
  - foundation and corporate annual reports, brochures, press releases, grants lists, and other announcements
  - IRS 990-PF forms from more than 35,000 U.S. foundations— often the only source of information on small foundations
  - books and periodicals on the grantmaking field, including fund raising and nonprofit management
- The Associates Program places this vital information at your fingertips via a toll-free number. The annual fee of $495 entitles you to 10 free calls of up to 15 minutes each, or 2 1/2 hours worth of answers per month.
- Membership in the Associates Program allows you to request custom searches of the Foundation Center's computerized databases, which contain information on some 35,000 active U.S. foundations and more than 700 corporate givers. There is an additional cost for this service.
- Associates Program members may request photocopies of key documents. Important information from 990-PFs, annual reports, application guidelines, and other resources can be copied and either mailed or faxed to your office. The fee for this service, available only to associate members, is $2 for the first page of material and $1 for each additional page.
- All Associates Program members receive the Associates Program quarterly newsletter, which provides news and information about new foundations, changes in boards of directors, and new programs and publications from both the Foundation Center and other publishers in the field.

For more information, call (800) 424-9836.

Foundation Center Databases

Foundation and Grants Information Online

The Foundation Center offers two important database files online. Perhaps the most flexible way to take advantage of the Foundation Center's vast resources, computer access lets you design your own search for the foundations and corporate givers most likely to support your nonprofit organization. Online retrieval provides information on funding sources, philanthropic giving, grant application guidelines, and the financial status of foundations to the following: nonprofit organizations seeking funds, grantmaking institutions, corporate contributors, researchers, journalists, and legislators.

The Center's up-to-date and authoritative data is available online through DIALOG Information Services, as well as through a number of other online utilities. For further information on accessing the Center's databases directly through DIALOG, contact DIALOG at 1-800-334-2564.

DIALOG User Manual and Thesaurus

To facilitate your foundation and corporate giving research in its databases, the Foundation Center offers the *User Manual and Thesaurus*.

December 1992/ISBN 0-87954-486-4/$45

Appendix D

The Foundation
Center Cooperating
Collections Network

The New York, Washington, D.C., Atlanta, Cleveland, and San Francisco reference libraries operated by the Foundation Center offer a wide variety of services and comprehensive collections of information on foundations and grants. Cooperating Collections are public and academic libraries, community foundations, and other nonprofit agencies that provide a core collection of Foundation Center publications and a variety of supplementary materials and services in areas useful to grantseekers. Presently, the core collection consists of:

The Foundation Directory

The Foundation Directory Part 2

The Foundation Directory Supplement

The Foundation 1000

Guide to U.S. Foundations, Their Trustees, Officers, and Donors

National Directory of Corporate Giving

The Foundation Grants Index

The Foundation Grants Index Quarterly

Foundation Grants to Individuals

Foundation Giving

Foundation Fundamentals

The Foundation Center's User-Friendly Guide

The Foundation Center's Guide to Proposal Writing

Literature of the Nonprofit Sector

Selected Grant Guides

Many of the network members make available sets of private foundation information returns (IRS Form 990-PF) for their state and/or neighboring states. A complete set of U.S. foundation returns can be found at the New York and Washington, D.C., offices of the Foundation Center. The Atlanta, Cleveland, and San Francisco offices have IRS 990-PF returns for the southeastern, midwestern, and western states, respectively. Those Cooperating Collections marked with a bullet (•) have sets of private foundation information returns for their state and/or neighboring states.

Because Cooperating Collections have different hours, materials, and services, IT IS RECOMMENDED THAT YOU CALL THE COLLECTION NEAREST YOU IN ADVANCE. To check on new locations or current information, call 1-800-424-9836.

REFERENCE COLLECTIONS OPERATED BY THE FOUNDATION CENTER

THE FOUNDATION CENTER
8th Floor
79 Fifth Ave.
New York, NY 10003
Tel: (212) 620-4230

THE FOUNDATION CENTER
1001 Connecticut Ave., NW
Washington, DC 20036
Tel: (202) 331-1400

THE FOUNDATION CENTER
Suite 150, Grand Lobby
Hurt Building
50 Hurt Plaza
Atlanta, GA 30303
Tel: (404) 880-0094

THE FOUNDATION CENTER
Kent H. Smith Library
1442 Euclid, Suite 1356
Cleveland, OH 44115
Tel: (216) 861-1933

THE FOUNDATION CENTER
Room 312
312 Sutter St.
San Francisco, CA 94108
Tel: (415) 397-0902

Cooperating Collections

Alabama

• BIRMINGHAM PUBLIC LIBRARY
Government Documents
2100 Park Place
Birmingham 35203
Tel: (205) 226-3600

HUNTSVILLE PUBLIC LIBRARY
915 Monroe St.
Huntsville 35801
Tel: (205) 532-5940

- UNIVERSITY OF SOUTH ALABAMA
Library Building
Mobile 36688
Tel: (205) 460-7025

- AUBURN UNIVERSITY AT MONTGOMERY
  LIBRARY
7300 University Dr.
Montgomery 36117-3596
Tel: (205) 244-3653

Alaska

- UNIVERSITY OF ALASKA AT ANCHORAGE
Library
3211 Providence Dr.
Anchorage 99508
Tel: (907) 786-1848

JUNEAU PUBLIC LIBRARY
292 Marine Way
Juneau 99801
Tel: (907) 586-5267

Arizona

- PHOENIX PUBLIC LIBRARY
Business & Sciences Unit
12 E. McDowell Rd.
Phoenix 85004
Tel: (602) 262-4636

- TUCSON PIMA LIBRARY
101 N. Stone Ave.
Tucson 87501
Tel: (602) 791-4010

Arkansas

- WESTARK COMMUNITY COLLEGE—
  BORHAM LIBRARY
5210 Grand Ave.
Fort Smith 72913
Tel: (501) 785-7133

- CENTRAL ARKANSAS LIBRARY SYSTEM
700 Louisiana
Little Rock 72201
Tel: (501) 370-5952

PINE BLUFF-JEFFERSON COUNTY LIBRARY
  SYSTEM
200 E. Eighth
Pine Bluff 71601
Tel: (501) 534-2159

California

- VENTURA COUNTY COMMUNITY
  FOUNDATION
Funding and Information Resource
  Center
1355 Del Norte Rd.
Camarillo 93010
Tel: (805) 988-0196

- CALIFORNIA COMMUNITY FOUNDATION
Funding Information Center
606 S. Olive St., Suite 2400
Los Angeles 90014-1526
Tel: (213) 413-4042

GRANT & RESOURCE CENTER OF
  NORTHERN CALIFORNIA
Building C, Suite A
2280 Benton Dr.
Redding 96003
Tel: (916) 244-1219

RIVERSIDE CITY & COUNTY PUBLIC LIBRARY
3581 Seventh St.
Riverside 92502
Tel: (714) 782-5201

NONPROFIT RESOURCE CENTER
Sacramento Public Library
828 I St., 2nd Floor
Sacramento 95814
Tel: (916) 552-8817

- SAN DIEGO COMMUNITY FOUNDATION
  Funding Information Center
  101 West Broadway, Suite 1120
  San Diego 92101
  Tel: (619) 239-8815

- NONPROFIT DEVELOPMENT CENTER
  Library
  1762 Technology Dr., # 225
  San Jose 95110
  Tel: (408) 452-8181

- PENINSULA COMMUNITY FOUNDATION
  Funding Information Library
  1700 S. El Camino Real, R301
  San Mateo 94402-3049
  Tel: (415) 358-9392

  LOS ANGELES PUBLIC LIBRARY
  San Pedro Regional Branch
  931 S. Gaffey St.
  San Pedro 90731
  Tel: (310) 548-7779

- VOLUNTEER CENTER OF GREATER ORANGE
  COUNTY
  Nonprofit Management Assistance Center
  1000 E. Santa Ana Blvd., Suite 200
  Santa Ana 92701
  Tel: (714) 953-1655

- SANTA BARBARA PUBLIC LIBRARY
  40 E. Anapamu St.
  Santa Barbara 93101
  Tel: (805) 962-7653

  SANTA MONICA PUBLIC LIBRARY
  1343 Sixth St.
  Santa Monica 90401-1603
  Tel: (310) 458-8600

  SONOMA COUNTY LIBRARY
  3rd & E Sts.
  Santa Rosa 95404
  Tel: (707) 545-0831

SEASIDE BRANCH LIBRARY
550 Harcourt St.
Seaside 93955
(408) 899-8131

Colorado

PIKES PEAK LIBRARY DISTRICT
20 North Cascade
Colorado Springs 80901
Tel: (719) 531-6333

- DENVER PUBLIC LIBRARY
  Social Sciences & Genealogy
  1357 Broadway
  Denver 80203
  Tel: (303) 640-8870

Connecticut

DANBURY PUBLIC LIBRARY
170 Main St.
Danbury 06810
Tel: (203) 797-4527

- HARTFORD PUBLIC LIBRARY
  500 Main St.
  Hartford 06103
  Tel: (203) 293-6000

  D.A.T.A.
  70 Audubon St.
  New Haven 06510
  Tel: (203) 772-1345

Delaware

- UNIVERSITY OF DELAWARE
  Hugh Morris Library
  Newark 19717-5267
  Tel: (302) 831-2432

Florida

VOLUSIA COUNTY LIBRARY CENTER
City Island
Daytona Beach 32014-4484
Tel: (904) 255-3765

• NOVA UNIVERSITY
Einstein Library
3301 College Ave.
Fort Lauderdale 33314
Tel: (305) 475-7050

INDIAN RIVER COMMUNITY COLLEGE
Charles S. Miley Learning Resources
   Center
3209 Virginia Ave.
Fort Pierce 34981-5599
Tel: (407) 462-4757

• JACKSONVILLE PUBLIC LIBRARIES
Grants Resource Center
122 North Ocean St.
Jacksonville 32202
Tel: (904) 630-2665

• MIAMI-DADE PUBLIC LIBRARY
Humanities/Social Science
101 W. Flagler St.
Miami 33130
Tel: (305) 375-5015

• ORLANDO PUBLIC LIBRARY
Social Sciences Department
101 E. Central Blvd.
Orlando 32801
Tel: (407) 425-4694

SELBY PUBLIC LIBRARY
1001 Blvd. of the Arts
Sarasota 34236
Tel: (813) 951-5501

• TAMPA-HILLSBOROUGH COUNTY
   PUBLIC LIBRARY
900 N. Ashley Dr.
Tampa 33602
Tel: (813) 273-3628

COMMUNITY FOUNDATION OF PALM BEACH
   & MARTIN COUNTIES
324 Datura St., Suite 340
West Palm Beach 33401
Tel: (407) 659-6800

Georgia

• ATLANTA-FULTON PUBLIC LIBRARY
Foundation Collection—Ivan Allen
   Department
1 Margaret Mitchell Square
Atlanta 30303-1089
Tel: (404) 730-1900

DALTON REGIONAL LIBRARY
310 Cappes St.
Dalton 30720
Tel: (706) 278-4507

Hawaii

• UNIVERSITY OF HAWAII
Hamilton Library
2550 The Mall
Honolulu 96822
Tel: (808) 956-7214

HAWAII COMMUNITY FOUNDATION
Hawaii Resource Center
222 Merchant St., 2nd Floor
Honolulu 96813
Tel: (808) 537-6333

Idaho

• BOISE PUBLIC LIBRARY
715 S. Capitol Blvd.
Boise 83702
Tel: (208) 384-4024

• CALDWELL PUBLIC LIBRARY
1010 Dearborn St.
Caldwell 83605
Tel: (208) 459-3242

Illinois

• DONORS FORUM OF CHICAGO
53 W. Jackson Blvd., Suite 430
Chicago 60604-3608
Tel: (312) 431-0265

• EVANSTON PUBLIC LIBRARY
1703 Orrington Ave.
Evanston 60201
Tel: (708) 866-0305

ROCK ISLAND PUBLIC LIBRARY
401 19th St.
Rock Island 61201
Tel: (309) 788-7627

• SANGAMON STATE UNIVERSITY
Library
Shepherd Rd.
Springfield 62794-9243
Tel: (217) 786-6633

Indiana

• ALLEN COUNTY PUBLIC LIBRARY
900 Webster St.
Fort Wayne 46802
Tel: (219) 424-0544

INDIANA UNIVERSITY NORTHWEST LIBRARY
3400 Broadway
Gary 46408
Tel: (219) 980-6582

• INDIANAPOLIS-MARION COUNTY PUBLIC
LIBRARY
Social Sciences
40 E. St. Clair St.
Indianapolis 46206
Tel: (317) 269-1733

Iowa

• CEDAR RAPIDS PUBLIC LIBRARY
Foundation Center Collection
500 First St., SE
Cedar Rapids 52401
Tel: (319) 398-5123

• SOUTHWESTERN COMMUNITY COLLEGE
Learning Resource Center
1501 W. Townline Rd.
Creston 50801
Tel: (515) 782-7081

• PUBLIC LIBRARY OF DES MOINES
100 Locust St.
Des Moines 50309-1791
Tel: (515) 283-4152

SIOUX CITY PUBLIC LIBRARY
529 Pierce St.
Sioux City 51101-1202
Tel: (712) 252-5669

Kansas

DODGE CITY PUBLIC LIBRARY
1001 2nd Ave.
Dodge City 67801
Tel: (316) 225-0248

• TOPEKA AND SHAWNEE COUNTY PUBLIC
LIBRARY
1515 SW 10th Ave.
Topeka 66604-1374
Tel: (913) 233-2040

• WICHITA PUBLIC LIBRARY
223 South Main St.
Wichita 67202
Tel: (316) 262-0611

Kentucky

WESTERN KENTUCKY UNIVERSITY
Helm-Cravens Library
Bowling Green 42101-3576
Tel: (502) 745-6125

● LOUISVILLE FREE PUBLIC LIBRARY
301 York St.
Louisville 40203
Tel: (502) 574-1611

Louisiana

● E. BATON ROUGE PARISH LIBRARY
Centroplex Branch Grants Collection
120 St. Louis St.
Baton Rouge 70802
Tel: (504) 389-4960

BEAUREGARD PARISH LIBRARY
205 S. Washington Ave.
De Ridder 70634
Tel: (318) 463-6217

● NEW ORLEANS PUBLIC LIBRARY
Business and Science Division
219 Loyola Ave.
New Orleans 70140
Tel: (504) 596-2580

● SHREVE MEMORIAL LIBRARY
424 Texas St.
Shreveport 71120-1523
Tel: (318) 226-5894

Maine

● UNIVERSITY OF SOUTHERN MAINE
Office of Sponsored Research
246 Deering Ave., Rm. 628
Portland 04103
Tel: (207) 780-4871

Maryland

● ENOCH PRATT FREE LIBRARY
Social Science & History
400 Cathedral St.
Baltimore 21201
Tel: (401) 396-5430

Massachusetts

● ASSOCIATED GRANTMAKERS OF
   MASSACHUSETTS
294 Washington St., Suite 840
Boston 02108
Tel: (617) 426-2606

● BOSTON PUBLIC LIBRARY
Social Science Reference
666 Boylston St.
Boston 02117
Tel: (617) 536-5400

WESTERN MASSACHUSETTS FUNDING
   RESOURCE CENTER
65 Elliot St.
Springfield 01101-1730
Tel: (413) 732-3175

● WORCESTER PUBLIC LIBRARY
Grants Resource Center
Salem Square
Worcester 01608
Tel: (508) 799-1655

Michigan

● ALPENA COUNTY LIBRARY
211 N. First St.
Alpena 49707
Tel: (517) 356-6188

- UNIVERSITY OF MICHIGAN-ANN ARBOR
  Graduate Library
  Reference & Research Services
     Department
  Ann Arbor 48109-1205
  Tel: (313) 764-9373

- BATTLE CREEK COMMUNITY FOUNDATION
  Southwest Michigan Funding Resource
     Center
  2 Riverwalk Centre
  34 W. Jackson St.
  Battle Creek 49017-3505
  Tel: (616) 962-2181

- HENRY FORD CENTENNIAL LIBRARY
  Adult Services
  16301 Michigan Ave.
  Dearborn 48126
  Tel: (313) 943-2330

- WAYNE STATE UNIVERSITY
  Purdy/Kresge Library
  5265 Cass Ave.
  Detroit 48202
  Tel: (313) 577-6424

- MICHIGAN STATE UNIVERSITY LIBRARIES
  Social Sciences/Humanities
  Main Library
  E. Lansing 48824-1048
  Tel: (517) 353-8818

- FARMINGTON COMMUNITY LIBRARY
  32737 West 12 Mile Rd.
  Farmington Hills 48018
  Tel: (313) 553-0300

- UNIVERSITY OF MICHIGAN-FLINT
  Library
  Flint 48502-2186
  Tel: (313) 762-3408

- GRAND RAPIDS PUBLIC LIBRARY
  Business Dept.—3rd Floor
  60 Library Plaza NE
  Grand Rapids 49503-3093
  Tel: (616) 456-3600

MICHIGAN TECHNOLOGICAL UNIVERSITY
Van Pelt Library
1400 Townshend Dr.
Houghton 49931
Tel: (906) 487-2507

SAULT STE. MARIE AREA PUBLIC SCHOOLS
Office of Compensatory Education
460 W. Spruce St.
Sault Ste. Marie 49783-1874
Tel: (906) 635-6619

- NORTHWESTERN MICHIGAN COLLEGE
  Mark & Helen Osterin Library
  1701 E. Front St.
  Traverse City 49684
  Tel: (616) 922-1060

Minnesota

- DULUTH PUBLIC LIBRARY
  520 W. Superior St.
  Duluth 55802
  Tel: (218) 723-3802

- SOUTHWEST STATE UNIVERSITY LIBRARY
  University Library
  Marshall 56258
  Tel: (507) 537-6176

- MINNEAPOLIS PUBLIC LIBRARY
  Sociology Department
  300 Nicollet Mall
  Minneapolis 55401
  Tel: (612) 372-6555

ROCHESTER PUBLIC LIBRARY
11 First St. SE
Rochester 55904-3777
Tel: (507) 285-8002

ST. PAUL PUBLIC LIBRARY
90 W. Fourth St.
St. Paul 55102
Tel: (612) 292-6307

Mississippi

- JACKSON/HINDS LIBRARY SYSTEM
  300 N. State St.
  Jackson 39201
  Tel: (601) 968-5803

Missouri

- CLEARINGHOUSE FOR MIDCONTINENT
  FOUNDATIONS
  University of Missouri
  5315 Rockhill Rd.
  Kansas City 64110
  Tel: (816) 235-1176

- KANSAS CITY PUBLIC LIBRARY
  311 E. 12th St.
  Kansas City 64106
  Tel: (816) 221-9650

- METROPOLITAN ASSOCIATION FOR
  PHILANTHROPY, INC.
  5615 Pershing Ave., Suite 20
  St. Louis 63112
  Tel: (314) 361-3900

- SPRINGFIELD-GREENE COUNTY LIBRARY
  397 E. Central
  Springfield 65802
  Tel: (417) 869-9400

Montana

- EASTERN MONTANA COLLEGE LIBRARY
  Special Collections—Grants
  1500 N. 30th St.
  Billings 59101-0298
  Tel: (406) 657-1662

  BOZEMAN PUBLIC LIBRARY
  220 E. Lamme
  Bozeman 59715
  Tel: (406) 586-4787

- MONTANA STATE LIBRARY
  Library Services
  1515 E. 6th Ave.
  Helena 59620
  Tel: (406) 444-3004

- UNIVERSITY OF MONTANA
  Maureen & Mike Mansfield Library
  Missoula 59812-1195
  Tel: (406) 243-6800

Nebraska

- UNIVERSITY OF NEBRASKA—LINCOLN
  Love Library
  14th & R Sts.
  Lincoln 68588-0410
  Tel: (402) 472-2848

- W. DALE CLARK LIBRARY
  Social Sciences Department
  215 S. 15th St.
  Omaha 68102
  Tel: (402) 444-4826

Nevada

- LAS VEGAS—CLARK COUNTY LIBRARY
  DISTRICT
  833 Las Vegas Blvd. North
  Las Vegas 89101
  Tel: (702) 382-5280

- WASHOE COUNTY LIBRARY
  301 S. Center St.
  Reno 89501
  Tel: (702) 785-4010

New Hampshire

- NEW HAMPSHIRE CHARITABLE FOUNDATION
  One South St.
  Concord 03302-1335
  Tel: (603) 225-6641

● PLYMOUTH STATE COLLEGE
Herbert H. Lamson Library
Plymouth 03264
Tel: (603) 535-5000

New Jersey

CUMBERLAND COUNTY LIBRARY
800 E. Commerce St.
Bridgeton 08302
Tel: (609) 453-2210

● FREE PUBLIC LIBRARY OF ELIZABETH
11 S. Broad St.
Elizabeth 07202
Tel: (908) 354-6060

COUNTY COLLEGE OF MORRIS
Learning Resource Center
214 Center Grove Rd.
Randolph 07869
Tel: (201) 328-5296

● NEW JERSEY STATE LIBRARY
Governmental Reference Services
185 W. State St.
Trenton 08625-0520
Tel: (609) 292-6220

New Mexico

ALBUQUERQUE COMMUNITY FOUNDATION
3301 Menual NE, Suite 30
Albuquerque 87176-6960
Tel: (505) 883-6240

● NEW MEXICO STATE LIBRARY
Information Services
325 Don Gaspar
Santa Fe 87503
Tel: (505) 827-3824

New York

● NEW YORK STATE LIBRARY
Humanities Reference
Cultural Education Center
Empire State Plaza
Albany 12230
Tel: (518) 473-5355

SUFFOLK COOPERATIVE LIBRARY SYSTEM
627 N. Sunrise Service Rd.
Bellport 11713
Tel: (516) 286-1600

NEW YORK PUBLIC LIBRARY
Fordham Branch
2556 Bainbridge Ave.
Bronx 10458
Tel: (718) 220-6575

BROOKLYN IN TOUCH INFORMATION
    CENTER, INC.
One Hanson Place—Room 2504
Brooklyn 11243
Tel: (718) 230-3200

BROOKLYN PUBLIC LIBRARY
Social Sciences Division
Grand Army Plaza
Brooklyn 11238
Tel: (718) 780-7700

● BUFFALO AND ERIE COUNTY PUBLIC
    LIBRARY
Business & Labor Department
Lafayette Square
Buffalo 14203
Tel: (716) 858-7097

HUNTINGTON PUBLIC LIBRARY
338 Main St.
Huntington 11743
Tel: (516) 427-5165

QUEENS BOROUGH PUBLIC LIBRARY
Social Sciences Division
89-11 Merrick Boulevard
Jamaica 11432
Tel: (718) 990-0761

- LEVITTOWN PUBLIC LIBRARY
1 Bluegrass Lane
Levittown 11756
Tel: (516) 731-5728

NEW YORK PUBLIC LIBRARY
Countee Cullen Branch Library
104 W. 136th St.
New York 10030
Tel: (212) 491-2070

ADRIANCE MEMORIAL LIBRARY
Special Services Department
93 Market St.
Poughkeepsie 12601
Tel: (914) 485-3445

- ROCHESTER PUBLIC LIBRARY
Business, Economics & Law
115 South Ave.
Rochester 14604
Tel: (716) 428-7328

ONONDAGA COUNTY PUBLIC LIBRARY
447 S. Salina St.
Syracuse 13202-2494
Tel: (315) 448-4700

UTICA PUBLIC LIBRARY
303 Genessee St.
Utica 13501
Tel: (315) 735-2279

- WHITE PLAINS PUBLIC LIBRARY
100 Martine Ave.
White Plains 10601
Tel: (914) 442-1480

North Carolina

- COMMUNITY FOUNDATION OF WESTERN
NORTH CAROLINA
Learning Resources Center
14 College St.
P.O. Box 1888
Asheville 28801
Tel: (704) 254-4960

- THE DUKE ENDOWMENT
200 S. Tryon St., Suite 1100
Charlotte 28202
Tel: (704) 376-0291

DURHAM COUNTY PUBLIC LIBRARY
301 N. Roxboro
Durham 27702
Tel: (919) 560-0110

- STATE LIBRARY OF NORTH CAROLINA
Government and Business Services
Archives Building
109 E. Jones St.
Raleigh 27601
Tel: (919) 733-3270

- FORSYTH COUNTY PUBLIC LIBRARY
660 W. 5th St.
Winston-Salem 27101
Tel: (910) 727-2680

North Dakota

BISMARCK PUBLIC LIBRARY
515 North Fifth St.
Bismarck 58501
Tel: (701) 222-6410

- NORTH DAKOTA STATE UNIVERSITY LIBRARY
Fargo 58105
Tel: (701) 237-8886

Ohio

STARK COUNTY DISTRICT LIBRARY
Humanities
715 Market Ave. North
Canton 44702
Tel: (216) 452-0665

- PUBLIC LIBRARY OF CINCINNATI &
  HAMILTON COUNTY
Grants Resource Center
800 Vine St.—Library Square
Cincinnati 45202-2071
Tel: (513) 369-6940

COLUMBUS METROPOLITAN LIBRARY
Business and Technology
96 S. Grant Ave.
Columbus 43215
Tel: (614) 645-2590

- DAYTON AND MONTGOMERY COUNTY
  PUBLIC LIBRARY
Grants Resource Center
215 E. Third St.
Dayton 45402
Tel: (513) 227-9500, ext. 211

- TOLEDO-LUCAS COUNTY PUBLIC LIBRARY
Social Sciences Department
325 Michigan St.
Toledo 43624-1614
Tel: (419) 259-5245

YOUNGSTOWN & MAHONING PUBLIC
  LIBRARY
305 Wick Ave.
Youngstown 44503
Tel: (216) 744-8636

- MUSKINGUM COUNTY LIBRARY
220 N. 5th St.
Zanesville 43701
Tel: (614) 453-0391

Oklahoma

- OKLAHOMA CITY UNIVERSITY
Dulaney Browne Library
2501 N. Blackwelder
Oklahoma City 73106
Tel: (405) 521-5072

- TULSA CITY-COUNTY LIBRARY
400 Civic Center
Tulsa 74103
Tel: (918) 596-7944

Oregon

OREGON INSTITUTE OF TECHNOLOGY
Library
3201 Campus Dr.
Klamath Falls 97601-8801
Tel: (503) 885-1773

- PACIFIC NON-PROFIT NETWORK
Grantsmanship Resource Library
33 N. Central, Suite 211
Medford 97501
Tel: (503) 779-6044

- MULTNOMAH COUNTY LIBRARY
Government Documents
801 SW Tenth Ave.
Portland 97205
Tel: (503) 248-5123

OREGON STATE LIBRARY
State Library Building
Salem 97310
Tel: (503) 378-4277

Pennsylvania

NORTHAMPTON COMMUNITY COLLEGE
Learning Resources Center
3835 Green Pond Rd.
Bethlehem 18017
Tel: (215) 861-5360

ERIE COUNTY LIBRARY SYSTEM
27 South Park Row
Erie 16501
Tel: (814) 451-6927

DAUPHIN COUNTY LIBRARY SYSTEM
Central Library
101 Walnut St.
Harrisburg 17101
Tel: (717) 234-4976

LANCASTER COUNTY PUBLIC LIBRARY
125 N. Duke St.
Lancaster 17602
Tel: (717) 394-2651

● FREE LIBRARY OF PHILADELPHIA
Regional Foundation Center
Logan Square
Philadelphia 19103
Tel: (215) 686-5423

● CARNEGIE LIBRARY OF PITTSBURGH
Foundation Collection
4400 Forbes Ave.
Pittsburgh 15213-4080
Tel: (412) 622-1917

POCONO NORTHEAST DEVELOPMENT FUND
James Pettinger Memorial Library
1151 Oak St.
Pittston 18640-3755
Tel: (717) 655-5581

READING PUBLIC LIBRARY
100 S. Fifth St.
Reading 19602
Tel: (215) 655-6355

MARTIN LIBRARY
159 Market St.
York 17401
Tel: (717) 846-5300

Rhode Island

● PROVIDENCE PUBLIC LIBRARY
150 Empire St.
Providence 02906
Tel: (401) 521-7722

South Carolina

ANDERSON COUNTY LIBRARY
202 E. Greenville St.
Anderson 29621
Tel: (803) 260-4500

● CHARLESTON COUNTY LIBRARY
404 King St.
Charleston 29403
Tel: (803) 723-1645

● SOUTH CAROLINA STATE LIBRARY
1500 Senate St.
Columbia 29211
Tel: (803) 734-8666

South Dakota

NONPROFIT GRANTS ASSISTANCE CENTER
Business & Education Institute
Washington St., East Hall
Dakota State University
Madison 57042
Tel: (605) 256-5555

● SOUTH DAKOTA STATE LIBRARY
800 Governors Dr.
Pierre 57501-2294
Tel: (605) 773-5070
Tel: (800) 592-1841 (SD residents)

SIOUX FALLS AREA FOUNDATION
141 N. Main Ave., Suite 310
Sioux Falls 57102-1132
Tel: (605) 336-7055

Tennessee

● KNOX COUNTY PUBLIC LIBRARY
500 W. Church Ave.
Knoxville 37902
Tel: (615) 544-5700

● MEMPHIS & SHELBY COUNTY PUBLIC
   LIBRARY
1850 Peabody Ave.
Memphis 38104
Tel: (901) 725-8877

NASHVILLE PUBLIC LIBRARY
Business Information Division
225 Polk Ave.
Nashville 37203
Tel: (615) 862-5843

Texas

COMMUNITY FOUNDATION OF ABILENE
Funding Information Library
500 N. Chestnut, Suite 1509
Abilene 79604
Tel: (915) 676-3883

● AMARILLO AREA FOUNDATION
700 First National Place
801 S. Fillmore
Amarillo 79101
Tel: (806) 376-4521

● HOGG FOUNDATION FOR MENTAL HEALTH
3001 Lake Austin Blvd.
Austin 78703
Tel: (512) 471-5041

TEXAS A&M UNIVERSITY AT CORPUS CHRISTI
Library
Reference Department
6300 Ocean Dr.
Corpus Christi 78412
Tel: (512) 994-2608

● DALLAS PUBLIC LIBRARY
Urban Information
1515 Young St.
Dallas 75201
Tel: (214) 670-1487

EL PASO COMMUNITY FOUNDATION
1616 Texas Commerce Building
El Paso 79901
Tel: (915) 533-4020

● FUNDING INFORMATION CENTER OF
   FORT WORTH
Texas Christian University Library
2800 S. University Dr.
Fort Worth 76129
Tel: (817) 921-7664

● HOUSTON PUBLIC LIBRARY
Bibliographic Information Center
500 McKinney Ave.
Houston 77002
Tel: (713) 236-1313

● LONGVIEW PUBLIC LIBRARY
222 W. Cotton St.
Longview 75601
Tel: (903) 237-1352

LUBBOCK AREA FOUNDATION, INC.
502 Texas Commerce Bank Building
Lubbock 79401
Tel: (8O6) 762-8061

● FUNDING INFORMATION CENTER
530 McCullough, Suite 600
San Antonio 78212-8270
Tel: (210) 227-4333

NORTH TEXAS CENTER FOR NONPROFIT
   MANAGEMENT
624 Indiana, Suite 307
Wichita Falls 76301
Tel: (817) 322-4961

Utah

● SALT LAKE CITY PUBLIC LIBRARY
209 E. 500 South
Salt Lake City 84111
Tel: (801) 524-8200

Vermont

- VERMONT DEPT. OF LIBRARIES
Reference & Law Info. Services
109 State St.
Montpelier 05609
Tel: (802) 828-3268

Virginia

- HAMPTON PUBLIC LIBRARY
4207 Victoria Blvd.
Hampton 23669
Tel: (804) 727-1312

- RICHMOND PUBLIC LIBRARY
Business, Science & Technology
101 E. Franklin St.
Richmond 23219
Tel: (804) 780-8223

- ROANOKE CITY PUBLIC LIBRARY SYSTEM
Central Library
706 S. Jefferson St.
Roanoke 24016
Tel: (703) 981-2477

Washington

- MID-COLUMBIA LIBRARY
405 South Dayton
Kennewick 99336
Tel: (509) 586-3156

- SEATTLE PUBLIC LIBRARY
Science, Social Science
1000 Fourth Ave.
Seattle 98104
Tel: (206) 386-4620

- SPOKANE PUBLIC LIBRARY
Funding Information Center
West 911 Main Ave.
Spokane 99201
Tel: (509) 838-3364

- UNITED WAY OF PIERCE COUNTY
Center for Nonprofit Development
734 Broadway
P.O. Box 2215
Tacoma 98401
Tel: (206) 597-6686

GREATER WENATCHEE COMMUNITY
FOUNDATION AT THE WENATCHEE
PUBLIC LIBRARY
310 Douglas St.
Wenatchee 98807
Tel: (509) 662-5021

West Virginia

- KANAWHA COUNTY PUBLIC LIBRARY
123 Capitol St.
Charleston 25301
Tel: (304) 343-4646

Wisconsin

- UNIVERSITY OF WISCONSIN-MADISON
Memorial Library
728 State St.
Madison 53706
Tel: (608) 262-3242

- MARQUETTE UNIVERSITY MEMORIAL
LIBRARY
Funding Information Center
1415 W. Wisconsin Ave.
Milwaukee 53233
Tel: (414) 288-1515

UNIVERSITY OF WISCONSIN—
STEVENS POINT
Library—Foundation Collection
99 Reserve St.
Stevens Point 54481-3897
Tel: (715) 346-3826

Wyoming

- NATRONA COUNTY PUBLIC LIBRARY
  307 E. 2nd St.
  Casper 82601-2598
  Tel: (307) 237-4935

- LARAMIE COUNTY COMMUNITY COLLEGE
  Instructional Resource Center
  1400 E. College Dr.
  Cheyenne 82007-3299
  Tel: (307) 778-1206

- CAMPBELL COUNTY PUBLIC LIBRARY
  2101 4-J Rd.
  Gillette 82716
  Tel: (307) 682-3223

- TETON COUNTY LIBRARY
  320 S. King St.
  Jackson 83001
  Tel: (307) 733-2164

ROCK SPRINGS LIBRARY
400 C St.
Rock Springs 82901
Tel: (307) 362-6212

Puerto Rico

UNIVERSITY OF PUERTO RICO
Ponce Technological College Library
Box 7186
Ponce 00732
Tel: (809) 844-8181

UNIVERSIDAD DEL SAGRADO CORAZON
M.M.T. Guevara Library
Santurce 00914
Tel: (809) 728-1515, ext. 4357

Index